NO GREAT MISCHIEF
IF YOU FALL

NO GREAT MISCHIEF
IF YOU FALL

A Highland Experience

JOHN MACLEOD

MAINSTREAM
PUBLISHING

EDINBURGH AND LONDON

Copyright © John Macleod, 1993

All photographs courtesy of *The Herald*

First published in Great Britain in 1993 by
MAINSTREAM PUBLISHING COMPANY (EDINBURGH) LTD
7 Albany Street
Edinburgh EH1 3UG

ISBN 1 85158 540 0

A catalogue record for this book is available from the British Library

Typeset in Garamond Stempel by Lasertext Ltd., Stretford, Manchester

Printed in Great Britain by Butler & Tanner, Frome

Contents

For Derek and Graeme,
northern lights

Preface

So many books seem now to appear annually about the Highlands and Islands that my first instinct is to apologise for adding to their number. This book, however, is one written from within. I must qualify this; I have not lived in the West Highlands since my fifth year, though I hope shortly to return, and I am not a Gaelic speaker, and I am not the spokesman for any collective or party.

But I have been raised, throughout my life, amongst Highland people — in Lochaber, in the Hebridean diaspora of central Scotland — and, every year, I have returned for weeks on end to the island of my forbears, and in recent times I have been privileged to explore other and beautiful corners of the Hebrides. From early years I have been fascinated by my background. I have read, questioned, and dreamed of the Gaidhealtachd for as long as I can remember, with that peculiar intensity of the exile and the refugee, and much of this book is born in a pondering and probing that began many years ago — in a book devoured in the playground, in conversations with the old and wise.

This is an unashamedly personal book. It wanders from corner to corner of my interests, my obsessions, and now and again my prejudices. It asks hard questions. At times it asks unanswerable questions; yearnings and demands of Highland mystery and Highland tragedy that touch universal agonies of human experience. And if this book is at times most emotional, and anguished, and angry, must it be then condemned? For there is, I hope, a thread of hard and vital logic through all its polemic. In reason is knowledge; in knowledge, truth; in truth, freedom and peace.

The book falls in three parts. The first four chapters give a lightning-sweep through modern Highland history, concluding in my own experience of summer life through two decades in one Hebridean village. The '45 is assessed, and that luckless but strangely lovable man at the head of it; the Clearance Age — I would call it our Holocaust, at least in its psychological importance to Gaels today — is retold, or at least as much of it as I can bear to tell. But a broken people rose again, and I have told that too. I hope my childhood memoir does not repel. Shawbost *was* lovely in those days, and it is lovely still.

The second part of the book is an account of a collective Highland psychology in the light of our historical experience — to wit, the tale of the Free Presbyterian Church of Scotland, a uniquely Highland institution, and its spectacular explosion around a senior politician. In his agony, and that of his brethren, can be seen the dilemmas and rebellions of Highlanders today. And in the spring of 1993, the centenary of the Church's foundation, that story is not inappropriate. I hope my abiding respect for the Free Presbyterian Church is not overveiled by dark analysis of its internal politics; and that my version of the 1989 split causes no distress to those involved, on both sides — many of whom, like William Mackenzie and Angus Morrison, showed me great kindness in foolish youth.

The last third of the work addresses themes central to Highland identity — the land, Gaelic, change, conflict. And in order to give the whole epic a certain coherence and grandeur, I have tied these sections by episodes of dialogue. Though drawn in some respects from several remote but real relatives, the Cousin is in his history and setting largely fictitious. He plays devil's advocate; he anticipates external criticism; he deflates pretentiousness. He has no substance, but he wields power of words: he is my ally and my enemy, and a reflection perhaps of the darker side of myself. I must say I will rather miss him.

Neil Wilson, then director of the late and lamented Lochar Publishing, first suggested I write a book on the Hebrides. The ridiculous demise of Lochar in the autumn of 1992 put paid to his role in its appearance, but I am grateful to him and his former colleague Mike De Luca. Bill Campbell, Peter MacKenzie and others at Mainstream were glad to revive the project. Their energy and discipline have been most helpful.

In this and many other spheres I owe a huge debt to Harry Reid, deputy editor of *The Herald*, who has chivvied and nagged and flattered me through each kink and turn of the history of the work, and fought to promote its welfare as a she-wolf for her cubs. Arnold Kemp, editor of *The Herald*, kindly authorised access to the paper's magnificent picture-library; David Doig, keeper of the door, happily helped me loot the files. Harry read the finished draft and made many helpful comments; in this I am grateful too for the help of Norman Shaw, artist and co-pilot on assorted Highland jaunts. Dr Raj Jandoo, advocate, read the script and delivered me from a thousand defamations. It would be most unjust to launch my first book on the Highlands without mentioning *The Scotsman* newspaper and its editor Magnus Linklater, who first flamed my modest journalistic talent, and provided a regular weekend column for my Highland travelogues.

In researching the book I have shamelessly ransacked the work of Dr James Hunter, whose titles on the Highlands should be compulsory reading for every commentator on the region. I was also glad of articles by David Ross and Torcuil Crichton, published in *The Herald* on 15 and 16 October 1992. Over the last year or two many have patiently received me into their homes and suffered my questioning on assorted matters of local interest: among these I should thank especially Dr James and Sandra Finlayson, Harris; John Murdo Morrison of the Harris Hotel; Dr Sorley MacLean, Peinchorran, Skye; Kenny MacSween, merchant at Strond, Harris; Murdo and Neil Murray, crofters and so much else, New Shawbost; Isobel and Alasdair Nicolson, Raasay; and Dr James Tallach, minister at Raasay.

My grandmother, Alice Macleod, has down the years fed me family lore and history with forbearance and humour. My parents have borne my aging presence in their home with great charity, and been as ever a constant encouragement. Stephen Marshall ably guided me in the selection and use of suitable computer equipment. Other friends kept me happy. The Free Church kept me humble. Norman Wilson, most understanding of bank managers, kept me solvent. Some brave souls granted me board and lodging on tours for this book — Dr James and Sandra Finlayson (again), and Rev Norman and Catherine Maciver, Tarbert, Harris; Donald and Mary Anne MacDonald, Lingerabay, Harris; Derek Graham, Aberdeen; and — repeatedly, cheerfully and with every comfort — Derek's parents, Angus and Isobel Graham of Inverness. The Harris Hotel, Isle of Raasay Hotel, and Raebhat House at Shawbost are lodgings I recall with great affection.

What is the truth, the key to understanding the catastrophe of the Highland tale? Is it the thin poor weakness of the land? The rigours of the climate? Or the cultured savagery of the people of the south country? Was Gaelic itself a burden and a blocking on the might of the Gaelic people? Are we, ultimately, innocent victims of an alien mass to the south; a hostile satellite-universe beyond all our shores? Or are we ourselves, we Highlanders, we Hebrideans, agents and factors in our own downfall?

There are many truths. And I have many cousins.

John Macleod
Edinburgh
December 1992

Lionagaidh

The wind on the west of Lewis, sounding in the sea on the rocks by the shore; the wind that makes a sea of the corn and the barley, sending waves through them in high summer, and has the bog-cotton dancing fretfully on the moorland fringe. But this is not that wind, soft and warm and wet; this is the wind of a nervy autumn day, a north-wester, cold and hard, that speaks of showers of hail and rain, and sets a mournful whistle in the cables.

And so I walk through the township, northwards, to Lionagaidh by the shore where my people are. I have to brace myself into this wind, setting my shoulders into it, glad for the grip of tarmac under my boots.

Past the modern bungalows, with their pink pebbledash and mock-Georgian front doors, towards and past the church that stands high on my right as the fortress of God. The post-office and its house, and the old telephone-box, where Leod puts the papers for collection at the end of each day, if so-and-so has not come by.

The road to Carnan and the tweedmill, to Phibhig, where once (so I was told by Aonghas Choinneach Rod) there was witchcraft; this road I pass on my left. The marshy field that was once a football park, and had a sign on the fence hailing it as "Chirrapungi", because that was the wettest place on earth, except this.

The widow's cottage. A dead rabbit in the ditch; the burn going under the road to the loch of the mill. The road turns leftwards, upwards, in a newly landscaped corner; once there was a deadly bend here, when I was a boy, combining turns with gradient, but now the road has been broadened and straightened, with a crash-barrier, and yellow signs with the stars of Europe, announcing in Gaelic and English that these improvements are financed by the European Regional Development Fund.

The byre of the old manse, and windblown grass where once the old manse stood, and the new manse a broad white dacha well back from the road. The cattle-grid rattles behind me, and I step a little to the side, and a car rushes by, going for Stornoway.

The shower comes, as promised, and I stand in the fetid bus-shelter and watch the hail pop on the road, and it passes. Raebhat falls behind, Raebhat of the restaurant and guest-house and "Lewis Teddy Bear Centre", where the man from Nottingham hatches great schemes for the west side. Sometimes I stay there, valuing the privacy, and he talks aloud his dreams — the building of this, the opening of that — and his harsh vowels defy the realities about him. The bleak and windswept locale, with that relentless rain. The honed and hammered values of the community, the religion and the simplicity of the lifestyle, though the religion be more formal and the lifestyle more cluttered than once they were.

But he talks still. An adventure playground for the kiddies. A reconstructed black house, transported stone by stone from another township, to attract the sightseers. A public bar. A lounge bar. Self-catering chalets on the slope beyond. A hairdressing salon. A function suite . . . so he sits out here, safely insulated in his western bungalow, and occasionally thunders off to town in his fast car, where he has another guesthouse, and other schemes.

He knows nothing.

He knows nothing of this parish, and its townships, and its people, and its past. He has never walked in boyhood through those meadows, and dew on your bare feet, and the grumpy cow to be watched, and Granny sailing out to feed the hens in the byre that was once the old house; the hill Beinn Mhor on his elbow beyond the end of the street, craggy and benevolent, and the houses marching in line towards him. The old byre, with the thatch that my grandfather renewed in season, that was once the home of his father and his father before him, that had its thick double-walls of unmortared boulder, and little skylight deep in the hip of the thatch, and broad unhammered lintel, and the steps of stone set in so that we could ascend and sit on the broad grass verge — for there were no eaves on the old houses — and watch the hens by the rhubarb, and the grumpy cow, and finger the netting and weighted rope that kept the thatch snug, the ropes anchored on the wee pole at the top of the hip.

And still, in those days of twenty years ago, days of Heath and Wilson, one or two of the old houses occupied; one on this street, by the far end out the road, and one away to the sea, at the far end of the Baile an Stigh. Where a fire still burned to warm old fingers; where they would sit, the couples, by the wireless or with the Bible, and where they lived at the end of their streets and the end of the world of the old Gaels.

All gone.

Iain Og, that Maclean from Uig of the hills to the south, from the eighteenth century, who was evicted by the minister of the place for poaching deer, and set in a boat with all that was his; so he waded up the coast, an open boat on the coastal swell, and came to Shawbost, and settled there; and his son, Murchadh Iain Og, that kept the Shawbost croft, and went away to the fishing, and came back with a wife from Fraserburgh that had not a word of Gaelic (now there was a scandal) and you can still see the stone folds and shielings he made for sheep by the back of the Beinn, though they say herself was useless at the crofting, and there was a song made about that which old men have in Shawbost yet; and his son, Angus Maclean, who was granted a fine new croft in Park Shawbost, when that tack was divided a hundred and fifty years ago, and built dykes about his wide acre, and the old house on which I played; and his son, Malcolm Maclean, that built the new old house at the end of the old old house, with gable and felt roof and an upstairs, that was an elder in the church, and precentor too, and we have a photograph of him by Dr Norman, the Bible open in his lap, and shaded eyes looking at you over the beard, herself beside him in white lace, and daughters behind and granddaughter before and a cat on the ledge of the window.

And his son, Murdo, my grandfather, that was in the Great War as a gunner on the trawlers, and was then all over the world, to Singapore and Australia, and Hong Kong, but most of all to Canada and America; always he kept in touch with home, and sent money, and once a ham from Belfast, and then he came back and married Mary with the broad lovely face and blue eyes, and wanted to go to America for good, but she would not. But he had saved much money in America, and so he bought a bus; the chassis came on the boat from Kyle, and Stornoway craftsmen fashioned a timber body, and he prospered in the carriage of people and tweeds, and bought another bus, and a lorry — a great lorry, with tailgate and hydraulic tipper — and built the big house.

It was of Dalbeg granite, roughcast and whitewashed, with solid walls, set well away from the road and facing south, fashioned by men of Ness with a loan from the Board, of stout timber and tiled roof and mighty windows and sturdy doors; and it is there yet, renovated, with pink pebbledash, the house of my uncle the minister on the other side of the island, and still a haven from wind and land.

My grandfather, who was very old when I was small, round and stolid and not to be trifled with; but he stirred black treacle into his porridge each morning, a ritual of relish, and he would pull funny faces for me, and occasionally would sing in a craggy baritone, "Oh, it's nice to get up in the morning, But it's better to stay in bed." Once I ran in with a huge one-clawed crab a disappointed lobsterman had left on the shore, still alive, and I clutched a leg or two triumphantly and dangled it before Grandpa, and he raised his hands in mock-terror. "Oooh, oooh..."

All gone. The old houses, levelled for nearly a decade, broken down by Council labourers; demolished because they were a hazard to sheep and children, and unsightly. The lorry with the hydraulic tipper, sold to Domhnull Easy the car-trader, who is now Convener of the Comhairle; it rusts at Bragar, a store for creels and boxes. And my grandfather and grandmother, and all their fathers and mothers: they lie at Lionagaidh.

Past Loch an Duna, splashing below the road, with its rubble of broch, and into Bragar: past one or two good houses, to Doune Bragar with its sleazy council-houses and bad reputation — a drunkard in that house, ne'er-do-well youths in those houses, girls of easy virtue in the place they call "Red Square". And then, a little beyond, turning left and down to the sea, the road to Lionagaidh.

Bragar falls behind as I walk, the wind now coming at an angle to me, no longer shrieking in my ears. An older better Bragar, or its remnants, lies about: a byre with the thatch still intact, two men gathering sheep, the clean ruins of old homes set by their crofts. Labost to my left, in the southern shore, its Decca mast knifing the sky. And the Atlantic before me, down the road.

This road is narrow, the tarmac a little broken: grass and docken grow in the middle. Down, down. The crofters straighten and stare; we raise hands in greeting. The road goes down into a dip, and then up again; you think you are about to walk straight into the sea, but then you come over the blind summit, and the last descent to the bottom, where the waves pound a stony beach, and the cemetery road turns quickly right, along a low sea wall, weaving up a few hundred yards to the gates of the walled burial ground: as I come to this turning I see the burdocks, that bastard rhubarb, which grows high on these slopes in summer, but now slumps in the slime of its fall.

Lionagaidh.

There is a Gaelic song about this burial-ground, modern and sentimental: *Tom a Shearrach*, or The White Foal's Hillock. It was written by a Bragar man who had gone off to Glasgow and done well; he had retired as a senior policeman. "Lay me by my first love," he trills in conclusion, "by the white bed beside the sea."

But Lionagaidh is open, without shelter or cover and precious little whiteness, on a headland by Port Mhor Bragar, where the sea boils angrily at the cliffs, and the spray foams over the crags by the road. It is not pretty, not immediately warm; it has not the numinous beauty of other Lewis cemeteries, not the drama of Dalmore nor the mystery of Habost. But, unlike these, it is very, very old. Some say it was the dwelling of earliest Lewis man, for Iron Age pottery has been found here, and other relics of primitive times, and there is the ancient church in the corner, Teampuill Eoin.

A tiny chapel. It stands in the original corner of the ground; the whole park is enclosed by dry-stone dyke, save for a modern (and scarcely used) annexe at the back. Little remains of Teampuill Eoin except a little gable, with a hint of alcove, and three low crumbling walls. Mortar has been dabbed here and there to preclude further disintegration. But you could scarcely put a car in these precincts; it is more of a cell than a church, perhaps the sanctuary of a Celtic mystic, for it has stood for many centuries. Perhaps he celebrated here with the bread and wine; maybe, in some forgotten cranny, he hid paten and chalice. For those were the days of invasion, rape and conquest; the strangers from over the seas, the warriors of Norway, who battered at these western islands towards the end of the Dark Ages, who gave Lewis much of her blood and villages (like Bragar) their names. But not their language: they set their stamp on places, these adventurers, and found themselves women and clawed themselves land, and settled, and bred — yet Gaelic, at the last, subsumed them.

This part of the cemetery is not tended. There are some modern stones here — minor community gentry from last century, some casualties from the Great War, and the *Iolaire*; I must yet talk of the *Iolaire*. But most of the graves are anonymous; some are marked with little boulders or slabs set edge on into the ground and that bear no inscription, the great majority not marked at all and utterly forgotten. Here, for perhaps a thousand years, the people of this west have buried their dead, in the holy shade of Teampuill Eoin, and when the land was full they would dig again, and again, grave upon grave, dead upon dead, era upon era, so that now in all the rabbit-diggings and bare sandy soil of this corner of Lionagaidh, there lie exposed fragments of bone, smashed and churned into the earth by generations gone.

In summer the grass grows over; the nettles stand shoulder-high, and you cannot clamber about here as I clamber now. But this is autumn, cold, the nettles black and the grass going brown, and I glance at the horizon for fear of another shower, and I step through the lost graves and into the heart of the modern cemetery, where the turf is neatly cut, and there are paths, and the burials organised by township — here South Shawbost, there North Bragar, and that the graves of Arnol — neat rows of granite headstones, proud, lonely.

I am crouching to read the inscription over some long-gone great uncle when a deep voice bubbles, "Well, is it all mystical enough for you?" and I jump with fright. I spring about. It is a cousin.

Oh, never mind which one. I have dozens of the things, first and second and third and fourth, removed and re-removed. I see them when I am home on the island. I bump into them in the city. I send a few deserving such a card at New Year. I giggle with the nearer ones at family weddings. Cousins are strange relations. You are rivals, like siblings, but the difference is that you have to love siblings. Mind you, I have cousins of whom I am very fond. This is not one of them.

"Oh," I say stupidly, "what a shock you gave me." I straighten, meeting his eyes. They are grey, cold, unblinking. He is tall, this cousin. The blood-tie with him is very distant. He is a mainlander, anyway, who rolls his "r"s and stops his "t"s. The last time we met, in some grim student flat, we parted in mutual loathing. It occurs to me that I cannot even remember his name, though I could take a stab at that of his grandfather.

"You shouldn't be all alone in Gothic burial-grounds," says the Cousin, grinning at me. "You never know what you might meet."

I am afraid. I am afraid of him. I do not know why. I sense that there is something wrong. He should not be here. This is not his world. When I last met this fellow, he was a particularly odious nineteen-year-old who thought me quite mad. When I last saw him in the street somewhere, it was a Sabbath morning and I was heading for church. He was not. He was out with a girl on his arm and making for the park, though he had at least the grace to blush.

But why is he now so white? Why does he turn his head to look at me, and away, and around, without ever moving his eyes?

This is Lionagaidh; in the realm of the dead. So near the cliffs. The cruel cliffs. "He went out into the night after that," ran innumerable stories of village horror — after the fight, the betrayal, the breaking-off — "towards the cliffs . . . of course, the body was never found." With an effort I hide my fear; I treat him as real and unthreatening.

"I could meet worse," I say jocularly. "You look human enough to me. And how's herself? Her first time on the island?"

"She's not here."

"Lovers' tiff?"

He says nothing. I remember his name now. I plug him into place on my mental map; I do swift calculations. I compute that our last mutual ancestor died in 1900.

"Our last mutual ancestor died in 1900," I say, "and I dare say she's here somewhere."

"And I dare say you know where she is, but don't show off." He slots his hands casually in the pockets of his jacket, which would make him look like a chipmunk if he were not so big, and glances at the sky, and casually inquires, "Well, what are you doing here?"

"Och, like you said — refuelling on mysticism. Getting a bit of atmosphere."

"Just as well," says the Cousin, "if you're still smoking these things."

I flick my cigarette towards America. The wind whisks it off to the mainland. "Fuel, you silly fellow. That's what a writer is. I'm a machine for converting nicotine and caffeine into prose. Anyway, I'll stop before I die."

"Death isn't so bad, when you get used to it," says the Cousin, with a curious solemnity. I overlook the bad joke, and continue, "Anyway, right now I'm working up a book."

"Oh? What's it called? *Write Your Way To Terminal Cancer?*"

I choose to ignore this remark. "*No Great Mischief If You Fall,*" I say importantly, "that's what I'm calling it." He stares. The phrase means nothing to him. "You see, it's a quote from General Wolfe — Wolfe of Quebec. He had been Cumberland's adjutant, or something, at Culloden. He was only eighteen then. And they asked him — in Canada, I think — where were good sturdy men for recruiting into the forces. And he said, 'The Highlanders. They are a hardy and intrepid race, and no great mischief if they fall'."

The Cousin snorts. I am not sure if it is General Wolfe that annoys him, or myself. Perhaps he does not understand.

"Exploitation, you see. The Highlanders in modern history — as victims, as fodder, utilities . . . always expendable, just pawns in other men's schemes . . ."

"It's too long," says the Cousin. He smiles; not pleasantly. "You should shorten it, John. You can always call it" — and he pauses, pretending to be lost in mystical thought — "I know. *Pawn Cocktail.*"

I feel my jaw clench. "Very funny, ha-ha. But it is a very serious . . ."

"Yes," says the Cousin, and lectures me in governessy tone, "very serious. A typical Macleod production. Calamity, disaster, catastrophe. *Eich, eich, eich, bhobh, bhobh, bhobh,* like some old Lewis granny with awful rheumatics. How very Teuch. Like those silly Mod songs. Always about the '45, or the Clearances, or unrequited love…Come to think of it, often all three."

"I know, cousin," says myself. "Celtic Twilight, Patience MacStrong. But not this book. This is a serious quest for our spiritual inheritance!"

"*Your* inheritance," says he, with sudden vehemence.

"Ours, surely," I say, faintly rattled. For have we not the same background, the same people, the same kirk? Did we not see birth in the same landscape, that great mass of mountain and moor and forest that is the Highlands and Islands, almost a third of the British landmass, and with a smaller population than the average London borough? The fracture-points of our history: the year of Charlie, of the great Rising, and the failure, and the savageries that followed? Genocide and emigration, and forced emigration, for sheep, for deer, to the colonies, to the great southern slums? And the struggle to survive in a culture despised and forgotten, its language suppressed, its landscape ravished, and the people themselves scattered like birds before the guns?

Survivors, who remained. But survivors burdened with inculcated inadequacies, their ruinous pride broken, the merry chuckle of their arts distorted and denied; who divided amongst themselves, who became the most vicious foes of each other. And though at last the worms turned, and wrought concessions, and won a wee victory or two, what were they but subjects of a smiling but haughty empire? From warriors to ghillies. From kinsmen to cannon-feed. From my land, your land, to a view; a park; a reservation; a rocket-range.

But still we toiled for the tide to turn.

"You are a fool, cousin," I say, "if you deny what you are. You remember the rock from which you were hewn. You remember your people and your place. You have roots here. There's many in the world would give much for such roots."

"Turnips," says the Cousin, and smirks. He tucks his hands in the pockets of his coat, and looks to the sky.

My temper is going. I must not lose my temper. I force a smile. "But you didn't tell me yet what you're doing here yourself."

The head declines, and he looks at me, and there is something in those eyes, something of incredible hostility, and emptiness.

"Come on," I coax. "Why, if you're really nice to me, I might even use you for a literary device . . ."

He strides suddenly away, over the park, up the slope, into the Shawbost graves. I puff after him, determined to win this one. "History," I snarled, "the past . . . if you don't understand it, boy, and what it's done to us, then you will surely repeat it."

He stops. He turns. Eyes blazing, like chips of grey-green ice, eyes of loathing. "That is your tragedy," he says, in low lethal tones, "and the tragedy of all you people, in the old paths. Always in the past. Always, but always, churning over and brooding on and scheming in the past." He laughs. "Yours included. And I don't wonder."

He is gone, into the cold air of the day, the clouds racing overhead. Shafts of sunlight slicing into the sea. I blink uneasily, and the shower comes suddenly battering. I dash for the gate and to shelter in the lee of the shed, wedging uncomfortably in a half-crouch, the water dripping off jacket and wicking into my trousers. I feel, suddenly, very stupid. And very afraid.

CHAPTER ONE

Culloden

The world of the Gael has languished because it has never made a state. For many centuries the Highlanders have existed on the fringe of several worlds: as far-flung possessions of Norway and the Norsemen, as an itching nuisance at the edge of the grubby Scottish kingdom, as barbarians that might threaten Britannia and her Teutonic monarchy, and at the last — for the culture, when you think of it, the language and the music and the agronomy and the society, held up remarkably well — they have been slowly crushed to conformity in the modern, centralised, overgoverned Britain of the last hundred and fifty years.

It was not always thus. There was a day when Scottish kings spoke Gaelic; but James IV was the last, and (in high irony) Portree, the port of kings, is named for his son James V, who dropped by on a Highland slumming-tour. But Margaret, that sinister Saxon, consort of Malcolm Canmore, had romanised the faith of the country, turning Scots away from the Celtic church and its oddly presbyterian values, abandoning the warm ideals of Iona. And the Lords of the Isles, those mighty chiefs of Clan Donald who were the last to give Gaeldom some unity of leadership, could never establish total sovereignty on the western seaboard. The kings in Edinburgh detested them, and laboured to destroy them; and the saga of grubby tricks employed, tactics of hostages and blackmail and divide-and-rule — it was then that the Campbells of Argyll, those scum of Highland history, became great — is a wearying one.

You can see fracture-points in all this, those moments when history turns and changes all irrevocably. The Synod of Whitby in 664 AD anticipated Margaret, and would bring all Christendom in the British Isles under the Roman whip, the mainland turning its back on the spirituality of Columba, the wisdom of the isles and Ireland. The Gaels had made Scotland, the great Gaels of Ireland that had come to Argyll, to Dalriada; they unified the landmass, and subjugated her peoples, and gave her a dynasty. There was not then a sense of Highlanders as people apart.

But by 1380, after Margaret, after Walter the Steward (whose children's time would come), an Aberdeenshire priest could write, "The Highlanders and people of the islands, however, are a savage and untamed race, rude and independent, given to rapine, ease-loving, clever and quick to learn, comely in person but unsightly in dress, hostile to the

English people and language and, owing to this diversity of speech, even to their own nation." They were also, he said primly, exceedingly cruel.

A battle once known to every Gaelic bard, and of which scarcely a schoolchild in Scotland has ever heard, was fought at Harlaw in the priest's county, in the summer of 1411. One Donald, Lord of the Isles, moved to add the rich lands of Ross to his dominions. Scotland's boy-king, James I, was a prisoner in England. His uncle, Duke of Albany, was regent: he had designs on the Earldom of Ross himself, for the little female heir was his ward. And so Donald marched from Morvern, and against the Scots executive; Inverness fell to him, and then he crossed the Spey, scything through the north-east, to Harlaw by Inverurie. There the Earl of Mar was waiting, northern hit-man for Albany.

Donald was a grandson of a Scots king. He was the pre-eminent power in the Highlands, and feared across the Scottish landmass; he came from a line of brave men and doughty fighters. "What did he seek at Harlaw?" asks James Hunter rhetorically in *Scottish Highlanders: A People And Their Place*. "Perhaps he aspired to rule all Scotland — if not in his own right, then possibly with the absent King's tacit connivance, as regent in Albany's stead. That, of course, is speculation. But what is certain is that victory that day for Donald would once more have enhanced the influence and status of Scotland's Gaelic-speaking people."

Donald lost. A monument at Harlaw today commemorates burgesses of Aberdeen who were drafted to serve with Mar "against the caterans". A cateran, says Hunter, was "a freebooter, a bandit . . . The Gaels were considered aliens now in Aberdeen; uncouth and uncivilised aliens at that." And the boy-king, James I, would come into his own and begin the final destruction of the Lordship of the Isles, the polity of the Gaels. The Mac-Donalds did win Ross. But renewed power over the north-east Lowlands, and even central Scotland — once theirs, so briefly a possibility at Harlaw — was denied them. The Lords of the Isles could hope only to defend themselves against the encroaching might and ways of the south. In 1460, feeling vulnerable, one even made a formal agreement with England's King Edward IV. Its benefits never materialised, but now the Scottish Crown could arraign him as a traitor. James IV would destroy the family of Argyll. He would forfeit the lands. He would jail the Lord himself. And the Lordship, then and to this day, was contemptuously appended to the courtesy titles of the heir to the throne.

Much remained (and still, in echo, remains) in the Lowland Scots world of the Gaelic input. An essential egalitarianism, for one; there were no class-tensions here, nor peasants' revolts, and the bloody battles and vendettas were between dynasties and princelings, not social groups. But Margaret, and Walter, and that trendy vicar John of Fordun, presided over a shift, a cracking. The Gaels had become *different*, quaint — rather amusing, my dear, aren't they? — but also alien, other, perhaps very dangerous. Different tribes: Highlander and Lowlander moved apart on different roads, to bloody rendezvous on the bog of Culloden.

We have made too much of the Stewarts — or Stuarts, as the later line styled themselves — in our Scotland. A stateless nation has seized on the luckless race for props and ikons, as kings and queens and princes that were once our own. Shortbread and liqueur-makers plaster their tartan-bedecked images on tins and bottles. From Sir Walter Scott, through an ongoing succession of literary midgets, the history of the Stuarts and their unhappy realm has been reduced to a pageant of cute stories. Hugely complex events are reduced to the sugary gloop of Hollywood legend. The role of religion is distorted and belittled; her finest minds in Scotland dismissed as gloomy bigots, tiresome thunderers. The horrendous political philosophies, the absurd will-to-power that stalked the dynasty from birth to fall, are scarcely understood.

Queen Mary, that inadequate and completely passive ping-pong ball amidst the currents of Reformation, has become the strange Mary-Queen-of-Scots, gorgeous and fragile, wronged by all and quite without sin, whom nasty John Knox reduced to tears. (Contemporary records show she gave as good as she got.) Charles I is the Martyr King, for whom High Anglicans to this day hold soft Mass. Charles II we are taught to regard as a cheerful old rascal, like a randy uncle who pinches the maid on the bottom; not as the treacherous and syphilitic traitor he was. James VII had "piety for a disease"; but then, he had mistresses of such ugliness that a bishop could wickedly wonder aloud if the King's priests had prescribed them as a penance. His son, warming-pan baby James Francis Edward, Old Pretender, the "best king we never had": a dark melancholic who alienated his sons and brought his wife to insanity.

And Charlie. My Darling. Young Chevalier. "We will meet in the palace of St James yet." Lochaber No More. Will Ye No Come Back Again, tra-la. Innumerable images, tableaux, slushy songs and improbable gallantries clutter his place in the Scottish psyche.

The Stewarts (the spelling was changed by Mary, who married her cousin Henry Stuart, and took on his French spelling) were the seed of Walter the High Stewart. He married Marjorie, daughter of Robert the Bruce that was perhaps the greatest leader this country will ever see. Her son duly took the Scottish throne as King Robert II, for David III — Bruce's son — died childless. And so the line went on, on the throne, off the throne, on two thrones and three thrones, on and off, from triumph to tragedy and disaster to debacle, to end on the edge of our own era in a mincing homosexual prelate who collected antiques.

There are only three things that need to be said about the Stewarts. In the first place, they were highly charismatic, endowed with good looks and poise and dash, and though they had the occasional breakdown (like that repulsive pedant, James VI) they could, right to the last, long after history had despairingly discarded them, rouse thousands of men to march forth and die for their honour and cause. In the second — famously — they were incredibly, appallingly, quite supernaturally unlucky.

Poor pregnant Marjorie fell from her horse, gave birth to Robert, and promptly died. Robert II was a weak silly fellow bedevilled by his sons. Robert III, lame from youth, once described himself cheerfully as "the worst of kings and the most wretched of men in the whole realm". His son James I was a prisoner in the Tower of London on accession — after a reasonably competent reign on return, he was messily murdered in Perth.

The Stewarts, and Scotland, suffered a long succession of child-monarchies, regencies and entailed instability. James II was six — grew up, killed by an exploding cannon. James III was eight — grew up, overthrown and murdered with the connivance of his heir. He was James IV, fourteen, quite a geriatric. A rather good reign was abruptly ended when he went to war on brother-in-law Henry VIII and fell with Scotland's finest at Flodden. James V was one year old. He combined Stuart guile with Tudor obstinacy; hugely unpopular, he died miserably after the battle of Solway Moss in 1542.

Mary was seven days old. She duly became Mary-Queen-of-Scots and had her head chopped off. Her story needs no retelling; by the time of her execution at Fortheringay she had been deposed and in exile for nearly twenty years. Her son sat on the throne of Scotland, and made some show of annoyance.

It is fashionable to describe King James VI as one of the best Scottish monarchs, whose competent rule and sagacious cunning in the things of state are overshadowed by his less successful rule in England. It is debatable, though he was certainly one of the best educated kings, being taught from infancy by sensible Presbyterian sages. James was but a few months old when his mother was deposed; the diminutive sovereign was raised by nurses and good Protestant tutors, though they did not always grant the child the respect he felt he deserved. Once a horrified courtier heard the boy howling after a vigorous spanking; was this the way, the man demanded, to treat the Lord's anointed? The master snorted, "I have skelpt his airse; you may kiss it if you like!"

James was very clever, very well read, and replete with natural slyness. He also overate, overdrank, stammered badly, slobbered at the table and dribbled in bed. He wrote learned and weighty monographs on everything from theology to smoking, and also (an omen) on the divine right of kings. James was a homosexual, a state which — if it is not a contradiction in terms — seems to have been a hereditary weakness in the Stuart line: James III had gone in for low-life rent-boys. His great-great-grandson was seduced by a French princeling at the age of thirteen; in London senescence, his cooing over choice favourites caused James VI much trouble. For yes, in 1603 Queen Elizabeth died, the last of the Tudors, and off sped James VI for London to become James I of England, and he never came back. He had little time for his native land — nor, come to think of it, any apparent affection for the one he inherited — and for the Gaels he felt only scorn and loathing. Still, though he knew little of their land, he thought it might be useful.

James set his eye to the "store of fischeingis" in the Minch, and dreamed of colonisation. He gave the remarkable opinion that the soil of Lewis was more fertile than any to be found on the mainland (and if that sounds stupid, scarcely less ridiculous pronouncements are made on the Highland economy today) and he decided to set "planters" on the island, as he later — with more success — put on Ireland. Clever and resourceful chaps from the Lowlands would be established on Lewis; they would take possession of the land, and if the natives were too vociferous in their objections the heroes had the King's leave to eliminate them.

The tale of the Fife Adventurers — for they were mostly down-on-their-luck sprogs of that county — is tangled and confused. Suffice to say that the whole project ground to a halt in the peat of Lewis. The islanders rose nearly to a man against it. Macleods resisted and did battle until the intruders were driven out, with many thanks to the Mackenzies of Kintail, who had begun to take deep interest in the Long Island; to no-one's very great surprise, save the Macleods, they eventually took possession of Lewis for themselves.

It was a classic Stuart folly. It bore witness to James' low opinion of Highland people and culture, and his cheap disregard for human life. But that was the third thing about the Stuarts — they had nothing but antipathy for the Gaels, their race and tongue. The Fife Adventurers fiasco was only the latest in a succession of schemes and plots against the far-flung tribes of the north and west. Some of Edinburgh's royal pronouncements ordered no less than common genocide. In the very year that James inherited the English throne, 1603, the kingdom in which he would defy family tradition and die in his bed at a good old age, a shocking proscription was passed against the clan MacGregor.

"It was enacted," writes Prebble in *Glencoe*, "that no man, under pain of death, might call himself MacGregor, nor his children and his children's children unborn. If he did so use that name he could be killed like a beast at the wayside, with all his lands and possessions forfeit to his killer . . . Death was the sentence if more than four of Clan Gregor met together, if they possessed any other weapon than a blunt knife to cut their meat, but only, said the Law in its clemency, if they persisted in calling themselves MacGregor . . . Many . . . died in brutish killings, or of starvation, cold and despair. Later Acts dealt with the branding and transportation of MacGregor women, and the Lords of the Privy Council discussed (and finally abandoned) a proposal to send all their children to Ireland . . . the lands they had once held passed to the Campbells of Glen Orchy who had been most active in executing Letters of Fire and Sword upon them. Nearly two centuries later the penal Acts against Clan MacGregor were still on the Statute Book, in the adult lifetime of Tom Paine, Edmund Burke and William Wilberforce."

From Finlaggan to Glen Fruin to Glen Orchy to — shortly — Glen Coe; race-murder masquerading as regrettable political necessity, commanded by a repellant old king playing at social engineering. But he died, at last, in 1625. And soon his house had other need of the Gaels.

Charles I was the last monarch to be born in Scotland, at Dunfermline, in 1600. His elder brother, Henry, died young; a pity, for the lad was well spoken of, and seems to have had gifts and sharpness lacking in the new heir. Charles I is a puzzle. He was a man of great personal piety. Uniquely for a Stuart, he reserved all his passions for his wife. He patronised the arts, commissioning or collecting some of the finest paintings of that generation.

Like his father, however, he took exception to the inconvenient democracies of Scottish Presbyterianism: both Charles and James were convinced Erastians, convinced that the Crown should be head of the Church, as was so acceptably the case in England. But Charles I lacked the old man's political aptitude, and was peculiarly stubborn; his wife, Queen Henriette Maria, was a French-born Catholic of the most pernicious variety. Repeatedly he tried to impose English episcopacy and English-style liturgy on the Scots: triggering first a riot, then the drama of the National Covenant, and finally two brief but vicious wars. Even as Charles wrestled to restore his grip on affairs north of the border, England itself revolted against him.

The Scots, even the Covenanters, were despite all, deeply attached to the monarchy and to the House of Stuart. But the Covenanters, groping towards the modern, were already formulating revolutionary new concepts: that Christ alone was head of the Church, and that the King must be under the law and not above it. After much agonising, the Covenanters cast in their lot with the English Parliamentarians after extracting assurances that the new order would establish a national Presbyterian church across the three kingdoms. Thus came the deliberations that produced the Westminster Confession of Faith (1647), ratified by Parliament in 1649 and again in 1690, still the central creed of Scottish Presbyterianism but made for a body that would never be.

Not all the Covenanters, however, put Christ before Crown. James Graham, Marquis of Montrose, repudiated the Covenant — the copy he signed hangs today in the Free Church College — and scurried into the Highlands to raise the glens for his sovereign. Montrose, so beloved of Scots romanticism, was a brilliant soldier grossly overrated as a human being. The army he assembled won some spectacular victories — at Inverlochy in 1648 Montrose and his men capped an extraordinary forced march by night over the hills with a devastating assault on the Argyll-led Covenanters, scattering the force with minimal losses — but contained unsavoury elements: assorted thugs, freebooters and very nasty Irish mercenaries.

Charles I, defeated and jailed, was at length tried and executed by the Cromwellian regime in 1649. Even the Covenanters were revolted; the beheading shocked Scottish opinion. All now flocked to a nationalist cause: the young Charles II was crowned at Scone — homologating enough Presbyterian formulae and catechisms to sink a seminary — and the Scots marched. Cromwell duly arrived at Dunbar and clobbered them. Another Scots-dominated army lost at Worcester (1651) and Charles II fled to France.

Cromwell occupied Scotland and governed it with grim competence for the rest of his life: he had little sympathy with Presbyterianism (being a Congregationalist) but spared the Scots the savagery he unleashed on the Irish. No arrangements, however, were made for succession. After his death his son governed miserably for a year or so, and the wily General Monck plotted, and in 1660 Charles II was invited to return.

No Stuart King was more debauched, more vicious or more unscrupulous than the Merry Monarch. But he was a past master at self-preservation. He had also conceived a deep loathing for the Scots and their democratic religion. Again — but this time with the fully savagery of the sword, the stake and the thumbscrew — the British state moved to impose episcopalian religion on the people of Scotland. The "Killing Times" — 1660 to 1688 — saw not only the torture and slaughter of thousands who sought only the freedom to worship God in their own way, but the incompetent rule of court-appointed commissioners, and a deep recession. Remote from the centre of power, cut off from the markets, governed by martinets (such as James, Duke of York, Charles' brother and later James VII) and ravaged by death-squads, it was perhaps the darkest and most miserable episode in Scottish history.

Charles II had many bastards, but no legitimate children. (His wife is often dismissed as barren, but by the time he married Queen Catherine syphilis had almost certainly rendered him sterile.) So James was his heir: a gloomy, stubborn, introspective man of some administrative talent but precious little common sense. Worse, James had reverted to Roman Catholicism, much influenced by his mighty mother. When Charles died in 1685 (receiving Roman rites at his last gasp) a nervous country consoled themselves in the knowledge that James at least had no male heir. Both his daughters, Mary and Anne, were Protestant.

This did not stop the Marquis of Argyll raising revolt on behalf of the Duke of Monmouth, illegitimate son of Charles II and ferociously Protestant (though, being Anglican, he shed Covenanting blood with much enthusiasm). The revolt collapsed at the battle of Sedgemoor (1686) and both lost their heads. James VII and II, for the moment secure, now sought to claim his realms for Mother Church. His bid to legislate for religious tolerance would, he hoped, placate Presbyterians as much as it would delight Catholics. But Stuart credibility in Scotland was at its nadir. When James' queen, Mary of Modena, unexpectedly delivered a healthy baby boy in 1688, the nation was swept by panic. Princess Mary and her husband, William of Orange, stood disinherited. At the invitation of anxious Protestants and Parliamentarians, the Prince of Orange sailed for England with a token force. He may not have sought the crown for himself, but rather to insist on a Protestant succession; he certainly had no designs on the life of his father-in-law. But James panicked. He packed up and fled the country with wife and baby, and handed England to William on a platter.

The "Glorious Revolution" was swift and bloodless. The English flocked with delight to the cause of William and Mary: Parliament drafted a new settlement, including a Bill of Rights. The Scots hesitated. A Convention assembled in Perth early in 1690 to consider the position: a letter of such insolence came from the exiled James that they promptly settled for William.

Such was lowland Scotland. The Highlanders, or at least their chiefs, rose for James: Viscount Graham of Claverhouse, that "Bonnie Dundee" of sickly song, led them to battle. These supporters of James (in Latin *Jacobus*, hence "Jacobite") won a smashing victory in the pass of Killiecrankie, but the death of Claverhouse in the action left them leaderless. The forces dispersed.

And so history marched against the house of Stuart. Irish revolt came to nothing. (William marched to the Boyne with the Pope's blessing.) Scotland was forced to heel: the MacDonalds of Glencoe were massacred, in a meagre but infamous slaughter, *pour encourager les autres*. Scottish aspirations collapsed in the swamp of Darien. Parliament wrote James and his baby son out of the succession, conferring the throne — in the event of no surviving heirs from the Princess Anne — to the seed of the Electress Sophia, first cousin of Charles and James, matriarch of the House of Hanover. James died in France in 1701, exhorting his son to adhere to the holy Catholic faith. William died the following year. Scotland entered into the Union of 1707, for the sake of open markets. Anne died in 1714, having survived all her thirteen children, so fat that her coffin was almost square.

And so George I, Elector of Hanover, became King. He could not even speak English, addressing ministers in a curious dog-Latin. At least three dozen others lived who were nearer the throne in strict primogeniture than he. But law was now King, the law of Parliament and Constitution. As the Whig Ascendancy built a new world of capitalism, the Crown fast declined in importance.

James Francis Edward, the Old Pretender, for a time dreamed and schemed. Louis XIV had proclaimed him as "James III and VIII" in 1701. But the continental powers had no real interest in a Stuart restoration: for Spain or France, Jacobite hopes were useful in fuelling internal British revolts that might tie down her arms. And these risings were beaten, again and again, by human and providential factors — sudden howling storms, leaked intelligence to government, military incompetence, Jacobite cowardice, and sheer ill luck. Of all the scutter of risings between 1701 and 1745, only those of 1715 and 1719 had any significance. But for an astonishing lack of leadership, the '15 — which had all Scotland at its feet, and generated great support in northern England — would have swept James onto the throne. Yet his commander, the Earl of Mar, dilly-dallied in Perth and let the whole thing slide away. The '19 involved Spanish troops, a landing in Kintail and Rob Roy MacGregor; it collapsed almost immediately in the battle of Glen Shiel, and Eilean Donan Castle was reduced to ruins.

James fled France for Rome, where he lodged as a pensioner of the Pope; a huge publicity coup for Hanover. He now resolved to make babies. After a succession of hair-raising adventures, a Polish princess — Clementina Sobieski — was safely delivered to her wedding in Rome. A year later, on 31st December 1720, she produced a prince. The child was named Charles Edward Louis John Casimir Silvester Severino Maria Stuart.

Scots have never rationally assessed the hero of the '45. Charles Edward Stuart is popularly prettified and romanticised: a powerful selling tool of the tourist industry. Intellectuals, naturally, have reacted against this tradition. For most of our own era — at least, until the advent of such historians as Frank McLynn and Bruce Lenman — Charles Edward has been deplored as an egotistical and irresponsible popinjay who roused the Highlands to march in his suicidal folly.

But Charles Edward was a very gifted man. To be sure, he was no Scot: he was half-Polish and half-Italian, and spoke English with a strange Irish-Continental brogue. His spelling was atrocious; he was probably dyslexic. He had, undoubtedly, grave weaknesses of personality. He lacked the patience for diplomacy, the gifts of negotiation in a hostile arena. He could not abide the crossing of his will. He was quite unable — and this shows repeatedly in his career — to relate to elder father-figures. His relationship with his own father was appalling; after 1744, he never saw him again. Charles' childhood had been miserable. His mother, neurotic and unstable, fought epic battles with her husband and finally retreated into a convent to starve herself to death. His younger brother grew up introverted, effeminate and homosexual.

But Charles was very handsome. (He is ill-served by his most famous portrait, which actually shows him as a boy of twelve.) He was tall and supremely fit; only someone of exceptional athleticism could have survived the post-Culloden privations. He was a fine horseman and a superb shot, able to bring down birds on the wing, time after time, with the crude flintlocks of the day. He spoke French and Italian and Spanish, all fluently. By the end of his crusade in Scotland he had mastered Gaelic. He liked tennis and badminton. He played the cello, well. He enjoyed theatre and opera; he had vast reserves of physical courage, dash, style and optimism. There was but one accomplishment lacking that nearly cost him dear: the Prince never learned to swim. And, even in adolescence, he showed a worrying taste for alcohol.

Yet, after the stubborn futility of the grandfather, and the descent into sanctimonious pessimism of the father, here now was one of sufficient impudence and oomph to inspire the Jacobites. And the young man who at length, after much frustration and difficulty, landed on the shores of Eriskay on 3rd August 1745, was embarked on no rash adventure. However irrational or ill-considered his aspirations may have been, he succeeded in launching a crusade that came to pose a threat to Britain's ruling establishment and order unmatched until 1940, and perhaps not even then; a crusade that came within a turn of success, and that drew deep from wells of frustration and anger in Scotland and the Highland hills.

Charles Edward Stuart, about 1744

The Highlands of 1745 remained a realm apart. The area had fully a third of Scotland's population. (Today it has not one-twelfth.) It was never, in any real sense, under the rule of law; the writ of Westminster ran not in the glens. As the new capitalist world wrought form, the Highlands remained a patrimonial order: not feudal, but patriarchal, the clan chiefs, with their heritable jurisdictions. To these magnates — Seaforth, and Cluny, and Macleod, and MacDonald — London left almost all aspects of government, administration and law, like the client-kings of ancient Rome.

The land was poor, and grossly overcrowded; even in 1748, after the slaughter, the Highlands and Islands held an estimated population of 652,000. Food was scarce, meagre and frequently expensive. Every visitor, without exception, wrote in shocked terms of the abundant poverty. The people lived in crude dry-stoned bothies; they worked thin land in common, and in winter when times were hard they might bleed their cattle and mix blood into their oatmeal. But they were sustained, in all their apparent misery, by the richness of their culture: songs, stories and music. Family and kinship were important to them.

It was a strange order, strikingly similar in many respects to that of pre-Second World War Japan. "Honour" was a powerful concept, that shed much blood. Highlanders were bound to the chief by supposed kinship, the belief in a common ancestor. This was, indeed, largely myth. Even before the '45 many chiefs showed precious little paternalism for their people: in 1739, MacDonald of Sleat and MacLeod of Dunvegan were caught arranging the capture and sale of tenantry as indentured labour for the West Indies. (Hence that shrewd man, Duncan Forbes of Culloden — to whom the Hanoverians owed everything in 1746, though they never thanked him — was able to blackmail them into staying out of Stuart aspirations.) The chiefs operated with savage efficiency: they had the power of pit and gallows, and used them. Yet they excited admiration from the south as "noble savages". A typical Highland chief spoke several languages — certainly English, Gaelic and French — sent his sons on the Grand Tour, drank fine port and claret and brandy, cultivated music and the arts, and dressed in grand apparel. Only the *plebs*, those without horses, wore the kilt; the chief wore tartan trews, and plaid, and buckled shoes, and jewels, and garters, and kerchiefs — he would "corruscate in green, yellow, blue and scarlet", writes McLynn acidly, "like a South American parakeet".

But the Highlands were run by tacksmen, the middle-tier in the hierarchy; they held large areas of land, and worked some themselves, and sub-let the rest. A tacksman's importance came in wartime. His kind were the officers of Highland armies, and it was their job to call men to the colours. He would order out his tenants, and if they showed reluctance he would fire the roof over their heads. There is no truth in the romantic view that the Gaels flooded gladly of their own will to the Stuart cause — but none either in the notion that they entered the '45 only for plunder.

The Highland remoteness from government, and this ability to produce a large army at the call of its chiefs, made it a favourite launching-pad for Jacobite operations — the English Jacobites, of course, having no such power to wield. Had all the pro-Jacobite clans come out in 1745, 30,000 men might have composed that host for Charlie, and it would surely have been unstoppable. For the Highlanders, though unruly, were brave and fearsome fighters. Their weapons were the broadsword (the true claymore, a massive two-handed thing, was long obsolete), the dirk and targe (a small leather shield), the pistol and Lochaber axe. There was also a psychological weapon: the bloodcurdling howl of the war cry. Highland warriors fired their pistols at the enemy, ducked to dodge the first musket-balls, cast aside pistols and raised targe and sword and flung themselves at the foe with a wild Gaelic scream. Many an army, even the cream of George II's, simply turned tail and ran before this onslaught. On territory that suited them — at the top of a rugged slope with the enemy below — Highlanders were formidable opponents.

Many forces fuelled Jacobitism in 1745. The Hanoverian monarch and royal family, Teutonic and stupid, were not popular; the Whig ascendancy in London was enmired in corruption. There was economic recession. In Scotland, a ruling clique ran an incredible web of patronage. Resentment against the Union was high; there were detested taxes, and tariffs, and customs-barriers. Some of the Union agreements had been blatantly broken. Scottish nationalism — a force, in truth, for which the exiled Stuarts had neither understanding nor sympathy — ran high. Add to this other powerful elements. Catholicism was of little account in Scotland — superstition was as much the Highland faith as Popery — but Episcopalianism had many adherents, long friends of the Stuart cause, and the north-east counties of Banffshire and Aberdeenshire were warmly Episcopalian and Jacobite. Yet it is important to stress the intense divisions of the Scots at this time: most were still devoutly Presbyterian, and viewed Rome with the same horror as Americans in 1950 viewed Communism. And many, probably the majority, prayed for the failure of the '45.

But the Highlands were, at least in sentiment, a Jacobite stronghold. Partly this was cultural: the '45 as the last desperate march of chiefs and men defending an old system and an old world, one that was already showing visible cracks: patriarchal tradition against modern efficiency. But this grew from real and practical issues, and the central problem — then, since, now, always — was the ownership and use and sharing of land.

The Highlands had a barter economy, with cattle as the soundest currency; this was under increasing threat from encroaching capitalism in Glasgow, Edinburgh and the south. But the short-term menace was that old villain, Clan Campbell. The Whig regime had made the Campbells great. It had also added to their impressive list of enemies. By 1745 Clan Campbell haters included the MacGregors, the Stuarts of Appin, the MacLeans of Duart, the Camerons of Lochaber, and the MacDonalds — all the MacDonalds. It was not merely a coalition of old scores that marked the Campbells down. Argyll was wading deep into land-reform. The second Duke had decided to create a new feudal order, abolishing the elements of patrimonial society. Old ways vanished. Papers and charters assigned land to individuals. The tacksmen were eliminated. All this was a naked threat to Highland tradition; one which might be infectious. Besides, the Campbells had much commerce with smaller clans: there was a clear pattern of debts to them by 1745 — which would be liquidated if the rising succeeded.

Romance may be forgotten. All who at length cast in their lot with Charlie — at least, the chiefs: mere men had no choice — gambled on his cause because it offered the chance of new fortunes and new standing, and could eliminate various unpleasant threats. Even so, they hedged their bets. "Gentle Lochiel" only joined up after he had secured financial guarantees from Charles if the rising failed — a promise, it must be said, the Prince honoured, for Lochiel in exile received a regiment paying much more than his Lochaber estates. Likewise Clanranald and others sought indemnity.

The dismal tale may be briefly told. The extraordinary truth is that, having raised the standard, all Charles Edward had to do to take Edinburgh and Scotland was to start walking. Hanoverian home-defences were in shocking disrepair. Repeated warnings from Duncan Forbes and the Scottish commander — Sir John Cope — had gone ignored. And the second Duke of Argyll's great leap forward, one the third Duke had begun too late to repair, had immobilised the mighty pro-Whig Campbell fighting machine. The tacksmen were gone; the system destroyed. For all their might in history, the house of Argyll played no part in the last drama of the '45.

After the '19, Marshal Wade had built magnificent roads for the better corralling of the Highlands. Charles Edward and his small army — a few thousands, short of monies and artillery, but in good heart and under the brilliant command of Lord George Murray — marched along these to Edinburgh. Already there was a price on his head; Forbes toiled night and day to threaten and cajole clans into quiescence, and Britain's armies were moving. But Cope, speedily trapped in the north, dashed for Inverness and shipped his forces to Aberdeen. One little strategem to open the gates of Edinburgh, and Scotland — to mingled glee, fear and incredulity — was Stuart once more.

For a few weeks Charles held court in Edinburgh. The dark Palace of Holyroodhouse rang again with dancing and cheers. It was the high point of his career, perhaps the happiest of his life. But Scotland was not enough. The Treaty of Union was now airily abolished by decree. A stubborn garrison and its bestial old commander were left unmolested in Edinburgh Castle, after he threatened to shell the city if supplies were stopped. Cope's army landed by sea at Dunbar and marched to Edinburgh: at Prestonpans, on 20th September, the Hanoverians sustained a humiliating defeat. Most of the army fled for their lives.

After much anxiety and whispering — what of the French aid which Charles had so gaily assured them was coming? — the Jacobites marched into England. On and on, with remarkable speed and discipline, with neither atrocity nor significant desertion, the army marched. Nearer and nearer, with Wade and the Duke of Cumberland — corpulent young son of George II — hopelessly at sea in the north, and the Jacobites found themselves in Derby. There was no significant opposition. All local militias thought better of battle. There were cheers, encouragement, some hospitality. But few rallied to the Stuart banner. No one appeared with armies or supplies. Billeting became difficult. And there was still no sign of the French.

It was perhaps the biggest single blunder of French foreign policy in that whole century not to appreciate the magnificent opportunity of the '45 — a chance on a plate to deal a shattering blow to their chief foreign rival. On 4th December the Prince and his men reached Derby. Unknown to them, no armed force lay between them and London. The city was only four days' march away. And it was already seized in panic. "There never was so melancholy a town . . . nobody but has some fear for themselves, for their money, or for their friends in the army . . . I still fear the rebels beyond my reason," wailed diarist Horace Walpole. For there was no enthusiasm to fight for the House of Hanover. All assembled forces of loyalty had melted away at the first prospect of serious action. George II himself wondered if he should call on Austria for help. And the French, at long last, now assembled an English invasion under Marshal Richelieu.

But of this the Jacobites knew nothing. Charles, young and happy, certain of success, had not stopped to carry his council. On the night of 5th December they demanded answers. Lord George Murray — whose relationship with the Prince was always brittle — painted a worst-case scenario, with every doubt in Hanoverian favour. An aghast council now learned from the Prince that he held no written guarantees from English or Welsh Jacobites, nor one from Louis XV. At a crucial moment, one Bradstreet was admitted to the room to tell of a third 9,000-strong army between Derby and London. There was no such army: Bradstreet was a spy.

And so the Prince was ordered to turn right round and march back home. Even then he could have done many things — gone over their heads to the clansmen, marched on alone — tactics that might have shamed his council into following. But the collective loss of nerve exploded only the demons of his soul. He lacked the psychological resources, the wiles, the belief in himself necessary to carry his cause. The Prince fell in with melodramatic bitterness. The following day, the rising made for home. And from then on, Charles Edward Stuart began to disintegrate as a human being.

"No-one," wrote a delighted Walpole, "is afraid of a rebellion that runs away."

An establishment breathed again. From cowardice, London and its rulers swung to vengeful hatred. When they caught up with this crew, terrible would be their judgement and most severe their deserts. Tired, hungry, demoralised, and with the smell of death already sinking over their whole crusade, the Jacobites marched back to Scotland. News of retreat reached Richelieu as he loaded his force at Boulogne: he paused, wondered, decided, and called the whole thing off.

Back to Scotland, by Glasgow, after a brief skirmish at Penrith: successful, but not the severe victory that might have been theirs if Charles had not insisted on headlong flight. Now, he hardly spoke to his commander. He slept late. He drank a great deal. Into Scotland, and to Falkirk: a battle with the force of Hawley, which again the Jacobites won, and again were not given the leadership to land a smashing blow on fleeing foes. And back, northwards, to Inverness, as Cumberland closed in, and cold winter became cruel spring: and Charles's incompetent Irish adjutants fumbled the commissariat, and more and more starving ragged men deserted. So Cumberland closed in, through Moray, to Nairn: and the Jacobites decided on a forced march and a night-attack. Too hungry, too weak, too slow: the dawn was high before the staggering force were within sight of Cumberland's tents. They were ordered to turn back. Charles, now almost insane with resentment and arrogance, countermanded the order. He was ignored. He trotted his horse alongside the men, berating them, his shrill voice proclaiming the utter doom of his cause, loud and demoralising.

CULLODEN: 26TH APRIL 1746

A crazy place for a Highland army, Drummossie Moor. A high plateau, smooth and level, with woods and a dyke that cramped the lines and blocked room for manoeuvre. There was a better place, the slopes by Clava, and here his officers beseeched him to position, but he would not listen. Were not his men invincible? Some dropped dead of sheer starvation as they assembled on the moor. Others fell and slept where they lay, to wake as a Hanoverian bayonet skewered them into eternity. The men of MacDonald of Keppoch demanded their time-honoured place on the right of battle, and were denied it, and so subsided in mulish sullenness.

And Cumberland came up. Cumberland, who had alone of Whig commanders studied Highland tactics: who had retrained his men in use of sword and pistol, left rather than right, to stab under the targe. Cumberland with ring-bayonets and muskets and artillery and grapeshots, younger even than Charles himself. So the Hanoverians lined up, and the shooting and shelling began, and where Charles stood he could not even see the field, and more and more of the Gaels dropped dead as they stood, under the shot of fire and lead, even as they screamed for the order to charge. It came, at last, and they charged; but most fell before they reached Cumberland's lines, and others only slammed into a wall of bayonets, and still others wallowed amongst a sea of the dead, and the men of MacDonald of Keppoch would not fight at all, until he at length burst forward imprecating them for cowards, and was then slain before them. The wall, and the trees, and the powder, and the blood; and Cumberland's men held firm, and for all the reckless courage of that day, the Jacobites soon turned and bolted as they could, the Prince standing aghast as they stumbled past him, exhorting them plaintively, until at last someone took his horse by the bridle and led him away.

Leanach cottage, by Culloden battlefield. This restored dwelling was inhabited in 1746

There was a rendezvous at Ruthven, in Badenoch, but it was a battered little group that assembled there some days later, without money or food, nor the Prince, who sent them word that the enterprise was off and he was returning forthwith to France to rouse His Most Christian Majesty for the next attempt. And so they went home, and soon he was on the run for his life, on islands inner and outer, in caves and coves, soaked and verminous and nearly starved, and a bounty on his head and a carnage around him; but brave and kindly people preserved him and lied for him, and on 20th September a little French ship sailed into Loch nan Uamh to take him away.

The adventure was over. After such calamity at Culloden, there was little else to be done; there was no concept of guerilla warfare in those days, nor the resources to maintain one, such as a politically sophisticated peasantry, and a friendly border-state, and a ready supply of food and arms. And yet it was not the end, not for some years yet, for so brutal was Cumberland's occupation and so ravaged were the Highlands that

Charles Edward in old age, given up to bitterness and booze

the land soon seethed with rage; the French, even as late as 1750, would have sponsored another rising, if Charles had settled for a landing in the Highlands and a bid alone for Scotland. But he would not. There had to be an invasion of England, and England alone, he screeched; and it was perhaps not egotism that drove him in that regard, but a rising awareness of what he in innocence had brought upon the Gaels.

An awareness that grew and grew, never ceasing, through all his adventures to come, his fevered plottings through the courts of Europe, his dramatic disguises and flights, his womanising, the final collapse of his dreams and his psyche. The bottle. The kindly bottle.

The day came, at last, when he could not bear to be reminded of Scotland and the Gaels, the glens of soft morning, and the sea and the shore; only to harangue and to belittle all who had failed him, in reality or fantasy, in that strange time that seems now so like our own, an age without real ideals or heroes, where all told lies and hedged their bets, and so many gave fair words and pledged their hearts and stayed at home. "I shall do for them what they did for me," said Charles of such in bitter old age. "I shall drink their health."

The Old Pretender died in 1766. Charles, obese and alcoholic, followed him in 1788. His marriage to a German princess had proved short and barren. His illegitimate daughter, Charlotte, survived him by only a year; her illegitimate son was killed in a Perthshire coach-crash in 1854, and is buried at Dunkeld. But the last of the Stuarts, Prince Henry, became a priest and then a Cardinal; a sheep-faced collector of bibelots and boyfriends, he died in 1807.

The tragedy of the Stuarts ended with him. The tragedy of the Gaels had just begun.

CHAPTER TWO

Clearance

Even in a savage age, the young Duke of Cumberland was a notably savage commander. In almost every regard he compares badly with his cousin and rival, save for a certain stolidity. Charles did not murder or torture; he shied from the task of disciplining soldiers, and after Prestonpans personally tended some of the wounded of both sides: he genuinely believed that all who fought were his subjects, and counselled humanity at every stage, even if his carelessness came to squander lives. Cumberland had no such scruples. He used lash and noose with gusto on his own men; and the greater part of them press-ganged from the urban stews, ill-fed and badly paid. After Culloden, he found himself in the heart of the Highlands with a large victorious army. There were also two substantial militias, and the full might of the Royal Navy. "For the first time," writes a sombre Bruce Lenman (*The Jacobite Risings in Britain*), "the Highlands and Islands were at the mercy of the British government."

And that government, the administration of Newcastle, the regime of the Whigs about George II and Hanover, thirsted for blood. Behind them brayed all the fury of the London mob, and the stern wisdom of the intelligentsia of that great city, where there were operas and oratorios nightly, where writers and artists met at the salons and coffee-houses, where the Gospel was freely preached. Yet, the threat of the Highlands must be "absolutely reduced", ordered Newcastle. Says Lenman: "Lord Chesterfield, the Lord Lieutenant of Ireland, was much more explicit. He was for genocide." And genocide he duly outlined. A naval blockade, to cut off supplies from the starving barbarians. A bounty on the heads of chiefs; the peasantry to be massacred. And Chesterfield put as much of this in practice as he could.

In mid-rising, Chesterfield banned the supply of all food from Ireland to Scotland. As far as he was concerned, all Scots were traitors and the more that perished the better. All London thought likewise. The absurd thesis that every Scot was a Jacobite gained general acceptance. The National Anthem was rewritten to contain (and until the 1980s still contained) a verse calling on the Most High to grant the King power "rebellious Scots to crush". To this day, quite falsely, popular historians talk of "Scots" and "English" forces at Culloden. That is the way now; then, in the mad spring of 1746, the generalisation inspired mass-murder.

"I like not this place," said Cumberland gloomily, and "this barbarous country" was another favourite phrase, and even as the rebels fled Drummossie field the atrocities had begun. The wounded, the comatose were bayoneted where they lay. Some schoolboys from Inverness had played truant to come and watch the battle; they were flushed from behind a wall, and brought down as they scurried. A rumour was put about that written orders had been found from Charles Edward to his men, that no mercy nor quarter should be given to the foe; the lie roused the Hanoverian dragoons to righteous wrath. On and on, through the field, towards the town, shooting and stabbing, butchering as they could, firing the thatch over a house of wounded and dying men.

A proclamation was made by the Duke that all who had taken up arms for the

William Augustus, Duke of Cumberland. After Culloden, he never won another battle

Stuarts must now come to surrender these and throw themselves on the King's mercy. Few paid heed. Of the clans, only the MacPhersons gave over their weapons. So Cumberland gave the nod. Rebels found in arms, naturally, were shot out of hand; that such often included clansmen trudging towards authority to surrender weapons when surprised by Hanoverian troops was, of course, an unfortunate consequence of the fog of war. Others ran away. But their homes were burned, crops wasted, utensils smashed, beasts driven away.

But what price the word of Cumberland? In May 1746 sixteen Grants of Glenmoriston and sixty-eight of Glenurquhart surrendered to Sir Ludovic Grant; they were forthwith taken prisoner and driven to Inverness, in complete violation of the terms agreed, and in due time (such as survived jail) transported to the Caribbean; two and a half centuries later, their Highland names still christen Rastafarian descendents. Amongst their ranks were men who had campaigned for the Hanoverian cause during the Rising, such as James Grant of Sheuglie; he died of fever on a Tilbury hulk. At home, the killing went on.

With hellish enthusiasm the militia and the Royal Navy established the sovereignty of George II throughout the Highlands and Islands. The most strikingly vicious amongst these were not English but Lowlanders, captains such as Dalrymple, Hay and John Fergussone. The latter — "that cruel, barbarous man" said a luckless captive — launched a reign of terror on the western seaboard that would match any atrocity of our own day. Fergussone and his dragoons descended on Raasay in the late summer: green Raasay with its trees and cattle, and the fine mansion of MacLeod, the island which unwittingly hosted, for two July nights, Charles Edward in his flight through the Hebrides.

So Raasay paid dear. Fergussone's men destroyed every house, overturned each stone, lit each thatch, casually killed every beast and fowl they could find, removed or polluted all food and water supplies. MacLeod of Raasay had been out for Prince Charles, but signed all over to his son before leaving; hence his estates were not forfeit, but his house was flattened and its contents looted. The soldiers raped "a poor girl that was blind, and most unmercifully lashed with cords two men, one of which soon after died". By the end of September, with Charles safely in France, nothing remained to wreck or burn. Bewailed one Donald MacLeod, "The whole island of Raasay had been plundered or pillaged to the utmost degree, every house and hut being levelled to the ground; and there was not left in the whole island a four-footed beast, a hen or a chicken." As a final touch before departure, the dragoons smashed every single boat.

HMS *Furnace* moved on. The island of Eigg too was laid waste. Repeated operations were launched on the coasts of Arisaig, Morar and Moidart; not only were the mansions of Jacobite leaders destroyed, but many humble and harmless villages put to fire as well, some never to be rebuilt. Captain Caroline Scott had proved a hero in defending Fort William from Jacobite siege. He promptly defiled his place in history by feral scourings through Lochaber and Appin. Going on a jaunt to burn the house of MacDonald of

Keppoch in June, Scott paused to hang three peasants with the ropes of a salmon-net; they had been on their way to surrender weapons in obedience to Cumberland's decree.

These were Cumberland's men. Like him, they were driven by a crazed anti-Highland racism that is hard to fathom today: for such, the Gaels were not remotely human. Neither the Duke nor his minions could distinguish loyal from disloyal Highlanders; they despised the few wise voices calling for moderation. For the penalties after the '15 and '19 had been temperate (another mitigation for Charles Edward); these bestial activities were without precedent. But, "that old woman dared to talk to me of mercy", sneered Cumberland of Lord President Duncan Forbes, "as arrant Highland mad as Lord Stair or Crawford", saying that all three seemed to think the shell-shocked Highlands as harmless as a dispersed London mob. But they were right.

On 23rd August Cumberland quit Scotland, yielding place as Commander in Chief to the Earl of Albemarle. Albemarle saw the posting as a great imposition, far from kith and kin. And he shared every whit of Cumberland's views, that an iron hand must now impose law and order on the northern lands. But the repeated killings, firings, drivings and confiscations had the opposite effect entirely. Far from restoring them, law and order broke down all together. Private vendettas flourished in the blood-soaked atmosphere. The chiefs who had maintained stability before were scattered, dead, or too shaken to govern. They had neither troops nor weapons. Thieving and banditry were rife. Over the winter, there was much suffering. None stood to protect the innocent and vulnerable. Where guns are outlawed, as Americans have said in more recent times, only outlaws have guns.

There was endemic unrest. Social cohesion fell away. The purge of Jacobites real and imaginary continued. Occupying commanders continued to distrust even the most senior statesmen in Scotland. Magistrates were harassed and harried. Then and now, senior soldiers have been too prone to see a situation as black-and-white, them-and-us: and at the bottom, there is one psychology from Raasay to My Lai. The Earl of Ancram, in charge of Aberdeen, ordered general illuminations on 1st August 1746 to mark the birthday of the late George I. That night, drunken soldiers took exception to the host of darkened windows; they went on a smashing spree, and even Albemarle had at length to apologise to the douce magistrates of the city.

In a sense the occupation of the Highlands has never ended. There was no formal departure, no lifting of the shroud of disgrace and suspicion that hung over the glens. Shame fell over the land of the Gael in those days, shame and fear, and a wracking guilt that was palpable in all that has followed. Great new fortifications were built, like mighty Fort George, garrisoned to this day. A Disarming Act was passed, of course, and Parliament also legislated to outlaw tartan and Gaelic and bagpipes — "engines of war" — the very symbols of Highland culture, and indeed of Scottish identity.

By 1767 there were a thousand miles of new military road. Regular military patrols moved through the glens, in the long term serving to reduce cattle-rustling from the

'A Real "Scottish Grievance"': The Clearances in a contemporary cartoon

eastern counties, for a watch was kept on critical mountain-passes. The barbarians were quiet — were the ringleaders not exiled or dead, beheaded, hung and drawn and quartered by the powers of gentle Albion? — the heritable jurisdictions no more. Proper courts of law were established, and county administrations, and the rising tide of evangelicalism began to swell the sails of the national Church in the Highlands. There were one or two embarrassments. The "Appin Murder", of Colin Campbell of Glenure, and the rigged trial that followed, brought little credit to the new administration. Euan MacPherson of Cluny skulked in his cave for years, until he unhurriedly chose to go abroad. And an overzealous military intelligence gave the Scottish authorities some agreeable entertainment. Wrote Commissioner Campbell solemnly to Lord Milton, of one fatuous report from General Bland — Albemarle's successor — "one Bethune a Tidesman at Inverness and Said to be a Highland Poet . . . This Genius is informed against for being suspected for author of ane Irish [Gaelic] Ballad in praise of the Clans at the Battle of Culloden."

Cumberland lived to be godfather of George IV, the monarch who would live to drape himself in tartan. The Duke never won another battle. But the Queen's cousin, the Duke of Gloucester, still bears "Baron Culloden" as a courtesy title. And on such aristocratic lines, in a new order with all the privileges of the old and none of its obligations, the Highland chiefs could now be remodelled.

The dark and noble saga of the '45 seems remote to us today, and much removed from the modern Highlands of our time: the West Highlands of meals-on-wheels, and fast carriageways, and bedenimed youth. But in the furthest corners of the west —

especially the Catholic west, Morar and Moidart — the anguish of the Rising and its aftermath still echoes in local memory. There is a hatred yet of the English and the British government, still there after all these years. And once in a while, despite the centuries, a window opens in the cloud of time to bring these horrors very close. Only three weeks ago, I met a man whose brother had known an old man in the Wester Ross hamlet of Drumbuie: he had known a very old man, who had known a very old woman, who had as a little girl watched the far flicker of the houses fired by Fergussone on Raasay.

In 1773 that sturdy old Tory, Dr Samuel Johnson, joined James Boswell on a famous Highland holiday. They travelled to Glenelg, abode a night in squalid lodgings, and then crossed to Sleat in Skye; at Raasay they were received graciously by the laird in his rebuilt manor, and Boswell climbed Dun Caan to dance his jig. Johnson was sixty-three. The Highland roads were bad, and there were precious few of them; straits had to be crossed in open boats, and the weather was not clement. "A testimony," writes Hunter, "to the curmudgeonly old writer's physical stamina as well as to his insatiable inquisitiveness about the world around him."

Johnson had come in search of those famous noble savages: that pastoral arcadia of which many had spoken, land of heroes and gallantry, whose aid to Charles Edward in flight despite the huge reward for his capture now belatedly excited southern admiration. But, less than three decades after Culloden, that whole order had all but gone. Even the boozy delights of Raasay House — "This is what we came to find!" — did not hide the truth from him. "The clans retain little now of their original character. Their ferocity of temper is softened, their military ardour is extinguished, their dignity of independence is depressed, their contempt for government subdued and their reverence for their chiefs abated . . . As they [the chiefs] gradually degenerate from patriarchal rulers to rapacious landlords, they will divest themselves of the little that remains."

All seemed calm, all seemed bright. Even in 1773 the mighty forts and broad soldiers' roads now raised a smile. The King's law and the King's peace prevailed. The Society for the Propagation of Christian Knowledge opened schools throughout the Hebrides. A cash-economy rapidly formed. Like sheep without a shepherd, the Highlanders milled in a brave new world; they would never again draw swords and march against the might of Britain. But Johnson had met their new chiefs, and judged their stamp; and his wise old eye could see the future. Indeed, the Gaels would not again raise armed rebellion. "But it affords a legislator little self-applause to consider that, where there was formerly an insurrection, there is now a wilderness."

Social change gathered pace in the north. The population was rising steadily, more than the land could properly support, though many began to drift away in voluntary emigration — Glasgow and the south, the Americas. The Government began increasingly

Dunvegan Castle, Isle of Skye

to harvest the fighting strength of the clans: the French force overwhelmed at Quebec in 1759 contained many exiled Jacobites from Scotland, but these were greatly outnumbered by Highlanders under the Hanoverian colours. (That was the day, of course, that Wolfe fell: Wolfe who had served at Culloden, Wolfe of our title.) Flora MacDonald had famously sheltered the Stuart fugitive in 1746; some years afterwards, she and hers left for America, where her sons would fight for George III against the forces of modern revolution.

The potato came to the Hebrides. After much suspicion, it was enthusiastically adopted as a staple food-crop, too much the staple of a top-heavy population. Presbyterianism marched apace, encouraged by the explosion in education and the wide availability of the Gaelic scriptures; in Ross-shire and much of Inverness-shire, Episcopalianism and Catholicism rapidly shed their adherents. Various thoughtful landlords experimented in schemes to support their communities: linen-growing prospered for a time in the north-east, but soon dwindled. It proved hard to generate enthusiasm for the coastal fishings, which remained largely the preserve of vessels from Europe. And the culture continued to strangle, with Gaelic officially proscribed, and the clan-chiefs and their heirs targeted by powerful and half-conscious conspiracies from London.

Slowly the princes of Gaeldom turned their backs on their heritage and their people. Within a mere decade or so of Culloden, they had begun to ape the monied nobility of the great southern cities, where the likes of MacDonald and MacLeod now spent a great deal of their time. They lost Gaelic from their tongues and the tongues of their children — whom, increasingly, they sent away for education. They repudiated their warrior pasts. If the chief maintained a *tail* of followers, it was only to impart glamour at a Belgravia ball. They now lived high, these princes: maintaining Edinburgh or London houses, inhabiting the salon or the boudoir or the banqueting-hall, travelling abroad. "The number and bravery of their followers no longer supports their grandeur," Johnson said of such, "the number and weight of their guineas only are put in the scale."

To support such greatness — spectacular clothing, beautiful furnishings, busy social lives, schools for their sons and gowns for their women — the new generation of chiefs had to raise money. The rent-roll would not buy such things for them, so rents were raised and raised again. Acres and acres of old Highland forest were felled, to be sold for charcoal for the burgeoning iron industry. They invested in spectacular schemes abroad: something in the West Indies, or in Canada, or in other corners of the New World. Much of what they made was squandered in high living or ridiculous projects. The last MacLeod of Raasay, for one, decided to tart up his policies with two elegant Mediterranean sculptures: when at length he received by sea two quite hideous stone mermaids, he went to law. The litigation ruined him and he was forced to emigrate.

New breeds of sheep had come to the Highlands: not the small scraggy beasts of traditional keeping, but the hardy Blackface and the plump North Country Cheviot. The first were in Dunbartonshire before 1760; by 1782 they had reached Ross-shire. Hardly anyone noticed.

Nothing in all of Scottish history arouses such passion as the Highland Clearances; and no period is more shrouded in confusion, blurred by propaganda, or distorted by plain old-fashioned lies as the critical eighty years between 1780 and 1860. There are still those who live but one remove from these ghastly events; old people who learned of those times from old people who had endured them. And there are still those who make apology for these events; who argue that comparable agrarian upheavals struck every country in Europe, that the land of the north could never sustain its people, that the events (however unpleasant for those concerned) were the unfortunate but necessary fruits of the inevitable march of history.

Some of these people profess themselves radical. (It is the Left, after all, which likes to talk of "historical inevitability" rather than the moral responsibility of individuals in a time and place.) Others are academics, too far removed in experience from the Highland people; and many are the dregs of our aristocracy, the braying descendants of those who, in Hugh Miller's savage words, "improved into a desert". But the Clearances were marked by a callousness, a stupidity and a ruthlessness that still shocks the student today. They were enforced without regard for the feelings (or property, or health, or even the very lives) of the people involved. They were not even good for the land vacated, which in most districts has never recovered from the new use to which it was put.

There is now a Highland radical establishment, which has done much good in chronicling these days and forcing the Clearances back into public consciousness, and drafted them into service for its own political agenda. Yet the insanity of the Clearances was not the work of ideological Tories: certainly not in the sensible, paternal vein of Dr Johnson. Greed, self-interest and expediency certainly drove the sails. But the logic was one of "improvement" and "progress"; in short, the Clearances were justified as a vital and invigorating act of social engineering. And our own century has seen comparable action on an even more inhuman and wicked scale: the grand agricultural projects of Stalin, Mao Tse Tung and Nicolai Ceaucescu, great ships of change on seas of blood.

Terrible the fate of those who oppose the march of Progress.

The Clearances, however, were much later than the vaguely comparable changes in agronomy which had swept the Continent. This imparts one aspect of their darkness, that they were "sins against knowledge", the conscious policies of cultured men in an age of professed enlightenment. But, too, these men were the supposed fathers and kinsmen of the people they wasted, people to whom they stood in huge advantage; it was perhaps the greatest gulf, socially and economically, between ruler and ruled in the Highlands that history has seen. For the virus of Cumberland had spread. The chiefs of the people now saw them only as a capital resource: sub-human, perhaps a liability, certainly expendable.

So they moved to exploit. There was first, in the Hebrides, the boom and burst of the kelp industry, from about 1796 to 1825. The harvesting of this thick, brown, woody seaweed fathered the crofting economy and brought most of the West Highland population from the hills and straths to the coast. There were hundreds of miles of suitable rocky seaboard, where the kelp grew profusely, and the cowed population provided abundant labour. So rocks were hauled inshore as seedbeds for the weed. It was gathered in summertime with metal implements, dried and burned in kilns, until the cold slag formed a blue clinker full of chemicals — salts, potash — with useful applications in industry, for the manufacture of glass and gunpowder and cleansers. During most of this period Britain was at war — with the French, with Napoleon — and the supply of continental barilla, a readier source of these substances, was cut off; besides, there was a tax on imported salt.

So in Orkney, in the Uists, in Skye and down the west coast, the chiefs and landlords encouraged the people to settle by the coastline and breed. Crofting communities were born: small linear villages, each house at the head of a long narrow strip of land, on which the family kept a cow or two and some sheep and fowls, and grew potatoes and oats and bere, but spent most of their time at the harvest of kelp. As the old great trade in black (in truth, more brindled) cattle slid away, kelp briefly became the mainstay of the West Highland economy and paid the rents.

The gathering was nasty work. You waded chest-deep in cold water, and the horny weed hard on the hands, and then the piling and drying and burning. Hence, afraid there would be little enthusiasm for the toil, chiefs made sure to remove alternative means of subsistence. The common holding and working land vanished in the crofting order. The crofts themselves were tiny; a share in the sour hill pasture, and perhaps two hectares of allocated land a hundred yards broad, drawn in a strip on the map, and often unbroken bog. To support your own and pay increasingly steep rent from these meagre plots was impossible. So all gathered kelp. "By limiting the amount of land at a family's disposal, by charging a high rent for that land and by paying extremely low prices for kelp, island lairds provided themselves with a workforce which was as much at their mercy, and as firmly under their control, as any set of slaves on a colonial plantation," says Hunter.

Not all were prepared to live this life. Many chose to go to America. By 1803 it was whispered that perhaps two-thirds of Lord MacDonald's Skye tenantry planned emigration. MacDonald, judging by his peeved communications, was profoundly hurt. He also panicked for his revenues. Swiftly he plotted with some fellow landlords; legislation was drafted, and passed, that immediately raised the cost of an Atlantic passage beyond the means of all crofters. MacDonald's factor could happily write, "The emigration is entirely stopped now, by Act of Parliament which puts it out of the poor people's power to pay the increase of freight."

Between 1790 and 1800, kelp-gathering on Orkney generated thirty thousand pounds in revenues each year: this was four times the entire annual rental of the islands. The Hebrides alone exported twenty thousand tons of kelp annually, worth seventy thousand pounds. Huge fortunes were generated for the landlords, perhaps twenty pounds a ton, for which the harvesters were paid two pounds or less. None of this money was invested in the West Highland economy: it did not go on poor-relief, nor fertilisation (indeed, the processing of seaweed deprived crofters of an important manure), nor piers and harbourworks. It was, said a disgruntled observer, "bartered for the merest baubles . . . residences, dress, equipages . . .". The kelp boom typified a greed without forethought, the greed of small-town profiteers — the half of them permanently resident in the south of England — without regard for the land or concern for their people.

The Napoleonic Wars ended in 1815; supplies of barilla resumed, industry found new techniques, and in 1825 the salt-tax was abolished. The bubble burst. Clanranald, another MacDonald chief who held the Uists and Barra, and had milked his people dry for kelp, now went spectacularly bankrupt. The prop of these overcrowded communities disappeared. With many children and cattle to feed, crofters recklessly turned to the one crop that might sustain them: the potato. In 1846 the West Highlands were struck by blight. The potato yield failed. A huge population faced famine of biblical proportions.

Scurvy, typhoid and cholera descended on the starving. In the Uists, an appalled clergyman chronicled months of wrenching misery. "Deplorable, nay heart-rending. On the beach the whole population of the country seemed to be met, gathering the precious cockles . . . I never witnessed such countenances — starvation on many faces — the children with their melancholy looks, big-looking knees, shrivelled legs, hollow eyes, swollen-like bellies. God help them, I never did witness such wretchedness."

Some moved to help as they could. A very few honourable landlords created relief programmes that should properly have come from central government: they hired men to build "destitution roads", or doled out corn. Some went bankrupt. Others carried on in the same old train. One sent his factor to buy grain and meal in the south: he bought it, and then re-sold it for a fat profit, and brought none back for the hungry. The newly born Free Church bought a yacht, the *Breadalbane*, and raised funds to load this with supplies which she landed where she could. But most of those in authority looked to Sutherland.

In Sutherland, as one euphemistically puts it, the ruling house had "advanced pastoral farming and consolidated extensive areas into sheepwalks under single managements". The south-country stockmen had arrived, energetic Lowlanders who powerfully sold the nostra of modern farming. Clear the straths of people. Turn each into a single sheepwalk. Install a single tenant, and he could do well from his sheep, and pay a rent far higher than the combined tithes of the former population.

It is a tale one can hardly bear to tell at this point. A saga of such unremitting cruelty and woe that you recoil from it; your stomach knots with anger, and you break away, and you pace the room, but you must come back unflinchingly to write what should never be forgotten.

In 1811 Sutherland had fifteen thousand sheep. In 1846 there were over two hundred thousand. For this we must credit Patrick Sellar, a son of Moray, factor to the Countess of Sutherland and her husband, that most liberal Marquess of Stafford. Sellar had little time for their tenantry. "Aborigines", he said, and a "parcel of beggars", he said, who spoke a "barbarous jargon . . . savages", he said. In the lovely green vale of Strathnaver lived such aborigines; they tended cattle and sowed crops, and though poor in many respects their houses — as Hunter points out — were larger and more comfortable than some inhabited in the Western Isles in our own time. But Sellar wanted Strathnaver for himself. In the frigid spring of 1814, after serving papers on the tenants, he cleared them from their homes. Some of the houses were burned down, to preclude their return.

The people were forced to the coast, to tiny villages they had to carve from rock and heath — Strathy, Bettyhill, Dunbeath — and deliberately given very little land, the better to motivate them for the fishing-industry of which the Countess had high hopes. And what happened to Strathnaver was repeated in scores of communities through that whole great northern county: the serving of writs, the firing of thatch, hard men with guns and dogs, and episodes of singular brutality: beatings and kickings, the cry of "Let the witch burn!".

"I presume to say," wrote Sellar, "that the proprietors humanely ordered this arrangement, because it surely was a most benevolent action to put these barbarous hordes into a position where they could better associate together, apply to industry, educate their children and advance in civilisation."

"One could scarcely hear a word," remembered an old mind of those days, "with the lowing of cattle and the screaming of children marching off in all directions." "All was silence and desolation," wrote another, "blackened and roofless huts still enveloped in smoke, articles of furniture cast away as of no value to the houseless, and a few domestic fowl scraping for food among the hill ashes were the only objects that told us of man. A few days had sufficed to change a countryside, teeming with the cheeriest sounds of rural life, into a desert."

"Something very similar to the Clearances," read Sutherland estate-publicity of the early 1980s, and this is as true as you are reading, "is still done today by local councils."

Harris, in the Outer Isles. Similar Gaels lived in a measure of contentment on the fine green *machair* lands of the Atlantic coast. They were cleared, and driven to the east, the savage east of Harris, bare gneiss in a desert of stone; in that dead landscape they clawed for a living from the sea, and the stockmen descended on what had been theirs.

The oceanic island of Pabbay: grassy and pleasant, cleared for a sheepwalk; its people dumped on the barren hump of Scalpay and told to become fishermen.

Benbecula and South Uist, sold in Clanranald's indebtedness to one Colonel John Gordon, then the richest man in Scotland, and his new tenants perhaps the most impoverished. He gave nought of his fortune on relief when the potatoes failed, but resorted to eviction. "Redundant", he said of the people, and so in their thousands they were removed, with arms and dogs and even policemen, chased into the hills and caught and trussed and hauled to the boats, and taken to the cities of Glasgow and Liverpool, and many put to Canada. The emigration ships: the most leaky, rotten, worthless craft at sea, unable to carry cloths or spices or precious goods, but held fit for human beings. To Glasgow, and to Quebec, where even the toughest officials revolted at the spectacle of ragged and verminous arrivals, squatting hopelessly in the gutters, with nothing in the world but in what they stood.

"Many a thing have I seen in my own day . . . oh Mary Mother," remembered old Catherine MacPhee, "I have seen . . . the people being driven out of the countryside to the streets of Glasgow and to the wilds of Canada, such of them as did not die of hunger and plague and smallpox while going across the ocean. I have seen the women putting the children in the carts which were being sent from Benbecula and Iochdar to Lochboisdale, while their husbands lay bound in the pen and were weeping beside them . . . the women themselves were crying aloud and their little children wailing like to break their hearts. I have seen the big, strong men, the champions of the countryside, the stalwarts of the world, being bound on Lochboisdale quay and cast into the ship as would be done to a batch of cattle or horses in the boat, the bailiffs and the ground-officers and the constables and the policemen gathered behind them in pursuit of them. The God of life and He only knows all the loathesome work of men on that day."

Between 1847 and 1853, at least forty-nine ships laden with forced Highland emigrants were lost at sea.

Raasay. A bewildering succession of landlords: by 1922, old islanders of eighty had been the tenants successively of a MacLeod chief, a West Indian sugar planter, his son, a land-speculator, a southern romantic, a *nouveau-riche* industrialist, a Lowland iron-firm and at last Her Majesty's Government. In those years the little villages of Inbhir, Balmeanach, Balachuirn, Hallaig, Screapadal and others were amongst many more cleared of their original inhabitants.

Lewis. Uig. Park, the strath of Dalmore, the vale of Galson — cleared. Inhabitants forced to emigrate.

North Uist. Sollas, 1849: thirty-three constables arrived from Oban to oversee the expulsion of six hundred people, from Sollas itself and from the near townships of Middlequarter, Dunskellor and Malaclete, on a promontory bounded on three sides by tidal sands. They were poor people; wet summers made unreliable harvests. Lord MacDonald and the Highland Destitution Committee had agreed to assist their removal. But the people refused to go. There was a scene; four men were arrested, some houses de-roofed, and at length the parish minister arrived to persuade the inhabitants to peace. They agreed to leave for Canada the following year. The four men of Sollas were tried at Inverness and found guilty of various charges, but the jury appealed for leniency, and the judge — Lord Cockburn — agreed. They got four months. The Sollas people were removed to the south of the island, and later to New Perth — the land poor, the crops bad. In December 1852 a ship took the young and fit away to Australia, leaving only the old and ill. The community of Sollas had ceased to be.

Mull of the MacLeans: cleared, and cleared again, and left massively depopulated. Today, flooded with English settlers, it is surely the least Gaelic of the Hebrides, its identity swamped and its soul long gone.

Skye. Skye of the Clearances, many clearances, throughout the parishes of Sleat and Strath and Bracadale and Duirinish: people driven to the most inhospitable parts of the coast, and to the mainland and the cities, and then to Canada and the Americas, South Africa and Australia and New Zealand, and all the places where wandering Gaels have found their homes. In 1801, Lord MacDonald moved out two hundred and sixty-seven tenants. In 1826 and 1827, perhaps twelve hundred people left for Nova Scotia, and others filed for government-assisted emigration as their landlord evicted them in the enthusiasm of the new farming. Meadal, Sumaradal, Teangue, Druimfearn, Dalavil, Caradal; and the clearing of Suisnish.

The people of Suisnish, on good land by Loch Slapin, were amongst the last Highlanders to be cleared in a large-scale operation. The due papers were served on them. The factor announced that Lord MacDonald's action was "prompted by motives of benevolence, piety and humanity". They were too far from church, felt he — "in serious want of proper spiritual guidance", writes a sardonic Hunter. Of course, Suisnish was to be a sheep farm. And most of its people were destined for the Australian and Canadian colonies.

The ships came to Broadford Bay. After some futile resistance, soon the people trudged through Strath Suardal; on the slopes above a young geologist, Archibald Geikie, watched them go, and fifty years later — a very old man — he recalled the scene in words that almost all writers on the Clearances quote, and so shall I:

"A strange wailing sound reached my ears at intervals on the breeze from the west . . . I could see a long and motley procession winding along the road that led north from Suisnish . . . There were old men and women, too feeble to walk, who were placed in carts. The younger members of the community, on foot, were carrying their bundles of clothes and household effects, while their children, with looks of alarm, walked alongside. When they set forth once more, a cry of grief went up to Heaven; the long plaintive wail, like a funeral coronach, was resumed . . . the sound seemed to re-echo through the whole wide valley of Strath in one prolonged note of desolation."

No more. Write no more.

The Gaelic world was broken, crushed beneath the southern boot. A people had been slaughtered, their leaders removed, their lords corrupted; a new generation, and generations after that, had been worked and exploited and at last scattered across the landscape, and beyond the seas under the whole wide canopy of Heaven. The Gaels are a merry folk, a race of song and dance; and it was not the Gospel that took that from them, but the almost unremitting century of calamities that befell them after 1745. The songs forgotten, the communities destroyed, the language cursed; and a breaking of such threads as the extraordinary line of the MacMhuirichs. Eighteen generations of MacMhuirichs, hereditary bards to Clan Donald, seed of a thirteenth-century Irish progenitor, a family of extraordinary learning and erudition; they ended in one Lachlan MacMhuirich of South Uist, still alive in the 1790s, who could neither read nor write his people's tongue; and he told how with his own eyes he had seen the ancient manuscripts in the care of the family cut up for a tailor's patterns.

The new heads of Clan Donald had shredded their people and devoured their heritage. And why, you ask, did the people not rise? Why no massive and organised resistance, a call to arms, an explosion of Gaelic wrath against the forces bearing to destroy? But that has always been the way in history, when oppression has been sufficiently huge and savage. Persecutions inflame; pogroms paralyse.

The old order was broken after Culloden: all lines of resistance, all chains of command, all structures of leadership. There followed a litany of horrors on a battered race; but as infamous as were these sufferings, and as broken was the Highland will, these were only the short-term faults of an acutely unusual period of history. By 1860, with sheep-farming in recession and land-use veering to sport, the great Clearances were over. Learning and the Gospel had come, and the healing of a people's nerve; though oppression continued, there gathered a mind for battle.

CHAPTER THREE

Conflict

After 1854, when Suisnish and the Easter Ross district of Greenyard were so brutally swept of their people, there were no more large-scale evictions. By mid-century such events attracted odious publicity; progressive opinion would no longer tolerate forced migrations at the whim of a landlord. Besides, barely a century beyond Culloden, the Highlands and Islands had been swept to the bosom of the Empire. A capricious ruling class had swung from fear and loathing of the Gaels to a fascinated regard for what they took as their ancient way of life. Had not Sir Walter Scott popularised Highland legend in best-selling novels, and personally stage-managed the triumphant descent of George IV on Edinburgh? Had not Felix Mendelssohn, William Wordsworth, William Daniell, Edwin Landseer, Lord Byron and famous practitioners of every art tramped into the north and west, seeking inspiration in new romanticism?

Highland tourism was born. The industrial revolution enmired much of England, but the lovely northlands beckoned, the groves and hills and sparkling rivers. By 1820, thirty coaches were arriving in Edinburgh each day. By the 1840s, the railways had reached Scotland. The construction of civil roads began in earnest. With the rise of steam, and the burgeoning of fervour for the isles, shipping-companies sprang up to furnish the west with efficient communications; before the end of the century, the railways would rip through the most arduous terrain to seafall on the remotest coasts. For the Highlands had become fashionable — and, after Queen Victoria herself had planted her *schloss* at Balmoral, well-nigh compulsory.

Victoria and her Albert fell in love with the woods and hills of Deeside; they had toured the western seaboard, in the most appalling weather, and taken a permanent aversion to that area of the country. The groves and peaks of western Aberdeenshire, however, were reminiscent of the Coburg fatherland; and in those days there was still Gaelic in Deeside and a Gaelic culture. And where Queen Victoria went, all must follow; her large family grew up to acquire their own castles and lodges about Braemar, and they were eagerly pursued into the Gaidhealtachd by anybody who was anybody; the landed gentry of England and the Lowlands, statesmen and bankers, judges and churchmen, and the swelling tide of rich *parvenu* businessmen, princes of industry and heroes of the Empire, and all seeking a bit of glen and mountain to call their own.

Much of the fabulous prosperity of Great Britain in the last century was founded on textiles, and particularly the production of wool and the manufacture of woollen products. Hence the flood of sheep into the north at the turn of the century, and the clearing of the people; but in 1830 the wool market slumped, and though there was some recovery after 1840 (with Scotland contributing a quarter of Britain's wool) the trade was soon in evident decline. New Zealand and Australia, rich in year-round grass, soon supplanted the home country as the chief wool-growers of the world. The price of the British product crashed in 1874, and again in 1880; at the same time, the advent of refrigerated cargo-ships allowed these lands and Argentina to launch a price-war in the British market for mutton.

Yet again a new Highland economy, based overmuch on a single industry, slumped and died. Stocks dwindled; the value of sheepwalks plummeted, and rents fell and fell. In any event, the farmers had presumed too much on the capital left by those expelled — the rich green land of lost communities, tilled and manured over decades and even centuries, could not long support the continued grazing of voracious sheep. Stockmen did not dig, nor drain, nor fertilise. After a decade or two, their walks' capacity to support beasts rapidly declined.

Wonderful then was this timely rise of a new bonanza: gold-laden industrialists seeking socially acceptable ways to spend (and display) their wealth, and the burgeoning of sportsmen hungry for game. There were salmon in the Highland rivers, trout in the lochs and pools. The thick heather abounded in things shootable and baggable. There were deer: and there could always be more deer. England had all but destroyed her woodlands, and new farming methods the long stubble beloved of game-birds; filthy rivers were bereft of fish. So the sporting of England headed north.

The landlords, besieged by the whims and tempers of the agricultural economy, could scarcely believe their luck. In a former day clan-chiefs had hired servants to catch their food, never thinking that the pursuit could be fun, never mind fun people would pay for. But new revenues were eagerly welcomed. So moors and glens and hills and rivers were parcelled into lets and beats, and sold or rented to the highest bidder. Still, and for decades to come, Scottish sport was cheap: the proprietor of barren Harris valued its sporting-worth at twenty-five pounds in 1833. By 1885 its rents for game totalled two thousand pounds a year.

All this brought changes to the Highlands. Continued pressure for improved access hastened the revolution in transport; by the 1880s, many islands and western districts were indeed more accessible than they are today. The sporting estates brought jobs: bailiffs, ghillies, guides, stalkers, beaters, boatmen were directly recruited for the harvest of things finned and furred and feathered. But more. Lodges and big houses and shooting-boxes must be constructed, and then furnished; and so there were jobs to build, decorate and staff these premises. And then, further jobs to build and craft and sell the tools of sport — boats, rods, nets, sticks — and to breed and tend the animals — ponies, dogs;

and beyond that the burgeoning labour-market for the crewing of those steamers, the construction of the roads and railways, and the servants and shopkeepers who sprang up about the noted ports and towns, their hotels and stations.

People who had benefited little from the arrival of the great sheep did rather better in the rise of the sporting Highlands. But those who had been driven out did not return. It was not until the following century, after the Great War, that some communities — Dalmore, Bracadale, Fearns — were repeopled. And the great deserts of the Clearances, the straths of Skye and the vales of Sutherland, are deserts yet.

The middle and later decades of the last century form an era of Highland history within, or just beyond, the memories of some still living. To be sure, there had come great changes and much violence since the collapse of the Jacobite enterprise: much that was destructive, hypocritical and cruel. But the new communications created for the Victorian travellers were an omen for good. And other changes slowly brought a measure of stability to the Gaels of shattered spirit. The fires of a new evangelical religion had always smouldered in Easter Ross, and especially in the Black Isle; but in the latter decades of the eighteenth century, Evangelicalism began to spread through the Highlands in great and powerful revivals. Sutherland and Caithness glowed with the new fervour, and after the turn of the century so did Skye; in 1828, the ministry of Rev Alexander MacLeod in Uig ignited Evangelicalism in Lewis, and that whole great island was soon aflame with the Gospel.

Less than a century after the passion of the Covenanters, the Church in Scotland had decayed into a cold and lifeless orthodoxy: the age of the Moderates. A system known as patronage — depriving the people of a parish the power to elect a minister, and instead conferring that right on the feudal superior or landlord — had been specifically forbidden by a clause in the Treaty of Union. But the Parliaments were not long one when patronage was imposed again on Scotland. Landlords, rulers and Crown saw the selection of clergy as their lawful duty: and a useful instrument of social control. The inevitable result, of course, was the corruption of the Church. Livings were bestowed on men without wits, industry or grace. The landlord's creatures frequently led lives of farcical sloth, even immorality. Others spent their days in pleasant pursuits: farming, entertaining, private hobbies. Congregations dwindled to nothing. In the Outer Isles especially, a lazy and often drunken minister might have charge of a vast parish containing thousands of souls, most of whom never set eyes on the one with the cure of their souls.

Evangelicalism blew this petrified edifice sky-high. To be sure, it made little impact in the southern Uists and Barra, which the Roman Catholic faith had recovered by Irish missionaries, nor in Arisaig and Morar, which the Roman Catholic faith had never left. But the new Gospel was water for the thirsty souls of the crushed people of the

Highlands. Energetic and powerful new preachers — men like Roderick MacLeod, Robert Finlayson, John MacRae, John MacDonald — attracted huge outdoor congregations. The movement was only swelled by the Clearances. Many saw in the Scriptures a picture of their own sufferings, a vindication of their plight. And the Moderate ministers who had said nothing, not a word against the evil of that day were abandoned by their people. (But do not forget that some of our most important and incensed accounts of the Clearances, like Donald Sage's *Memorabilia Domestica*, were penned by Highland clergy.)

Pressure grew to build new churches, and form new parishes to supply this hunger of souls. Various 'Parliamentary' parishes were created, to be financed by the givings of the people rather than the funds of the landlords; these congregations were invariably Evangelical, and called Evangelical ministers. The Parliamentary churches, and the financial system devised to support them, also served as a blueprint for what loomed. For Scotland and her Presbyterians were now convulsed in battle against a repressive Establishment and Crown to abolish patronage and restore the liberty of the Church and the democratic rights of her members. A foolishly counselled Government refused to accede; Sir Robert Peel and his Cabinet lamentably failed to appreciate the strength of feeling. In May 1843 the Evangelicals gave up on them. The Established Church tore asunder in Disruption. The Evangelical ministers, in their hundreds, decamped to found the Free Church of Scotland. Many, perhaps most, of the people followed them. In the Highlands, only a very few remained in the Established Church.

The new Free Church was a remarkable organisation led by resourceful and inventive people. It rapidly prospered. Despite many difficulties — many landlords refused sites to build churches and manses, and some molested worshippers in the open air — the Free Church, within a decade or two, had constructed new buildings across the country. Colleges were set up to train her ministers. Foreign missions were developed. And the Church had a powerful social conscience. It devoted itself particularly to the construction of schools, and Free Church schools mushroomed across the Highlands and Islands, and were run by the Church until the state took over in 1872.

The Free Church was the first organisation to comprehensively cover the Highlands, and the first since the Jacobites to offer any focus and cohesion to her people. Much has been mockingly written of the eccentricity of Highland worship (though what would a Raasay crofter have made of Matins?) and the perfervid frenzy of these revivals (though can the burning of fiddles compare to the firing of thatch?). But the Free Church brought morality, cleanliness, and dignity; where the Gospel took hold, drunkenness vanished and the family unit strengthened. The Free Church gave dignity to a people: in her services and on her courts, Highland men might lead and worship with wisdom and much scope for oratory. The Free Church brought learning. It taught the Gaels to read, and to read in their own tongue, but also to draw on the culture (and politics) of other lands and peoples. The fashionable Highland Left of today has often despised Presbyterianism and exalted Catholicism. But it was in the hotbeds of the new faith that social agitation would begin: not in Barra of the priests, not in "blessed Morar, where no Protestant minister ever preached a sermon".

Once Evangelicalism, and the Free Church, had taken hold and reanimated the Highland identity, the will for reform was inevitable. A people's might was rising. And there was much to rise against.

By now we talk of landlords, not clan-chiefs. Most chiefs were gone: bankrupted by their social excesses, exiled in England or beyond. Others lived in England, or the Lowlands, of choice. Scarcely any remained with a word of Gaelic. Most of the land in the Highlands and Islands was in the hands of men of another stamp: the Lowland gentry, the successful entrepreneur, the scrap-merchant made good.

That most of the landlords were insensitive, and some positively wicked, should not obscure the memories of more honourable examples. The Earl and Countess of Dunmore created and sponsored Harris Tweed. Sir James Matheson ran Lewis with wisdom and general benevolence, spending far more of his fortune (won peddling opium in the Far East) on the island than he ever recovered. The MacKenzies of Wester Ross — Sir William, Osgood — are fondly recalled. But every landlord, without exception, dominated and occasionally evicted as it suited him. Most were tyrannical. And a few were utterly vicious.

For all landlords had power, far more power than was good for them; powers which, possessed, will inevitably be abused. To be sure, there were no more heritable jurisdictions. But at times it was hard to see the difference: so often were landlord and police and sheriff united in friendship and collusion, so frequently was the landlord or his factor endowed with an astonishing array of civil offices and authorities, and so powerless were the crofters and people on their estates to resist them.

There were no more Clearances, but the power of eviction remained. And it was a good weapon for keeping a people in check. An individual who threatened the system could be readily picked off; and so none dared to call meetings, or petition, or pamphlet. Others who were faithful to the powers-that-were — loyal workers, willing agents of the factor — could be promoted to better holdings. And this had one very serious effect. From the squalor and poverty of their dwellings in these days, and their lack of endeavour to improve what they held, the Gaels acquired a completely unjust — but lingering — reputation as a people of indolence quite lacking in drive.

But why invest your labour and time in improving your house, your holding? The next thing you would be knowing, the factor would be along and saying, "Well, that's a fine place you have there — and what is your rent? My! Is that all?" and, sure enough, up it would go. Or you might be evicted, if the factor happened to want a superior plot or house for someone he owed a favour. And if you were evicted — be it on a casual whim, greed for your house, or because you were causing trouble — there was nothing to do but pack up and go, and no hope of any compensation for the permanent improvements you had made. Hence thin, rank land remained thin and rank; and poor houses damp, reeky and fetid. From the day that security of tenure came in, West Highland housing began steadily to improve; it was not the fault of the people that their communities seemed backward, but of a fatuously evil system that stifled all initiatives of betterment.

Despots. That was what they were, many of these landlords and their agents. For the sake of sport, Raasay's proprietor Herbert Wood poured rabbits and more rabbits on to the island, forbidding the crofters to touch them, forbidding them to keep cats or dogs that might harm game. One of his predecessors had forbidden the people of Raasay even to marry without his consent; a young man who defied this law was put out of his house, and all forbidden to give him shelter. In Kilmallie, the people came out in 1843 for the Free Church. Cameron of Lochiel, that benevolent Episcopalian, refused a site for a new church and manse, or even a place to worship in the open air; the congregation had to meet on the foreshore at low tide, below the high-water mark, where his writ could not run, and when at length they were granted land for their buildings it was a bog so bad that men had once used it to trap wild horses.

And throughout the western coasts and islands, similar men ruled as petty potentates. Donald Munro, a most frightful factor in Lewis, was the Chamberlain of that island. He was also Baron Baillie, Procurator Fiscal, Justice of the Peace, Commander of the Local Volunteers, Commissioner of Supply, Chairman (and legal advisor) of the island's school boards, Commissioner for the Revenue, Director of the Gas Board, Director of the Water Board, and Collector of Poor Rates. Against such massed civil and military power, what chance had tenants-at-will? But there were others of his breed. In Skye, Alexander Mac-Donald served as factor to Lord MacDonald, administering not only his enormous estates but those of three others: and he was clerk to seven school boards, one of Skye's three bank-agents, the sole tax-collector, captain of volunteers and distributor of postage stamps.

Though the sheep had gone, deer and grouse brought worse impositions on the tenantry. Further grazings were annexed for sporting use — a moor, a park — and forbidden to the beasts of the people. Many landlords forbade all measures by crofters — fences, dykes — to protect their crops from the ravages of vermin. (Raasay's epidemic of rabbits so destroyed the grazing that soon many tenants faced virtual famine: Wood imported more rabbits.) Some went so far as to ban the gathering of rushes and heather for house-roofs: reaping might disturb the grouse. In January 1882, the proprietor of Glendale and district announced yet further rules for his miserable tenants. Dogs were now forbidden. All driftwood cast up on the shore was forthwith held to be the exclusive property of the estate. The ukase was duly posted up at the village store. "Notice is hereby given that the shepherds and herds on these lands have instructions to give up the names of any persons found hereafter carrying away timber from the shore, that they may be dealt with according to law."

But, a day or two later, another announcement was there beside it. "We, the tenants of the estate of Glendale, do hereby warn each other to meet at Glendale Church on the seventh day of February, at about one p.m., for the purpose of stating our respective grievances publicly."

There had always been some patchy, isolated resistance to evictions and to the excesses of landlords: the odd crowd of women hurling stones, a broken head or two. But the serious tide of the crofting struggle — it culminated in the Crofters' War, the formation of the Highland Land League — began in Lewis. In 1874, Donald Munro served eviction papers on fifty-six families in the villages of Tobson and Breaclete, hamlets on Bernera in the west of Lewis. The news was not received placidly; the Sheriff Officer returned to Stornoway alleging an assault. Some weeks later a Tobson man arrived in Stornoway on business. Munro promptly ordered his arrest. A brawl broke out as townsfolk hurried to the scene; the Riot Act was read. The news came to Bernera, and a great crowd of men marched across the moor to enter Stornoway and demand an audience of the proprietor.

Matheson was genuinely shocked to hear of his factor's folly. When three crofters went to trial for assault, their crafty defence lawyer used the occasion to pillory Munro. The men were acquitted, and a town baker who had intervened in their arrest; but the Sheriff Officer was heavily fined for brutally assaulting a detainee in the police-station. Munro was shortly stripped of almost all his offices. In broken old age he would limp through town, the little boys skipping about him to chant mockingly, "I'll take the land from you!" — "the threat", writes James Shaw Grant in *Highland Villages*, "with which he had terrorised the crofters for so long".

In the Park Deer Raid some years after, crofters from all over the eastern fjords of Lewis marched into the deer-forest of their detested landlords, armed with guns (some, they say, hidden in the thatch since before Culloden) and playing the bagpipes. They built a great camp-site and lived in the open for some days, hunting and roasting venison over big fires, only fleeing when the rain came. The authorities panicked; there was silly talk of despatching gunboats to arrest the ringleaders. Instead they were taken in by a tactful constable, sent for trial in Edinburgh, acquitted by a sympathetic jury, and entertained in high style by island students before touring the city in triumph.

But it was in the district of Braes in Skye, in 1881 and 1882, that the first serious blow was struck for the people of the Highlands and Islands. The Braes villages — Penifiler, Lower Ollach, Upper Ollach, Gedintailor, Balmeanach, Peinchorran — run down the Trotternish coastline south of Portree, by the Sound of Raasay, to end at the foot of Ben Lee by the waters of Loch Sligachan. They were then part of Lord MacDonald's estate. And he had just seized the valuable Ben Lee grazings to rent to a tame sheep-rearer. When that lease expired, the men of Braes offered Lord MacDonald a better rent. The landlord refused. But Braes men were fishing in Ireland that year, and came home with word of the success of the Irish Land League, whose boycotts and rent-strikes had forced concessions from the government of mighty Gladstone.

The rents were not paid in November of 1881. And a dignified little deputation marched to Portree to advise factor Alexander MacDonald that there would be no more rent until Ben Lee was restored to them. Lord MacDonald's response was typical of his kind. He promptly sent the Sheriff Officer with eviction-notices for twelve tenants: easily done, for that official was his deputy factor. Back came the worthy, bruised and shaken, whose papers had been ripped from his hands and burned in front of him. This was too much for his legal superior, Sheriff William Ivory, virtual viceroy of Inverness-shire. Ivory, a Border Scot, ordered a mass of Glasgow police and put himself in personal charge of an expeditionary force. On the morning of 19th April 1882, fifty surly constables marched from Portree in the face of driving rain, with Ivory in the rear in a rather comfortable carriage.

It was a dawn raid: the people were to be surprised, and the miscreants arrested. Sure enough, there were no sentries, and the first part of the mission was readily accomplished. Five wanted men were seized, but now the taskforce had to bring them home. And the people were roused. In a narrow gorge the invaders found their way blocked by a furious crowd. Fighting began in earnest; police with truncheons, crofters with flails and stones. Had most of the young men been home and not at the Irish fishings, lives would certainly have been lost. But the police made a determined baton-charge, and as officers and oppressed tangled in battle, sheriff and prisoners crossed the river under the confusion.

Yet they still had to negotiate the steep high road above the Narrows of Raasay, with a sheer cliff below and another above. To this some of the Braes men had doubled back. There were rocks piled above the road as a munitions-dump, and more men were now hastening up from the melee at the gorge, and women too. Great jagged rocks rained down on the police; the air was thick with screams, cries and Gaelic denunciation. Somehow, the police broke away and at length reached Portree with their prisoners; a Braes crowd marched after, but was persuaded to turn back by a minister.

Sensation. Gunboats and troops were melodramatically despatched. But in the power-centres of Britain, concern took hold of the intelligent classes. What had driven a peaceful people to this, and what men were in charge who sent such absurd expeditions forth? And even the Government now sensed the truth of the matter, that in the Highlands a society without just and effective law was collapsing upon itself.

The Braes men had a small victory: they had been seen to stand together and powerfully resist, and their grazings were restored to them — though at a steep rent — after Cameron of Lochiel, politically astute, had intervened with Lord MacDonald. And the Glendale men too had acted. They signed a compact with one another, and petitioned the estate for the restoration of grazings at Waterstein. The land was denied to them: they went on rent-strike, and drove their sheep on to the Waterstein farm. Against such united force, the authorities could not execute even writs from the Court of Session in Edinburgh. The police were driven from the glen. Again Ivory and his serfs clamoured for military action and the arrest of ringleaders; again, nervous rulers thought better of it. A diplomatic Gaelic-speaking official persuaded the Glendale leaders to recognise the rule of law and go of their own will to court in Edinburgh. And they left, not on HMS *Jackal*, but on the mailboat *Dunara Castle*, a "victory for tact and common sense". Three of them were eventually sentenced to two months' imprisonment; the news was greeted with dismay in Glendale, but then — a day or two afterwards — word came that the Government was to create a Royal Commission to tour the Highland and Islands and investigate all crofting grievances.

The concession had come after a move by Charles Fraser Mackintosh, Member of Parliament for Inverness Burghs; he and twenty other Scottish Liberal MPs had signed a memorial to the Home Secretary. And he was duly called to serve on it. So were Cameron of Lochiel, Sir Kenneth Mackenzie of Gairloch, Alexander Nicolson (Skye-born Sheriff of Kirkcudbright) and Donald Mackinnon (Colonsay-born Professor of Celtic at the University of Edinburgh). Malcolm MacNeill, who had mediated in the Glendale crisis, was appointed secretary to the Royal Commission. And Lord Napier and Ettrick, the only non-Highlander selected, was made chairman. Two of the Commission were major landlords, three spoke Gaelic, and all were men of substance and intelligence. Mackenzie, to his credit, refused to serve until he was allowed to minute that in his opinion no landlords should be on the Commission at all; in Parliament, a voice or two bewailed the absence of any crofting representative.

The Napier Commission held its first meeting in Braes on 8th May 1883. Over succeeding months, amidst much mishap and adventure (including a spectacular shipwreck), they visited Skye, the Outer Isles, Orkney, Shetland, western Sutherland and Ross and Inverness-shire and Argyll, the north and east Highlands, and a scatter of very small islands ranging from Foula to St Kilda. In every community they hosted a public meeting, in church or schoolhouse, and heard shattering tales of hardship and exploitation from spokesmen who impressed them by their remarkable candour and bearing. (It must be borne in mind that these testators were frequently describing local conditions as recalled half a century before: some stories may not be entirely reliable.)

Afterwards, Lord Napier and his colleagues received expert witnesses in Edinburgh. Their report was published on 28th April 1884, with five volumes of their gathered evidence. The Royal Commission recommended the creation of regulated crofting townships, recorded and fenced, with roads half-paid by the landlord, and full free access to all the peats, thatch, heather and sea-ware their crofters sought. If a Sheriff agreed that a township was overcrowded, the landlord would be compelled to enlarge its limits.

Government grants to the landlord could finance the creation of new townships if they were deemed better.

Security of tenure should not, thought the Royal Commission, be granted to crofters, save those with large holdings who paid six pounds or more in annual rent and entered on a thirty-year lease; they should also be fully compensated for permanent improvements. In this matter the Napier Commission was badly divided: Fraser Mackintosh wanted the rent set at four pounds, Sir Kenneth sought the abolition of common grazings, and Lochiel wanted reforming powers bestowed on the landlord. The people of the crofting districts, whose hopes had been raised high, were bitterly disappointed. Still, the Royal Commission had amassed priceless data, and had given frustration and anger a profitable focus.

The Highland Land Law Reform Association — the Highland Land League — revived its endeavours even before publication of the report. Members were recruited across the north, and branches established in every district. John MacPherson, leading "Glendale martyr", became a full-time organiser. Huge audiences turned out to hear him speak. At a Dingwall rally, Land League delegates rejected the Napier Report and demanded complete security of tenure, with fair rents assessed by land-courts. It was agreed to put up candidates for Parliamentary elections, taking advantage of the recent extension of the franchise. Within a year or two, the Land League organised massive rent-strikes; a convenient slump in the beef-market so impoverished crofters that they gladly participated. In Skye and South Uist, there were land-raids. On 30th October 1884, a posse of police set forth from Portree to Kilmuir to restore order; they were met, turned, and jostled all the way home by two hundred jeering crofters.

On 18th November a military force really did land in Skye: fifty extra policemen, armed with revolvers, and over four hundred Marines. They disembarked at Uig Bay. But the crofters were not fools. They knew better than to mob, or to oppose guns with sticks. So they assumed pleasant, polite, passive resistance, working on their crofts and waving cheerfully. The mystified troops marched through a friendly landscape. Six hundred Land League activists were meeting at Glendale; but they closed with prayer and drifted quietly away. The rent-strike in Kilmuir continued. But there was no more conflict. Braes and Glendale were the last battles. The Marines left Skye in the summer of 1885. In the General Election of that year, three of the five Highlands and Islands constituencies were won by Land League candidates. And Charles Fraser Mackintosh cast in his lot with their cause.

Their support was needed if the Gladstone Government were to carry his policy on Irish Home Rule. Using the Irish Land Act as a model, the legislation all sought was drafted. The Crofting Act was passed by Parliament on 25th June 1886. It bestowed upon all crofters the same benefits: security of tenure, the right to bequeath the land to another in the family, compensation for improvements if the tenancy were ever given up, and a new body — the Crofters' Commission — with the power to fix fair rents.

Contemporary sketches in the Isle of Skye

Marines on the march to the disturbed districts, Isle of Skye

Marines landing at Uig, Isle of Skye

The Act did nothing for those without land, nor cottars without title; nor did it transfer into their hands the empty acres still feeding grouse and sheep and deer. But it made crofters secure in what they held, at set and mostly lower rents. And it is crofting that has kept the people on the land to our own day.

Meeting of crofters: John MacPherson speaking, Isle of Skye

The age of cynical, brutal, state-sanctioned oppression was gone. But the age of hardship and suffering continued; and the patterns and techniques of exploitation have endured to the present, often changing, rather softer, but never ceasing. The people of the Highlands and Islands remained poor for many decades. They had little money, and few ways of raising it; in many districts, a true subsistence economy — people living largely on what they grew or caught for themselves — continued until after the Second World War. Compulsory education came in 1872; a change of some social benefit but with catastrophic impact on the Gaelic language. The earliest schools — "Society", Free Church — taught in the medium of Gaelic; the state-schools taught in English, and in many the use of Gaelic even in the playground was forbidden on pain of corporal punishment. And so generations of Gaels grew up once more illiterate in their own tongue. Since 1872 the Gaelic language has steadily declined.

The Gaels, a people of the land and its fruits, had been forced to face the sea. Untold thousands crossed it to the lands of the new world, never to return; others crewed the steamers of Hutcheson and MacBrayne. Thousands now found sustenance in fishing. Along the Moray coast, and the eastern seaboard of Ross and Sutherland and Caithness, fishing communities mushroomed through the decades of the nineteenth century. In the west, Stornoway and Castlebay jammed with the fleets following herring, and on the mainland Lochinver and Ullapool and Mallaig drew on the harvest of the ocean. In the eastern bays of Harris, and many other western districts, townships of the newly cleared turned to the sea because the new hard land could not sustain them. Island girls grew up to look to the herring-gutting for a living — the savage work of the gutting, the plunging of cut and gashed hands into barrels of icy brine. And the boys grew up to go to sea.

To sea, to fish; and, increasingly, to fight and die for the glory of the Empire. Hardy and intrepid, were we not? And the resourcefulness and skill of Hebridean sailors made them highly sought by the Admiralty; useful, brave, and eminently expendable.

Even near the end of this catalogue of tragedy, few Highland calamities have the pathos of the *Iolaire* disaster of 1919. In the last hours of Hogmanay 1918, with the trains disgorging hundreds of Lewis naval-ratings at Kyle of Lochalsh after the conclusion of the Great War, the authorities belatedly realised that the regular mailboat could not carry them all. And so they improvised, despatching the Admiralty yacht *Iolaire* from Stornoway, and she was filled to the gunnels with Lewismen and sailed for Stornoway before midnight.

A cold, dark night, with some sea running; but nothing a sound and competently crewed vessel had to fear. What precisely happened will never be known, but the *Iolaire* went badly off course; heading for what her officers must have thought was Stornoway harbour, she smashed into a reef — the Beasts of Holm — by a cove just north of the town and bay. There was a heavy swell. No orders were given. There were not nearly enough boats or life-preservers for all on board. The saloon doors jammed; the ship broke up and sank with speed, and of the two hundred and eighty-three men aboard, only seventy-five survived. The rest went down with the ship, or drowned in the seething seas, or were dashed to pieces on the cliffs and rocks; teenage boys home on their first leave, veterans who had survived four years afloat against the Kaiser's navy, and amongst them scores who could have sailed the *Iolaire* safely into Stornoway with their eyes shut.

Two men, John Finlay MacLeod of Ness and Donald Bruce Murray of North Tolsta, saved most of those who lived. Powerful swimmers, they struggled on to shore with ropes, and hauled in hawsers, and almost all the survivors made their way to life along those ropes. From Stornoway, where the heads of Admiralty and the operators of rescue vehicles were enthusiastically celebrating the New Year, land-based help took hours to reach the scene. On the town quayside, a large and puzzled crowd saw the lights of the *Iolaire* dip and disappear.

Every soul alive in Lewis then, and of age to be aware, has never forgotten that dreadful morning. My great-grandfather, returning from the war, who had been marched on to the regular mailboat and so did not die; my grandmother, a small girl in a Stornoway house, hearing the wails and cries in the room around her. My grandfather, in Ness, watching lorries and carts coming over the hill, six and ten coffins at a time. The old man weeping over the body of his son on the shore; the lad who was washed up at the foot of his mother's croft; and the woman who found a cap bearing her husband's name in the water, and went home keening for her loss, to receive a telegram from him in Kyle, for he had missed the boat and lived.

Iona Abbey, as restored. When it was built, the Hebrides were a beacon of light during Europe's Dark Ages

A Scalpay townscape

Miners' row, Inverarish, Isle of Raasay

Angus Macleod of Shawbost: a young medallist, National Mod at Govan, 1990

A Lord Chancellor meets the people

Washing on line, Isle of Lewis

An ever-youthful Donald MacLean: the minister of St Jude's arrives at the Southern Presbytery to try the Lord High Chancellor

Lord Mackay leaving morning worship at Gilmore Place, Edinburgh,
12th November 1988

Raasay's medic, Raasay's minister – Rev Dr James Tallach, outside his manse

The good life: "white settlers", Isle of Lewis

Feeding time on a salmon farm

Kyleakin, and ferry *Kyleakin*, 1990. Two new vessels took over the run in 1991. They, and the village itself, will be laid off when the Skye bridge opens in 1996

Winter evening: Sleat, Isle of Skye

Winning is a lot more fun: National Mod, Oban, October 1992

Boy, Eriskay, about 1935

Aignish, Lewis, 1888. The authorities often resorted to melodramatic force against crofting agitation

There was an inquiry, of course, but nothing could be proved. All the officers, and the ship's log, were lost. Some suggested a confusion of lighthouses. The Admiralty did not emerge well from the affair. A furious mob intervened when naval orderlies were found landing bodies on the quayside by derrick-and-sling. The wreck of the *Iolaire* was advertised for sale before most of the bodies had been recovered. The court reached an anodyne conclusion: lack of prudence, insufficient life-preservers, and so on. The persistent rumour that the *Iolaire*'s officers had been drinking was indignantly repudiated.

Most of the wreck appears to have been removed in the 1920s; so low was Lewis morale in that dark decade, that no-one noticed the operation. Papers on the disaster are still in classified files. The Queen's advisors, visiting Stornoway with her in 1956, dismissed a suggestion that she lay a wreath on the waters by Holm. When the Townsend-Thorenson ferry *Herald of Free Enterprise* sank in March 1987, with the loss of one hundred and eighty-eight lives, it was widely reported — causing great offence in Lewis — as the "worst peacetime British sea-disaster since the *Titanic*". But more died with the *Iolaire*, and their loss decimated an island and scarred its soul for a century. Then, and to this day, men like my grandfather would relate the tale to their children and children's children; but always they pronounced it *Eye-oh-lare*, not recognising the name for what it was. Perhaps some Greek deity? But *Iolaire* is the Gaelic for "eagle", pronounced *Yoo-uh-lurr*; the men of Lewis quite failed to recognise a naval nod to their own language and culture.

Nearly seventy years later, in the summer of 1988, three known veterans of the catastrophe were still living — Donald Morrison of Ness (who had clung to the masts of the wreck all night, until rescued at daybreak by dinghy), Neil Nicolson of Lemreway, and Donald Bruce Murray. One evening I went to visit him. He was an old man by then, ninety-three, and exceedingly deaf; but, even sprawled in a kitchen chair, you could see the power that had once been in his massive frame, and in the strong face with its bushy brows and disconcertingly dark hair. We talked for a little about the Great War, and about that night, until he became too distressed to continue; he had left good friends trapped in the ship, and had dived to bring one up too late, and it haunted him yet. "I could do nothing," he croaked, "there was not a thing that could be done," and we abandoned the subject.

My uncle was with me, minister in the village. He made a prayer, and we left Donald Bruce's house, and him sitting there by the range with wet blue eyes, and back in his mind in the cold and choking sea. He died in the early summer of 1992; Donald Morrison had passed away in 1990, and Neil Nicolson, last of all, survived Donald Bruce by less than two months. It is said that there may be another still alive, an island immigrant in Los Angeles. He would now be a very old man, far from the rocks and waves of the west, but whose eyes may yet be clouding on every Hogmanay.

CHAPTER FOUR

Changes

The Small Boy was scared of the cow. She was a strange old beast, with some Friesian in her, but more white than black, and she had crinkled horns and big hooves and a sour disposition, and these hooves — they were overgrown, Uncle Angus told him many years later — gave the cow a strange gait, for they flip-flopped beneath her like slippers when she walked. She liked grass. She disliked milking. And she had no time at all for small boys. So when Grandpa-in-Shawbost went out to milk the cow, morning and evening, the Small Boy and his smaller brothers were beckoned inside, and they would watch fearfully from the kitchen window as Grandpa-in-Shawbost and the cow made for the byre.

The byre was the old house, or more accurately the oldest house, for it stood in evolutionary end-to-end with a less-old house. They were both by the main road, with the block-built garage where Grandpa-in-Shawbost kept his pet lorry right on the roadside, and behind that the ruined barn — tumbled walls of boulder and turf and clay — and at the end of that was the byre, the old house, with its very thick unmortared walls, and the neat golden thatch sitting snug between the tops of them, tethered by netting that was anchored with rocks, and one small skylight in the hip of the roof, and around it — for the old houses had no eaves — a broad grassy ledge of turf, that sat on top of the walls, and here the Small Boy could sit on a summer day and watch the world go by. Climbing up was easy, because stone steps were built into the outer wall, and the house was so squat and low that even the Small Boy could jump down safely to the ground, landing by the rhubarb-patch.

In the byre were stalls for cattle, though there was just the one beast now, and tea-chests stacked on their sides as nesting boxes for Granny's hens, and they strutted in and out, not the homely brown things of story-books, but tall white ladies with hard yellow eyes. It was a dim, mysterious place, the byre; only the light from the one wee window, and the smell of cow and hens, and dust and cobwebs, and — incongruity — the black perishing wire to the electric light, a single bulb tucked abashedly where roof met wall. And sometimes the Small Boy — who was not supposed to be here at all, not supposed ever to wander on his own, lest he meet with some swift and grisly end — would sneak through the door at the end of the byre, into the less-old house.

A suspiciously neat black house, western Lewis, about 1950

The less-old house had been uninhabited for nearly forty years, since Grandpa-in-Shawbost had built his fine new house around 1933, and it now served as his barn. But in its day this house had been state-of-the-art for Shawbost domiciles; it was the first *tigh geal*, or "white house", in the street when Grandpa-in-Shawbost's father had built it in the 1890s. And it had solid mortared walls, squared and angled, and it had a framed window or two, and a gabled roof of black felt, and an upstairs. So the Small Boy would go carefully up the stairs, into what had been a bedroom but was now a loft, filled with more yellow straw for bedding the cow and mending the roof of the oldest house.

The golden sun of July would stream through the skylight, and make bright and precious the tousled straw, and as the Small Boy stamped about the loft the dust would rise, and dance in the beam of sunlight, a million tiny sparking particles, and he would watch this in wonder for a time, until he heard his Mammy's raised and anguished tones, and then he would scramble down the wooden stair and through the old house and into the oldest house and out the door and past the rhubarb and round the peat-stack and over the little bridge that crossed the ditch and into the house for tea.

Tea was always in the kitchen. The Small Boy liked the kitchen, because it was a warm and homely place, with a big peat-fired range puffing in the chimney-breast, and a granny-clock that had a pendulum and a slow tick-tock and hung on the wall over the fridge, and the black cat Sooty would slink in and out of the room in the contemptuous way that cats do, and there was a squashy couch under the window by the larder, most useful, so that Granny-in-Shawbost could sit there innocently and look on to the road, and not a thing nor a soul going in or out of New Shawbost could escape her big blue eyes.

But tea was always rather a fraught occasion for the Small Boy, because he was only six, and found cutlery difficult, and he was always being scolded for bad manners, and being told to eat things he did not like. Often there was fish, all bones, and sometimes salt herring — all salt and bones — or there was Granny's broth, which he loved, but the spoons were always worn silver plate, scratched and rough, that scraped his teeth in spine-chilling agony. Once he asked, "Granny, why are your spoons so rough?" and his mother scolded him, and his father cast him a black look, and Grandpa-in-Shawbost munched on without hearing, and Granny looked puzzled — she was not fluent in English, and the Small Boy had a thick Lochaber accent — and his small brothers writhed and giggled, but Auntie Chirsty — who was his very favourite aunt, glamorous and jolly — winked at him and said, "Oh yes, the spoons are rough, *a bhalaich*. Very rough."

Tonight there was no soup and no fish, salted or otherwise. There was a cheerful fry-up, sausage and black-pudding and tomato, and mugs of brave tea laden with sugar, and plates of good Stornoway bread, and Granny's pancakes, and *aran-eorna*, the barley-bread, in coarse triangles, that was filling and chewy, especially with crowdie-and-cream. And there was always a bowl of that on the table, and a plate of butter, and a jar of Robertson's raspberry jam with the golliwog on the label. So the Small Boy ate placidly and well, and his brothers also, and Granny — who was very large and red-faced, and could be fearsome when she lost her temper — beamed with pleasure, and said, "Now, boys! Clean plates! Clean plates!" And she said to Angus, who was only a toddler, plump and blond and pretty, "Now you eat up. Food's scarce! Food's scarce!", and winked at him, and the children gurgled at the joke.

The Small Boy was sitting across the table from Grandpa, and he watched him eat with awe. Grandpa was an old, old man, over eighty, slow and careful, and getting deaf, and he spoke little to his grandchildren, and they were all rather afraid of him. It was not a fear born of dread — Granny, her temper gone, waddling out to howl blue murder was a much more terrifying phenomenon — but of respect, for he was a good and wise man, and a deacon in the Church, and his brown eyes were deep and earnest, and his voice a gravelly rumble. He had a round craggy face, with broad mouth and deep jowls, and these bobbed as he swallowed, and the Small Boy watched Grandpa eat and swallow and the jowls bob, until the old man looked up from his fork and caught his gaze, and Grandpa's broad mouth parted in a dry but friendly smile.

Afterwards there was worship. The Small Boy and his brothers sank into tense silence on the couch, and Granny cleared the table and composed herself with a sigh, and Daddy — that was a minister, like Uncle Calum and Uncle Angus and Uncle Alastair — opened the big Bible, and made a prayer, and read some verses of a Psalm, and precented it, and everyone sang, and then he read a chapter, and asked Grandpa to pray, and they all knelt on the floor at their chairs, and the Small Boy squirmed into the stretch-cover of the couch, as Grandpa prayed in long and fluid and sonorous Gaelic.

There was much that was good and happy and comforting in Shawbost of the early Seventies, for in those days it still retained much of its old Gaelic culture, and the virtues of the dying subsistence economy, while enjoying most of the benefits of the age of affluence. Every home now had electricity, except for one or two eccentrics who would not have the marvel in the house, and most had running water, and almost all had a car or van or access to same — some, mind you, held together by rust and prayer, fearfully and wonderfully made. Many houses had television, though Lewis still enjoyed but a single channel — BBC 1 — and, insidious as were the effects of this air-lane for the joys of Anglo-American culture, it was to many a blessing and a treat. Grandpa-in-Shawbost had just acquired a set, a black-and-white ITT that stood on a tripod in the lounge, and he took to it avidly, enjoying especially the American cop-shows — *Cannon, Ironside, Kojak* and the like.

It was not a town, not like Stornoway and its suburban comforts, but Shawbost had an air of purity and innocence, and the Small Boy did not forget the Shawbost of those childhood summers. You ran about the croft in bare feet, through clover and grass and the silverweed that flashed in the wind, and you played hide-and-seek with your brothers, or your cousins, in the broad *feannagan* — raised growing beds — that scored the park from top to bottom. When Grandpa put away the bad cow at last, and let a neighbour graze his own beast on the pasture, milk was part of the deal, and each morning and night a big bottle — empty of squash, or pop, or whisky — was left at the head of the croft, full of new milk, still warm, and often the Small Boy was given the honour of collecting. So he would scurry out of the house, out of the big solid back-door, and past the zinc-house that stored coal and tools, and trek up to the head of the croft — and it was a huge croft, the size of a football pitch, climbing gently to the ridge of Druim Tortomar — an epic journey, and there the bottle would lie in the grass by the little galvanised gate on to the common-grazing, and the Small Boy would hug its hard cow-heat to him and make back to the house, proud as Ulysses from Troy.

When the sun shone, Shawbost smiled; at every croft a cow or calf or heifer munched contentedly at the fence, and the sea was blue and bright beyond Baile Stigh, and the gable of the big church glowed honey on the near horizon. Evening would come, the air still, the sun — reflected and re-reflected from the sea, enriched, burnished — would pour as gold over the land, in the green of the croft, in the yellow

Peats, tweed, crofter. Eoropie machair, Ness, Isle of Lewis

of thatch — and each sound carried like a bell over the township. There would be a going of tweed-looms, for the industry was strong in those days, and Shawbost had Macleod's big tweed-mill in by Loch na Muilne, that gave her people work and money — and so the looms clattered away in smug rhythm, clackety-*clack*, clackety-*clack*. There was someone on Church Street that had the pipes, and would stand outside to practise when the night was good; you could not see the house, nor him, but the skirl floated over the community, liquid and pure.

Cows came and went for milking, lowing in their way, and it was a good noise to a child's ears; a hen layed an egg, and cackled in joy to the cosmos, and a cock might crow and make her day. If there were still peats to be gathered out the road — and "out the road" meant to the moor; "in the road" was to the sea — then the tractors would grumble down the street of New Shawbost, and out to the moor and the Beinn, and back again, with a snorting of gears and clouds of fume. Blue was engine-smoke, and soft brown the reek of peat — for every house burned peat, and kept an immaculate stack by its gable or shed, peats built into a neat symmetrical bank as big as a black house. There would come the laughter of children playing, and the merry voices of mothers meeting in the road, except on the night of the prayer-meeting, when vans and cars would roll up the road to the Gate and the main road to church.

The Gate was the crossroads of Shawbost, and had once been a real gate, when

New Shawbost was not a village but one farmer's track. Through this junction ran the main road, Barvas to Garynahine, swooping down the hill to the river and over the bridge and up by the school and curving away to Carloway. Into the shore from this junction went Gearraidh a'Bhuidhe and Baile Stigh, the community of old Shawbost, when the sea had been its life, and the houses close to one another as those of fishermen are. And into the moor from this junction went the dead-straight road of Pairc Shiabost, or New Shawbost, three-quarters of a mile, by old houses and new houses, to peter out after the last house in a scrappy peat-road, that wound up to the foot of the Beinn, out to the reservoir and the shielings, for once Shawbost — like all the Outer Isles communities — had practised transhumance, resting the croft in summer from the greed of cattle, by decamping, children and cows and all, and heading out to the moor for some weeks to live in cosy bothies and treat the cattle to new moor grass and enjoy a general vacation. But this custom died, like so much else, with the onset of the Second World War.

Of this the Small Boy knew nothing, and the moor had a mysterious horror to him, but he knew Shawbost and he knew many of the people — Murchadh a'Ghobh, the bookish and merry crofter at the Gate, who read voraciously and argued gaily and never darkened the door of the church, but was the best husbandman in the parish; and Poko, the stocky man across the road; and old Craig, that was said once to have been Granny's boy-friend, until she met Grandpa; and Sine, Auntie Jean, in her little lime-cottage that was painted bright pink; and Morgan and his wife — *bean Morgan* — that kept a big black cow, and more official, the minister, the Rev Alasdair MacFarlane, with white hair and gold-rimmed glasses and a great white grin, who always came calling when the Small Boy and his family were home in Shawbost, early in the morning, bristling with humour and anecdote. And then, of course, there was the wider family: for Granny and Grandpa had had six children, and all had married, and four had children of their own — and, once every holiday, five or six MacLeans and their spouses and their broods descended on New Shawbost, in chaotic and whooping reunion, sisters and brothers-in-law, and the children quite forgotten, and shooed outside if the day was fine.

Once, the last summer that Grandpa was living, Mammy and Daddy and the wee brothers went off to town for the morning, and left the Small Boy to mind Granny and Grandpa. So he followed Grandpa about the croft that day; Grandpa was fixing fences with a hammer and staples, and murmured pleasantly when the Small Boy asked questions, but said very little. He worked along the fence, pulling and tapping, and the Small Boy sat playing in the grass beside him, making great adventures for the new Corgi car that Auntie Chrissie had given him the previous day; and he remembered, ever after, that day with his grandfather, the old man moving unhurriedly about with his tools, cloth bonnet on his bald head, shirtsleeves and braces.

The peace of the night. Sometimes Daddy went fishing, and took the Small Boy

with him, driving two or three miles to Arnol and Loch Urrahag, and they would sit
on its boulders with their rods and be men together, as Lewis gathered her skirts for
the half-night of summer, and the twilight would steal in, the drumming of snipe and
the keening of peewit; always, far away, the rumble of the sea, and sometimes (oh, woe)
the malicious squeak of midges settling about your ears. Rarely, they caught a fish. And
they came home in the night, headlights bobbing on winding road, the shining eyes of
outraged sheep in the beams, to New Shawbost and the house. Tea, and perhaps a
craggan — an extraordinary biscuit, unique to Lewis, a thick chewy round of bread as
big as a saucer and as thick as a thumb, and you spread it with butter and jam, and it
was a great treat for the Small Boy. And bed, in the room upstairs with the two big
beds; one for Granny and Grandpa, and one for the three grandsons, with the window
looking out to the twilit Beinn, and the tinny tick of a cheap but loyal alarm-clock.
And it was a place warm, and snug, and secure, in the stillness of the room and the
snoring of Grandpa, and his brothers warm in the bed beside him; unless the wind was
up, and the rain coming, and then the elements howled mournfully about the house and
its high defiant gables, and the Small Boy tightened his knuckles on the blanket, and
listened to the wailing of the night, and thought of bogles.

It was, he understood many years later, a place that then stood and looked two ways
in time. There still flickered the embers of an old culture and a dying poverty, but
too the brightening flow of alien ways and modern comfort. And that was how Shawbost
was in those days, at the cusp of mighty cultural change. So Grandpa watched television,
Ironside and the boxing, and when he put it off at night he picked up his Gaelic Bible.
Granny went forth to feed the hens, hissing to them to come — *ish-ish-ish-ish* — and
collected the eggs, and came back to put them in the humming fridge. By day the Small
Boy played with Iain Thormod, or Christine Anne and Joan, and highly coloured
FisherPrice toys trundled on the road, neat and plastic — and there would come by an
old woman, black from head to toe, in thick stockings and man's boots, muttering to
herself, and giving them one quick shy smile: a widow, of the Great War, or the *Iolaire*,
or the terrible tuberculosis.

The Small Boy went to church on the Sabbath, a long and dreary day for a carnal
child, and MacFarlane did not smile, and the Psalms were sung in Gaelic wild and free,
and then MacFarlane would preach — earnest, orating — as Granny pressed sweet
after sweet into the Small Boy's hands, and he sucked away and studied the ladies' hats
in the pew before, and peered round to watch the preacher giving voice in that
impenetrable tongue, light glinting on his glasses, voice popping in the pulpit-microphone.

Cars whizzed down the New Shawbost street, a Maxi, or an Allegro, or a Vauxhall
Viva — but one day all would be terrible silence, and hushed voices, and you were told
to play very quietly in the evening because so-and-so had died and there was a wake in

that house — and the next day men would gather outside that home, and MacFarlane emerge after the worship, and a coffin lifted on its bier, and the slow dark procession would march in the road to the Gate, and the road to Lionagaidh; the shuffling of feet, the steady shifting of arms to carry the burden of death.

Baths, grim baths on Saturday, with hot water and hard brushes and maternal hands without mercy; but the water always dark and peaty, a urinous shade. Reservoir there might be, but filtering was something for which the natives had to wait, and washing of clothes was made difficult, and the water made gritty thick tea. So, every so often, when Mammy had endured enough of authentic Hebridean tap-water, she called on the Small Boy and his brothers, and took with her an empty and mighty sweetie-jar, and they went out the road to her Uncle Angus and his well.

Uncle Angus was Granny's younger brother, a tall strong-featured MacAulay, with a mop of hair and strong booming voice and much kindly humour. He lived on the family croft out the road, where Granny had been raised early in the century with her four sisters and three brothers; their formidable old mother outlived three of them, dying in 1961 in her ninety-first year, and bedridden for most of the previous decade. A character. It was said that every spring she gave Angus orders for the planting of potatoes on the croft she had not seen in years. But now she lay at Lionagaidh, and Angus had inherited, and he stayed in the good stone house with his wife Annie and his son and his daughter, Margaret, who was still going to the school in town — for Angus had married late, in his forties, and Mammy had been a bridesmaid — and two grim purposeful dogs.

So Mammy and the Small Boy and the brothers and the sweetie-jar would reach the gate, and went down the path, and into the house with a loud call, and Uncle Angus would come laughing, and Auntie Annie glowing, and Margaret radiant and very Seventies, and the two dogs slid about them. The Small Boy looked on these nervously. One of the Border collies had strange eyes — one blue, one brown — and this gave the dog a villainous appearance. But island sheep-dogs seldom bark, and never bite, and attack only the hub-caps of passing cars, and those of obstreperous habit are either trained or destroyed, and until then tethered like a grazing horse.

There would be much Gaelic talk and banter that went over the heads of the boys, and then Uncle Angus, whistling — it was usually *The Lambeth Walk* — would take them down the croft to the well. There were several wells like this about Shawbost, dug deep into the rock where there would be a natural spring, and a stone cowl built over them, and the water clear as air and sweet as love. Uncle Angus cleared the mouth of cobweb and grass, and the jar was filled, and the lid screwed on, and that was the good water for Mammy's tea. But the Small Boy and the family never left without seeing Auntie Bellanne, who was a younger sister of Granny's, and a widow for many years, and she lived in a tiny cottage of her own which her brothers had built for her when she came home in her widowhood.

Harris Tweed on home-made barrow. These are still in use in modern Lewis

Auntie Bellanne was a very clever woman — and the MacAulays were clever people, but she was the ablest of that family. Yet, in the poverty of the Great War and after, only one child in such a family could be educated, and the fourth stood low in the pecking order; the oldest, Peggy, was kept at home to help raise the youngest offspring, and Doll was sent off to train for teaching in Glasgow, and the others put out as they were able to make their way in the world and send home a little money — domestic service in the south, or gutting herring round the coast. So Bellanne left school at fourteen, and went off to work, and in due time married, and a year or two later her man was taken by typhoid, and she was left alone in Glasgow with no husband, no livelihood, and a baby on the way. These days, of course, there are benefits and grants; and Bellanne would have stayed in Glasgow and found a job and dropped Baby off each morning at the registered child-minder. But this was the early Twenties, and widowed mothers did not work. She came home to Lewis, and took of her family's charity, and raised her fine boy in that humble little bothy, this delightful and witty and highly intelligent woman, and over the decades her intellect rotted and her soul grew dark.

Bellanne was a small, bright and bird-like woman, tall and thin and very different to Granny, with bright eyes and quick speech and hair that was quite white. And her son was in Glasgow now, master of a dredger, with a wife and daughter, and she went down every winter to see them; but she still lived here, and this was her home. It was very small, and kept neat, but it was a home of small and neat poverty, with little in the way of excess and luxury, except for an ornament the Small Boy cherished — a little plastic souvenir, clear, filled with water, and a plastic Scottish piper standing inside, and white plastic snowflakes on the bottom, so that when you shook the wonderful lump of kitsch the flakes blew about in the water, and fell in a gentle shower about the plastic piper. "Piper in the snow, *a ghraidh*, my love," Auntie Bellanne always said, beaming, when the Small Boy went to the brace and picked the thing off the mantle and happily agitated it. And she talked to Mammy, in Gaelic, and fed the boys biscuits, her eyes darting about, hands working in the black stuff of her dress.

At length the convoy made for home with the jar of water. And the tea was very good. And Granny found a jar of Creamola Foam, sugary crystals that made a pink fizzy drink when stirred into water, and you were fed mugs of this after your meal, and perhaps a chocolate tea-cake. And out to play for a while in the evening, to listen to the cows, and watch Sooty looking for shrews in the grass, and steal in to look at the hens; and the golden sunlight over Shawbost, in the new houses and older houses, and in the thatch of old houses kept as byres, and in the thatch of Oithrig Anna's house, which she shared with her sister, which was the last inhabited black house in the street, though it had a chimney, and was kept immaculately clean.

Daddy and Grandpa watching the news of Mr Heath and Mr Wilson. The lights gleaming in the half-night. A *craggan* with butter, and milky tea, and Granny ushering the cat outside. The cool thick blankets of bed. The bleating of sheep as the Small Boy slept.

Death came, in his soft insistent tap-tapping, mending the fences that bound the hubris of man, that keep his goings in the allotted land of life. Grandpa died, and was buried, and the Small Boy cried, and everybody cried, and when they came home that summer Granny-in-Shawbost was in black, and kissed the children when they came running in to hug her, and her eyes filled with pain and love. Nobody looked after the thatch of the oldest house now, for he who had been born in it was gone, and there was no more cow, and the hens had gone up to Auntie Shonnag in Ness. Granny had a bad heart, said the doctors, and could go at any time; but her children were good to her, and each winter she went to stay in three manses — two sons-in-law, a son — in turn, like a royal progress. And the younger women clothed her and styled her and scolded her gently and kept her on a good strict diet, and she shed weight, and felt better physically, and grew more mellow, and jolly.

One does not get over a bereavement. One learns to live with it, because one has no choice; and Granny learned to live as a widow, and to enjoy what she had, and to give thanks for what she had lost. Just once, a year after Grandpa went to Lionagaidh, she came to stay with Mammy and the small boys in Glasgow. One night the three boys, and Granny, sat before the television and watched *Lassie Come Home*, an old and very weepy movie, and the small boys duly cried, and Granny cried, for she doted on all animals, and could never eat a creature she had known personally: a hen would be throttled for some occasion, and the family would dine heartily on chicken, and Granny would sit dolefully picking over corned beef.

The years went by. The thatch on the oldest house was soon blown off, or in, and at length Uncle Calum smashed down the roof-timbers, for Granny had a nightmare of the ruinous canopy collapsing on her grandsons. All over the village, thatched roofs decayed, and were demolished, and some began to remove the stone walls themselves. Death came, again and again. Craig's wife died — she had gone quite senile, the Small Boy heard, and begun to wander, and she had latterly been tied to a chair — and then Craig himself, and Granny cried; Uncle Angus died, and Auntie Peggy died, and Auntie Bellanne died, all in one grim year. There came a succession of wet summers, that made the gathering of hay difficult, and many people gave up cows, for there were vans now with fine milk in plastic envelopes from Stornoway or Inverness, and besides, a cow tied you down; you could not go away, nor on holiday.

In 1961 the parish of Barvas had nine hundred and sixty milk cows. In 1971, Barvas crofters kept two hundred and forty-three cows. By 1981, there was one milk cow in all the parish from the Butt to Dalmore. And with all those vanished cows went much else; the growing of corn, oats and barley for winter fodder, the gathering of hay, the rituals of milking, the skills of producing butter and cheese, and the very heart of the crofting economy. Crofters became sheep-grazers and claimants of subsidy.

Television exploded over Lewis in 1976, with the opening of new transmitters: the big mast at Achmore, and the big mast at Melvaig on Wester Ross, so that now the islands had BBC 2 and ITV. The Gaelic radio-service went to VHF at five weeks' notice. There was a sensational new paper, the *West Highland Free Press*: it was really Skye-based, but its lively writing and radical politics sent a frisson of disapproval through the Hebrides. A big new car-ferry began sailing from Ullapool, and MacBrayne's old cargo-boat soon stopped sailing from Glasgow, and haulage firms in Stornoway began to import the joys of mainland consumerism. Roads throughout Lewis had to be widened, renewed. The passing-places disappeared; bends were unbent, bridges recast in concrete and aluminium.

The Shawbost manse caught woodworm, and was demolished, and a new manse was built above Loch na Muilne: a bungalow, squat and hideous. MacFarlane retired, and shortly died, not a very old man. A brash young minister came, a Stornoway lad, tall and puffy, the Rev Calum Matheson, but he was a preacher with a lovely nature, and Granny took to him, and everyone else. A housing revolution was now in full swing, for there were grants from the Board for new harling and pebble-dashing and double-glazing and loft-extension and sewerage, and so house after house was renovated, and Shawbost succumbed to a tide of pink pebble-dash and angular extensions and mock-Georgian front-doors. Oithrig Anna and her sister moved into a large modern caravan. The old house crumbled. The elderly inhabitant of the last black house in the district, at the end of Baile Stigh, died. The house, abandoned, mouldered away. The last cow was sold.

The Youth, approaching manhood, used sometimes to wonder why Shawbost had such a hold on his heart. It was not the place of his birth, for he had been raised on the mainland — childhood in Glasgow, now in Edinburgh — and it was not even the land of his father's people, which was Ness, the parish at the Butt of Lewis, the north-western tip of Europe; his father's parents lived by Laxdale, outside Stornoway, and they were most interesting and gracious people — Grandpa-in-Laxdale that had laboured on the Glencoe road, and in the Clyde shipyards, and worked at John Brown's on the Cunard liners; and Granny-in-Laxdale, who had been a housemaid in Kelvinside when she met Grandpa, an able woman, apple-cheeked and smiling, that had kept screeds of lore and tradition from her Thomson people, the seed of a Banffshire dominie, James Thomson, who opened a school in Ness in 1739, progenitor of the Thomsons of rural Lewis, and many of them scholars, poets. The Laxdale grandparents were rather younger than the Shawbost ones; they had lived in the urban grind of the Depression in a Govan single-end, and braved the unknown dread of the Second World War, with Grandpa in the Navy, and herself raising the little ones. They were more fluent in English; they had strong ties with Glasgow, and the mainland.

But Newmarket, that corner of Laxdale where they had settled after the war in 1945, was a new community, a village that had scarcely existed before 1939 — a straggle of houses and huts on the ridge of the Barvas road, home to a Lewis diaspora from Park and Ness and the West Side. Here there was no depth and no tradition; there was warmth and kindliness, and the neighbours were good neighbours, but there was not the tight bond that there was among the Shawbost people. And as for Ness, it was a great flat sprawling headland, crammed with crofts and people in a log-jam of townships, bleak and open, and yet most claustrophobic.

Shawbost was beautiful — Shawbost with its hills, and crags, and the river in its valley, and the winding road, and old dykes, and the going of looms and pipes in a still sunlit evening. And here, as the Youth dropped by each summer nearer to his coming of age, he grew more aware of the bubbling tensions and humours in the human entity of Shawbost. The land became precious to him, as he dug into the family past, and learned of the allotting of the croft to the Macleans, and how four generations had struggled to make it rich, and to feed their children: tearing great rocks from the earth,

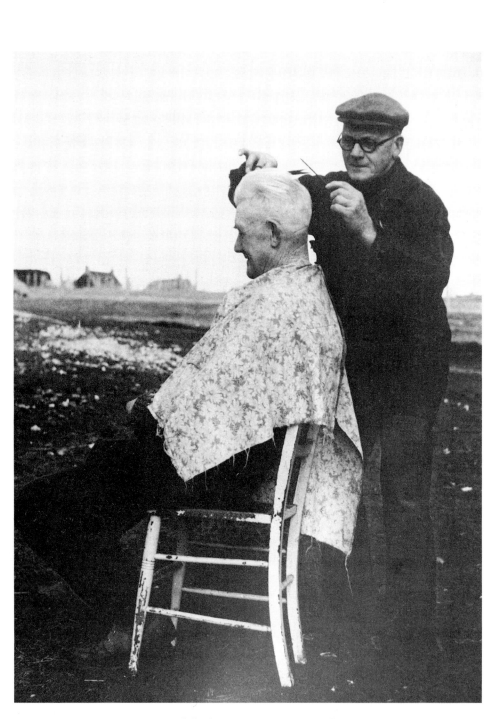

Community skills: haircut at Ness, Lewis, about 1935

and hauling them away to clear the soil, and staggering from the shore with creels of dripping life-laden seaweed to sweeten that soil, and the planting, and the reaping, and fear of the weather, and always that unease. Life that could end in a moment, on the rocks or out at sea, or the choking of a child with diphtheria, tetanus, and a host of slimy deaths.

The goodness of the people, in their fellowship, their concern for the poor and the widowed — and their own blind folly, their viciousness. The contempt for tinkers. The ferocious family and inter-family feuds that could span three or four generations. The ceaseless, swirling, searing thunderstorm of gossip, your every move and word being observed and noted, analysed; your character summoned up in a crude and enduring stereotype, that came to be held against your line. *Tha e anns an uil.* It's in the blood. They were always wild in that family. The great and true piety of the godly, and the church that was near to full each Sabbath — the Bragar people on one side of it, the Shawbost folk on the other; the good old elders, the wise and godly old women, the keen purity of the young convert. And the great bulk of the people, though they were not communicants, followed the faith afar off; they read a chapter each night, they said grace before meat, and the one greater disgrace than being denied baptism was in failing to apply for it. There were always, of course, one or two households that made mock of all this; perhaps the father was a drunkard, or had intellectual pretensions, but the electric-storm fizzed in understanding. "Ach, aye, indeed. Well, that was ever a dark home."

Goodness: real vital goodness, a village that knew you were sick and cared when you died. And yet there was the serpent, sliding in the night; little hints and glimpses of what was dark and squalid and vile. The human tragedies of which one heard, in the vague recent past — fifty years? a hundred years? "He went mad. He went quite mad, and one day he bolted from the house, and made for the shore, and walked straight into the sea, and he drowned." "She was never right. She did not mix at school, and people ignored her, and her mind went completely. Her mother is over eighty, and still looks after her, and she hasn't left the house in twenty years, and the girl is never seen." "Poor soul, when she was old she grew a beard! I suppose it would be the hormones . . . at last she wouldn't go out without a scarf covering her chin . . ."

Scandals. "She got into trouble — a baby, and they said her father had given it to her. Anyway, she never left the house afterwards . . ." "She was the most narrow self-righteous girl at school, and look at her . . ." "Aye, dead in the ditch — he must have fallen on his way home, unconscious, and the weather . . . drinking, of course, they had been drinking at that place all night."

Superstition. "Well, he was on the road at night, and saw the headlights suddenly coming straight at him, and before he could move they went right through him. He was terrified out of his wits. Wouldn't go out for days, and then a fortnight later he went out to so-and-so's, and in the dark he was knocked down and killed by a lorry." "There was a cousin of yours in Bragar, a long time ago, and he saw funerals — you know, he would go out of the house, and have this sudden vision of a funeral procession, and know whose it was, and sure enough there would be a death in that house . . ." "Loch an Coinnich. That's what they called the loch that was on your grandfather's croft — the loch of moss — and it was drained, of course, but it is said there was an *each-uisge* in it — a water-horse . . ."

You went to Shawbost, and thrilled to being sucked for a while into the bosom of this great warm wicked family of people. But living there, you sensed, you would be another proposition entirely. So the Youth reasoned. Either you accepted this gossip-frenzy, and revelled in it, and played the game of shredding your neighbour's privacy while shrouding your own — a colossal social fencing-match — or you stood away from it, kept to yourself, put others at a distance. A poor victory. "Strange, that one, he doesn't mix . . ." "I'm telling you, he is not normal. No-one from that house was ever normal." "Wasn't there a sister of his grandmother that was put away in the mainland, that was mentally ill?"

On a wild wet August day in 1982, Cousin Margaret had her wedding to Kye from Baile Stigh that worked in the mill. New Shawbost thrilled to the occasion; the women old and young flocked to her house for the show of presents, and Granny had her best suit pressed and ready, and when the day itself came the whole street put out the wedding-flags, the white cloths that ancient tradition posted at the gates. So when the big car left the house out the road, and bore Margaret to her marriage, at every gate and fence there flapped and fluttered a banner — dusters, teacloths, towels, handkerchiefs; and even old Annie a' Ghobh, Annie-with-the-purple-lips, stood at the roadside in the driving rain with a great white sheet billowing from a pole, her pinched face radiant with delight.

The winter came, and came again, and the Youth came to Shawbost in the summer of 1984, and spent a few nights in his grandparent's house. His uncle was home from Canada, to see Granny, his mother, who was now very poorly, her great heart rapidly failing. She slept most of the time now; she breathed heavily, and her face was grey and clammy with the struggle of living. She had had one or two minor strokes, and each had left her confused, but she had slowly recovered her wits and she missed little. She did not make meals now, nor go for coal and peat, nor waddle out to the van; but she peered from the window to the road, and not a morning nor afternoon went by without someone dropping in, and she was laughingly said to be the most visited woman in the island.

The Youth was shocked by the sight of her when he came home: the wheezing for breath, the evident pain whenever she rose or walked. But she was in her eighty-fifth year, an age the doctors would never have thought her heart would grant her; and he admired his aunts, who had looked after Granny assiduously, and Chirsty, who was staying with her now each night.

There came a Sabbath evening; the Youth had been to church in the morning, with his uncle from Canada, and that evening the Youth volunteered to Granny-sit. It would let Chirsty out to church, and in any event the evening service was to be in glorious and incomprehensible Gaelic, adding a new dimension of guilt to his public worship. So M.D. and Chirsty went out, and the Youth sat with Granny-in-Shawbost, in the lounge, and for a time she dozed and he read, and then she awoke, and took up the Free Church *Monthly Record*, and slowly read to herself the Gaelic sermon for the August issue.

It was another of those lustrous evenings outside, the sun still high, the land green and vibrant in the rich rays of light. A sheep or two munched beyond the window; a gull squawked angrily on the roof, and up the street little plumes and spirals of smoke rose to the sky. But there were no looms tonight, and no pipes; no cars on the road, no children at play.

Granny put away her magazine, and her glasses, and asked about the new assistant minister they were getting in Shawbost, and then how Calum Macleod the missionary was doing. He was a Shawbost man: did the Youth know that? And his wife, though born in Canada, was of island people. Like many she knew of in Canada, who had been born from people she had known, who had poured out of Lewis and over the Atlantic after the Great War, and never returned.

She was silent for a little while, and then she began to talk of her youth and of her century. The terrible War, that had taken the young men away, and some had not come back, and some had gone down with the *Iolaire*. The great migrations, and the huge ships that had sailed from Stornoway in the Twenties: the *Canada*, the *Marloch*, the *Metagama* . . . and there was an old man she had known in youth, who had come back to Lewis only a few years ago, after fifty years in Canada, and found nothing but changes: new houses, new people, new ways, and he had died, so said Granny, of a broken heart.

At the gutting. Following the herring-fleets down the east coast — Wick, Fraserburgh, Arbroath, Lowestoft — the laughter of the girls, the cruelness of the work — the hacked fingers and cut hands, and every morning you had to bandage them again, and go out in the frost to plunge them anew into fish and brine. And then there was service in Edinburgh — a maid, a cook, on Gilmore Place, on Morningside Drive — and then she had met Murdo. He had just come back from America, and of course he had known her all her life — the same street, were they not — but now there was love, and they were married by the minister of Leith Free Church at the end of 1924.

A small wedding. "Oh, she is still living, yes," said Granny, when the Youth asked about the bridesmaid, and then they had come back to Shawbost, herself and Murdo, and taken over the croft, and he had saved money, and bought himself the chassis of a bus on the mainland, and it came up by boat, and a Stornoway man built the timber body of it and put the seats in. And Murdo had done well with buses and lorries, the people and the tweeds. Though he could be so absent-minded — there were many jokes about that . . . And then, in the way of very old people, she talked of death: it made her sad, but not afraid, for it was the separation that moved her, the leaving of kindred and home. She had been to see Mor a week or two ago, the last sister she had, up in Brove on the west side. And she had said to Mor, "I'm afraid you'll not be seeing me again, because I am going to Bragar." And Mor, though not believing, had understood.

The sunlight was deeper, and lower. M.D. returned, and his wife Annie, and Chirsty, and Margaret came by with Kye. There was tea, and then there was more tea, and talk, and worship, and the singing of several Psalms. Granny could not sing, and could not carry a tune, but she sat with them and shut her eyes and droned the words softly to herself; at length the visitors left, and Granny — small, shrunken, very old — rose with much coughing; the Youth bent down and kissed her, and Chirsty guided her to bed.

Outside the night was cool, approaching dusk; new orange streetlamps glared balefully down on the main road. The Youth stood at the door for a minute or two, and watched the stars emerge in the sky, and listened to the distant roar of the surf in Dalmore. The summer was drawing in, the days lengthening, autumn approaching; the sea on the sand of Dalmore and the rocks of Bragar, by the bed of Lionagaidh. Ebbing summer. The guttering wick of time and life; the ocean of timeless death.

Arnol

The smoke of the fire before me is full and warm, hanging in the room of the old house, for there is no chimney; but it is the smoke of peat, a kindly fume, not sulphurous, and although it leaves the air heavy it does not clutch at the throat. There is soot thick on the links of chain hanging above the fire, and more soot on the roof-timbers above, and the smell of peat and smoke is in every cranny of the house, but the dwelling seems in no way unclean. It is all of a piece, this blackhouse in Arnol, except that it is perhaps a little too tidy, and sterile. Crockery and utensils sit on the dressers just *so*; assorted tokens of ethnicity — the coat-hooks fashioned from a thistle-stem, the tinkers' lamps hanging from nails — are neatly in their place. Plates, but no food; hooks, but no clothes; a Bible, but no spectacles.

No-one lives here, and no-one has lived here in my lifetime. The house is now a museum, in the care of Historic Scotland, near the end of the Arnol road and in sound of the sea; and it would be tempting to write of the lonely murmur of breakers in my ears as I sit staring into the fire and think of Clearance and the *Iolaire* and Grannies and death, but in truth I can hear nothing. Thick deep walls of boulder and clay see to that.

A remembering house. It sits by the sea and dreams to itself, of the people who were here once, sitting as I sit now, in their laughter and their troubles, and the house kept them as it now keeps their secrets. And perhaps it laughs itself, at the worthy purists who restored it and maintain it for the people of Scotland — the ones who came in the mid-Sixties, to purge it into political correctness, stripping it of wallpaper and electric wiring — and, no doubt, at the daft tourists that come off the coaches each summer day, to poke blue-rinsed heads about its corners, and ask the attendant where the last tenants had the video. So the house abides, and chuckles in tolerant amusement at the frailty of man.

"Done brooding?" asks the Cousin, and he is there beside me, as he is always there now in my mind, dark cynicism looming at those moments of reflection, like a spider on your shoulder, and it spinning in your ear its webs of arid snaring death.

"I was thinking," I say, "looking two ways in time. Seeing as how the history is done, or at least the big important bits, and trying to link it into the ongoing narrative;

the exploitations of this century, the troubles of the present. Do you understand?"

"Dearie me," says the Cousin, with his least nice smile. "Is your talent by any chance faltering?"

I stare at him coldly. "This thing is, basically, a Highland epic. Its scale has to stretch over centuries, and there must be a thread of continuity. And this is the difficult thing — linking something like Culloden and the Clearances, and those people, up to the BCCI crash and the kids of Stornoway in the Led Zeppelin jackets. Don't you see," and I force myself to pause, for fear that I might start to gabble, "we have a mental picture of those Highlanders in the 1700s — be-tartaned, Gaelic monoglots, superstitious, as remote from us now as the Red Indians, and a writer must bridge that gap?"

"Ah," says the Cousin, "so he's got to come to the native reservation, to visit the hut of the medicine-man and see mystical things in the sacred fire!"

I decide to forgive this provocation. "Looking two ways in time," I repeat, liking the phrase, "hence I look for details, vignettes, something that captures the present in conjunction with what is ancient or timeless. Weren't there jokes in the Fifties, when the Hydro came in many places before the water, about the old wifies hirpling out of the black houses to fill electric kettles at the well?"

The Cousin says nothing to this. He puts a hand to his mouth, as if hiding a secret smile, and the first two fingers straighten up to stroke the cheekbone, and the smile is wiped away, and he leans forward over the blue-red embers on the floor. He spreads his hands for a moment. The glow of fire glinting in his glasses.

"The old days are gone," he insists, "and good riddance. Look at that soot. Can you think what it was like to grow up with that filling your lungs, night and day? And the poverty? There's the byre on the other side of the door — in the same square of wall as the house — and the beasts were there through winter. And we — I mean, the ancestors of happy memory — that was their lavatory. Just the dung-heap of the byre. Oh, very romantic, I grant you, but who would want to stay in those things for the sake of Japanese tourists? Not myself. You might, I suppose. But you would."

I stand up and pace about the room with the fire; to the dressers, and back to the settle, and round to the chest, and to the door to the room of box-beds, and back to the Cousin. "Yes," I say, "you are quite right. The old houses had many serious defects. There was no sanitation, and seldom effective drainage, and the floor just stones on bare earth, so the water would often rise through it in very wet weather. And there wasn't much light — where were they going to get glass? — and weren't windows taxed anyway? And that thatch up above, barley-straw on turf, will be crawling with insects and fleas. And the houses were damp, despite the fire. You look in the bedroom there, and you see water trickling down a part of the wall, from the roof-valley at the corner of house and barn."

But I am yet loyal. "The black house had these defects, but they reflected the lack of good materials and the poverty of the people, and also the insecurity of their position — why improve your house, when you could be evicted at any time? Man, the basic black house design was a good one. It was windproof, and very aerodynamic. You would be in here during a storm and you'd hardly hear a thing; stay in that kit-house next door, and in a Force Nine you would think it was about to take off, and you with it. Everything to build this place came from the environment about it: stone, clay, turf, heather, straw. Everything was renewable. The soot-impregnated thatch could be recycled as fertiliser. And they looked good, the old houses; they seemed to grow out of the land itself, and not be as awkward and intrusive as a modern bungalow is. No eaves to catch the wind. No square corners for it to howl around. Single-level apartment. Even flowers growing in the roof come summer. There's an old tale about the islander in New York. He was told about their fancy houses by all he met, and he could say — quite truthfully — that his folk's place had central heating and a roof-garden.

"The fire in the middle of the floor," I add patiently, and the Cousin understands. "And they lasted a long time, you know. There were still a few inhabited in our own lifetime. This one was only vacated in 1964. And the last black house — the real, chimney-less thing — was in Carloway, and it was abandoned — good life, only in 1982." And I thought of that home, hard by the seedy hotel, and the little old woman who lived there alone; who would stand by the door in summer, in black-clad dignity, to marvel at the cars jamming in beside the pub.

"With some improvement," I continue, "like proper damp-coursing, and timber flooring, and windows, and sewerage and so forth, it's basically a very good design of Hebridean housing." I stop. I am beginning to lecture.

"There's still some in the Uists, the kind with chimneys," recalls the Cousin, and for a time we say nothing more, and we watch the fire, its warmth between us, that makes it hard at times to maintain animosity. I am glad of the fire. I feel, somehow, very cold in my kinsman's company.

"All a bit fake," giggles the Cousin. "I mean, it's obvious that no-one really lives here. No kid's toys lying about, or sewing-things, nor a newspaper. None of those typical signs of a Hebridean homestead. You know? A print of the Gospel ship, a plate on the mantelpiece with a coloured picture of Stornoway Free Church —"

". . . and a rented video of *The Texas Chain-Saw Massacre*," mock I, granting no monopoly of cynicism. "Ach, well, it's a museum-piece. Give the tourists what they want. The past remote, and hygienic, and safe, and not a hint of what the southerners and the Lowlanders did to the people that made these houses and worked this land."

"Is that what the book is all about? The untold cruelties inflicted on noble Gaels by the forces of Anglo-Saxon civilisation?"

"Aye, that, but also something a wee bit more original. Dangerous. What the Highlanders became in response to oppression — the dark, destructive side of Gaeldom; the negativism in us. Like that seedy side of Shawbost — sex and death, land of salvation and sin. And whence we found comfort. And what we have done to each other. Indeed, the extent to which the Gaels are responsible for their own plight and malaise today."

He shifts his feet, and I sense discomfort. "They'll not thank you."

"My cousin, they never do."

"Can't say I blame them."

Further silence. A peat shifts in the fire, the ash crumbling into the golden heat. I wonder where the attendant is. Not that there would be many visitors today, in this south-western rain, the steady downpour outside. Not in November. She came loping from her nice house next door, and sold me a ticket, and left me to dream.

"Well, they had that after Culloden and the Clearances," says the Cousin, "the consolation of religion."

"Aye," I say, "the Gospel, in full-orbed Reformation purity, though at length with a curious Gaelic spin on it. Pietism. Intensively introspective. That was not biblical, the stress on assurance, almost making out it was virtue to be uncertain of going to Heaven. It came in with Richard Baxter, the Puritan. And Archie Cook brought it to the Highlands. Oh, cousin — Archie Cook. He was a minister at Daviot, *and* the Free North. So Highland Christianity could become dangerously censorious, divisive. And in the small cosmos of Highland Presbyterianism, there was — and is — much good, but also the capacity for venomous dictatorship. And division. And heartbreak."

I am remembering it now, and it is coming back as if we were still in that little town in that long and dreadful summer. And he can remember it too: and perhaps he too then tossed awake in the northern summer nights that were never dark, keening for friendships made rubble, the tongues professing love under eyes that glowed malice.

"Mackay," he whispers. "You're going to write about Mackay?"

"Someone must," I say, "for it was very badly covered at the time, even by myself, for there was so much I did not understand, and so much to be learned. A very Highland church, and a peculiarly Highland calamity. And didn't the great wide world laugh and laugh? And didn't it all have something to teach us about our own world, the peculiar psychology of our birth and background?"

Moments pass, and he says nothing. There is an unease in the room of the fire, that hung about with the smoke, an unease without name or time.

"You fool," he says at length, "you utter fool." His face has gone quite white.

CHAPTER FIVE

Clear as the Noonday Sun

Sabbath, 9th October 1988. A crisp autumn evening in Edinburgh, still and cool, and in the suburbs of the city the first leaves were falling in the avenues. But there were no leaves crunching underfoot as you approached the big nondescript church on Gilmore Place, for Gilmore Place was in Tollcross, and Tollcross was a dull and dusty and barren corner of old Edinburgh, though Victorian, and very central. Gilmore Place headed in from the junction at the King's Theatre, and there was a second-hand bookshop there, and a grimy grocer, and an ice-cream parlour; the Convent of the Little Sisters of the Poor was there, and up a little road to your left was the Annexe of James Gillespie's High School, once Darroch Junior Secondary, which schooled the young Sean Connery. And on the next little road to your left was the Edinburgh church of the Free Presbyterian Church of Scotland.

A big, nondescript building on the outside: very grimy, the stonework in need of repointing. You went up the steps, and the stolid little elder smiled and nodded and grasped your hand, and his teenage son smiled and nodded and tugged the inner door open, and you went into the church. A large building indeed, far too large, with galleries on three sides: a thousand people could have sat in these pews, but the congregation rarely topped seventy.

Two elders sat murmuring in the enclosure below the pulpit, and you recognised them both: John Scoales, clock-repairer, and the other one . . . You realised that the fine young minister was away, and that tonight one of these elders would take the service, for the Free Presbyterian Church lacked ministers, and its pulpit-supply draws heavily on laymen. Not that a mere elder could preach from the pulpit: no, without Presbyterial ordination, and a collar, and a frock-coat, an elder preached from the lectern at the precentor's desk. Even this one.

A little frayed and shabby, this church, with some peeling paint and worn carpet. Yet it had its own simple dignity: the high plaster arch behind the pulpit, with its painted text: HIM THAT COMETH UNTO ME I WILL IN NO WISE CAST OUT — a slight misquotation of John 6:37, but then this church had once been United Free. It was pleasantly warm. It smelt of varnish and peppermints and old ladies. There was a pew or two of them to your left, in good coats and hats, their silver hair piled in buns, and they turned to beam as you sat down. Some young Highland women, down for nursing, in colourful berets and daring lipstick. Families. A mother with three very small children. Two fidgeting teenage boys.

The other elder came in, and the senior elder rose and began the service. It was an affecting thing to hear him, because of his great office and his fame, and him content to give a Gospel word to these people, in the near-empty church in dark Tollcross, and the clock-repairer leading the singing. He was a striking man, the preacher, with his keen features and soft cloud of white hair: the small bright eyes, and the dark brows that contrasted with the hair and seemed permanently, quizzically raised.

He preached from a verse of Psalm 46: "Be still, and know that I am God." His voice was soft, educated, but very Scots; it lilted logically through the simple heads. "Be still, and know that I am God in bereavement. Be still, and know that I am God in affliction. Be still, and know that I am God in injustice." He was a good preacher: understated, undemonstrative, but reverent and earnest.

He concluded in prayer. He read out the last four stanzas of the metrical version of the Psalm, to be sung in conclusion. The tall precentor stood, and began the tune in his high mild voice, and your voice rose with the other voices, to blend in that most fluent and Gaelic of sounds, the ornamented cadences of an old tune and eternal words, swirling and echoing in the depths of the building.

"May the Lord bless His word: we shall remain here no longer," said the preacher, and that sufficed for our benediction — which only a minister might give — and we relaxed, and stood, and made for the street, and shortly he was out among us, modest and affable, hands tucked easily in trouser pockets.

A few weeks later, they suspended him.

The Right Honourable Lord Mackay of Clashfern, M.A., LL.B., Q.C., was Lord High Chancellor of Great Britain and Northern Ireland, holding one of the most ancient posts in government; Speaker of the House of Lords, head of the English Bar, minister for all matters of jurisprudence and the judiciary in the United Kingdom, ahead even of the Prime Minister in the order of precedence, behind only the Royal Family and the Archbishop of Canterbury; sometime Dean of the Faculty of Advocates, Lord Advocate of Scotland, and Lord of Appeal in Ordinary in the House of Lords, one of the ablest Scots of his generation, and the most eminent alive. And, until 26th May 1989, he was a member and elder of that most distinctively Highland denomination, the Free Presbyterian Church of Scotland.

James Peter Hymers Mackay was born in July 1926 in Edinburgh, the son of humble but industrious Highland immigrants. His father came from the hamlet of Clashfern, by Scourie in west Sutherland, and had worked with the Caledonian Railway Company, though he retired on his marriage in 1920 and devoted himself to the duties of an elder in the Free Presbyterian Church in Edinburgh. His wife was Mary Budge, from Halkirk in Caithness. And James Peter would be their only child.

He came to them late in life; his mother was forty-one, and his father nearly fifty. There is a story that a pious old woman met the couple, when they were still childless though wed for some years, and assured them that they would yet have a son who would rise high in goodness and ability. But stories of this sort are so common in the Highlands, and so frequently retrospective that perhaps we should not believe this. (My grandmother speaks piously of seeing my father in the pulpit when he was yet in the crib, but fought ferociously to keep him out of it when he heard the call.)

It was a warm and kindly home, and Mackay grew up a warm and kindly person; he was ever at pains to destroy the image of Free Presbyterianism as something cold and legal. It was, he once said, a community of the "sweetest love", and he was only twenty-one when he was received as a member of the Church at a Communion season in Bonar Bridge. Also going forward that day for the first time, by the way, was a huge ex-serviceman called Alexander Murray. Murray, who was shortly to begin training for the ministry, became a firm friend; but Mackay had other friends, and was especially close to the doughty minister of Wick, Robert R. Sinclair, who was twenty-eight years his senior but shared his birthday. Every Saturday, the Lord High Chancellor would ring him for a chat.

Mackay married a cousin, Elizabeth Jane Hymers, quiet and lovely: they produced a son and two daughters. They lived in a gracious house in the Grange district of Edinburgh, and treasured their privacy in family life. Later, when he entered the Government, the Mackays moved to an exclusive address near Holyroodhouse.

The details of Mackay's spectacular career are well known; they stand testimony not only to his considerable mental abilities but to the virtues — industry, application, sobriety, seriousness — of his background, and it must have saddened him that neither parent lived to see him even take silk. The boy won a bursary to George Heriot's, one of Edinburgh's curious "Merchant Company" private schools. He studied mathematics at Edinburgh, and lectured at St Andrews before reading further at Cambridge. Returning to Edinburgh, he took another degree — in law — and went to the Scots bar, in 1955. He took silk a decade later.

Mackay specialised not as much in criminal law as in cases of corporate liability and negligence, where he had a depressing habit of appearing for the defence. Two cases, however, did him some damage in Free Presbyterian circles. He was involved in the sensational divorce-hearings for the Duchess of Argyll in 1963; contested, of course, and abundant in salacious detail. And, in 1973, he appeared for a huge multi-national oil-corporation whose proposals to develop Drumbuie in Wester Ross as a rig fabrication-yard had triggered a heated public inquiry.

The local councillor was none other than Alexander Murray, now minister at Applecross, and one of the central issues he pursued was the matter of Sabbath observance. At length Murray agreed to some Sunday work at the plant, accepting that concrete-pouring could not be interrupted without compromising the structure's integrity and the lives of men, and hence was a "work of necessity and mercy". But some Free Presbyterian colleagues were incensed by this concession to Mammon, and there was a cack-handed attempt to arraign him at Synod, the supreme court of the Free Presbyterian Church. It failed. So did the Drumbuie proposal, though a yard (since closed) opened soon after at Kishorn.

Mackay, universally respected by his colleagues, became Vice-Dean and then Dean of the Faculty of Advocates. In 1979 the Lord Advocate in Scotland, Ronald King-Murray, announced his retiral at the looming General Election; both Prime Minister Callaghan and Leader of the Opposition Thatcher were set on Mackay as his successor. Thatcher duly appointed him, and Mackay was installed with a peerage, taking title from his father's birthplace. The posting was greeted with general acclaim. He was generally held to be a man of no party loyalty: perhaps an old-fashioned Highland Liberal? And he was kindly, modest, soft-spoken: unlike many of his colleagues, there was no talk of drunkenness, nor of a mistress, nor of rent-boys. Though some resented his success, he was a man whose only enemies were among the people from whom he had come. (Mackay would still enjoy general goodwill in Scotland's legal circles when he entered the Cabinet in 1987: after five years in office, however, he was out of favour.)

He presided over Scots laws and lawyers with competent aplomb. In 1984 he quit the position, for a more important (if less visible) seat as a Lord of Appeal in the House of Lords. Mrs Thatcher had her eye on him for other things; he was fast becoming a favourite of hers, being unable to aspire to her position, and most honest. Yet, on the retiral of Lord Chancellor Hailsham in June 1987, Mackay was surprisingly passed over, and Lord Havers went to the Woolsack. Three months later, a bad heart-attack forced Havers to retire, and Mackay was appointed in his stead. Havers, rather a passenger in the Government, had left a great backlog of work which took Mackay months to clear.

He was not (a common error) the first Scot to be Lord Chancellor, but he was the first Lord Chancellor in modern times who had never served at the English bar. So the English bar made their displeasure plain. The Scots gloated. And the Free Presbyterians — indeed, evangelical Christians throughout Britain — were convulsed with delight and pride. The *Free Presbyterian Magazine* pronounced sententious blessing. "We know that it is the prayerful desire of the Lord's people throughout the Church that Lord Mackay be sustained by divine grace in this high office to which he has been called and in which he will exercise great responsibility . . . We would commend the new Lord Chancellor to the prayers of the Lord's people. Let them pray that he may be a witness for Christ in the high places of our land, as Daniel was in Babylon, and be an instrument for good in the hand of the Lord in promoting in the land that righteousness which alone exalts a nation."

Somewhere, the godly lit a fiery furnace.

The Free Presbyterian Church of Scotland has long been the smallest of our national Presbyterian denominations, overtaking only the tiny Reformed Presbyterian Church of the south country, and it has always been intensely Highland. Virtually all Free Presbyterians come from a Gaelic or crofting counties background; and until the Seventies the Church supported but four ministers south of the Highland line.

By some strange providence, the Free Presbyterians have always been strongest in the poorest districts of the north. Calum I. MacLean, a famous son of Raasay who converted to Roman Catholicism, made this point many years ago. "Adherence to a certain denominational group is an important determinative factor in the social grading of Highland communities. Members of the Scottish Episcopal Church . . . are on the highest social plain . . . the church of the people of quality in the Highlands . . . Next . . . come the members of the Church of Scotland . . . the church of the middle and professional class . . . the Free Church is more Gaelic than the Church of Scotland for the simple reason that a greater percentage of its adherents will understand Gaelic preaching, and one of the reasons why it is on a lower social level is that very same fact . . . The Free Presbyterians and the Roman Catholics constitute the lowest strata; the former because they have less tradition behind them than the Free Church and are numerous in the poorest and most barren areas, and the latter because they have had less time to overcome the disabilities of the Penal Laws . . ."

And indeed it is in rocky Harris, bleak Torridon, furthest Assynt, and in a dozen extremities and road-ends throughout the Highlands and Islands that the largest Free Presbyterian groups are found. If you were surprised, by the way, to find in the paragraph above that the Free Church and the Free Presbyterians are completely different denominations, you are not unusual. Confusion of the two is endemic.

In fact the Free Presbyterians separated from the Free Church in the last decade of the last century, unwilling to accept the tide of change sweeping that body. By the 1870s much of the evangelical fervour that had brought the Free Church into being had faded. Ministers and divinity-teachers began to dabble in the new theology dawning on the Continent: a theology that put the Bible on a par with all human writings, and no longer endorsed its integrity or inerrancy. The Church had grown rich; its people risen in society. And its new leaders were power-hungry and ambitious. Robert Rainy, Principal of New College in Edinburgh and fast emerging as virtual Pope of the denomination, dreamed of totally eclipsing the Established Church. Could not a super-church be created, a united body that would stand as the most powerful kirk in Scotland?

The obvious route was to forge a union between the Free Church and the United Presbyterian Church, a moneyed and decidedly trendy coalition of former Secession groups. The United Presbyterians were in the forefront of change. They built new churches of astonishing grandeur and opulence, commissioning such architects as Alexander "Greek" Thomson. And they were in the forefront of the anglicisation of

Scottish worship; the first denomination to replace metrical Psalm-singing with hymns, and precentors with organs and choirs.

Such practices were rapidly copied throughout the Free Church, except in the Highlands, which were now the conservative heartland of the denomination. But the primary obstacle to union was theological. Though the Free Church had left the Establishment, she still officially held to the "Establishment Principle" — that the state had a God-given duty to finance and maintain the Church in Scotland. The United Presbyterians, however, were "Voluntaries" in full accord with the Founding Fathers of the United States: they thought any state-religion or state-church was wicked. They also held to a curious view of the Atonement, contrary to historic Calvinist teaching. As both the Establishment Principle and the standard Atonement theology were specifically propounded in the Westminster Confession of Faith, to which the United Presbyterians officially adhered like all Scottish Presbyterians, this posed a problem.

The United Presbyterian Church had accordingly passed a Declaratory Act, in 1872, modifying the Church's stand on these matters and regularising the position of ministers who held to the new views. And if Rainy was to have his super-church, he had to persuade the Free Church to do likewise. A united body required a united theological position.

Rainy was a most gifted man, of impressive appearance and powerful connections: he was well known for his Liberal sympathies, had the ear of many important politicians, and was even a cousin of Gladstone. He also held high counsels in the body of Christ, in an age noted for sublime optimism in the Empire and serene faith in continuous human progress. Though himself most orthodox, he hated the Established Church with every atom of his being; and if it took some constitutional tinkering to engineer a union that would quite humiliate her, so be it. Hence he set the Free Church on a course that splintered Highland Presbyterianism from top to bottom.

The first push for a union with the United Presbyterians foundered in the 1870s; opposition within the Free Church was too strong, and many of the doughty Disruption leaders — like George Smeaton and James Begg — were still living. Rainy abandoned his efforts for the moment, and led a campaign for Disestablishment of the Church of Scotland. He waited for death to carry his adversaries away. By 1892, all the great Lowland conservatives of the Free Church were gone; so, too, was Dr John Kennedy, minister at Dingwall and the most influential of Highland ministers. Rainy surveyed the shrinking conservative bloc, and judged — correctly — that they were men without courage or gifts of leadership.

In May 1892 the Free Church General Assembly passed its own Declaratory Act, a most subtle document. Seven clauses of studied ambiguity set forth what purported to be but a clarification of Free Church teaching. In reality it was a virtual repudiation of the key doctrines of Calvinism and of the Establishment principle. And the Act — which is still a cornerstone of the Church of Scotland constitution today — concluded in a phrase that has become notorious: "While . . . diversity of opinion is recognised in this Church on such points in the Confession as do not enter into the substance of the Reformed Faith therein set forth, the Church retains full authority to determine . . . what points fall within this description."

What the "substance of the Reformed Faith" actually *was*, of course, has never been defined; ministers and professors of the national Church who deny the inspiration of Scripture, the Trinity, the Virgin Birth, and the Resurrection of Jesus Christ are the spawn of that vacuum today. The Declaratory Act was a charter for heresy; moreover, it ushered in profound changes for the Free Church and its successors. No longer was Christ the Head of the Church and the Old and New Testaments its charter of doctrine; the Declaratory Act conferred all doctrinal authority on the General Assembly, which would assume — and maintain — virtually Roman airs of infallibility.

To become binding law in the Free Church, the Declaratory Act had first to go through the procedures of the Barrier Act, a mechanism to preserve the Church from unwarranted policy shifts; hence, through 1892 to 1893, the Declaratory Act was referred to all Presbyteries of the Free Church for their approval. All save the Highland courts did so, and in the 1893 General Assembly the Declaratory Act was confirmed by an overwhelming vote. This was now the teaching and the constitutional stand of the Free Church of Scotland.

A great many Highland ministers, like Murdo MacAskill, had warned of the terrible things they would do if the new Act were confirmed. Many had spoken of a second Disruption. But, in the crunch, only one member of the General Assembly — and he a man of timid personality and no great learning — made any stand. As the Act was confirmed, the minister of Raasay, one Donald Macfarlane, rose from his seat and advanced to the Clerk's table with a handwritten document. He read this aloud — it was a formal Protest, repudiating the authority of the General Assembly to legislate thus — put it on the table, refused to withdraw his assertions, and left the building.

That Macfarlane would enjoy some popular backing was clear. Two huge public meetings in the Highlands, at Flashadder in Skye and Achnasheen in Wester Ross, had seen many Free Church elders sign a declaration that they would leave the Church if the Declaratory Act was made law. A large group of students had quit their studies in New College the previous year, and made alternative arrangements. But the thought of separation chilled most of Macfarlane's clerical colleagues. "You will compromise us," said Murdo Mackenzie of Inverness, and "I never thought or dreamt of a disruption," said MacAskill.

The Raasay minister addressed meetings in Edinburgh and Glasgow, and then sailed unhurriedly down the Clyde by paddle-steamer to take Communion services at Kames on the Kyles of Bute. After the Sabbath he held a lecture, and this congregation became the first to follow him out of the Free Church. On the second Sabbath of June it was the Communion in his own parish; again, a meeting was held, and out came almost all the Raasay people with their minister. And throughout the Highlands and

Islands, and in the large cities beyond, the Free Church was in uproar.

Later in June, at a meeting in Inverness, the minister at Shieldaig — Donald Macdonald — cast in his lot with his Raasay colleague. Two ministers could constitute a new Presbytery. On 28th July 1893, they met at Portree with one of the Raasay elders to form a "separate Presbytery, not owning the jurisdiction of the courts of the presently subsisting Church, calling herself the Free Church of Scotland". It was agreed that the Presbytery should be known and called by the name of "The Free Church Presbytery of Scotland". Afterwards, the brethren spent some days drawing up a splendid Deed of Separation, laying forth their grounds for departure; this was adopted by Presbytery on 14th August, and a copy lodged with the Register of Sasines in Edinburgh. In the summer of 1894 the Presbytery announced the provisional name of "Free Presbyterian Church of Scotland", and after a month to allow for objections the name was settled in August.

It is impossible to assess numbers at this distance in time, but perhaps thirty thousand people — almost all Highlanders, mostly in the Hebrides and northern districts, some in the biggest Lowland towns — left for the Free Presbyterian Church. Most joined from conviction. A few groups, particularly in Lewis, came out on account of local quarrels. In the north-east Highlands, Free Presbyterianism was grounded largely in the tradition of "North Country Separatism" — a long-standing movement of devout but at times censorious laymen, who jealously kept their own services and had a deep distrust of clergymen.

Though the new Church had only two ministers, there were many elders and deacons willing to maintain services in most districts. There was a good clutch of divinity students, a few on the brink of ordination. Still, many potential Free Presbyterian congregations melted away for lack of supply. With more ministers immediately available, the new body could have been much stronger.

"The sincerity of the Free Presbyterian leaders has never been called in question," wrote a Free Church minister in 1910. "Whether they were right or wrong in the course they adopted, they acted in accordance with their sense of duty . . . They believed that on various fundamental questions the Church of 1893 was a different body from the Church of 1843, and they were resolved at all costs to maintain the testimony of the Disruption . . . It is also a fact . . . that many of the most pious and loyal of the Highland people connected themselves with the Free Presbyterian Church. It was poor in supporters of wealth and in leaders of ecclesiastical experience, but it was rich, within the limits of its sway, in those things which form the true glory of any Church — men and women of believing hearts and godly lives."

But the general reaction in 1893 was one of mingled derision and anger. Public and ecclesiastics joined to shower ridicule on the new body, to proclaim for it a short life and a miserable end. And the Free Church was swift to act against the brethren. Macdonald and Macfarlane were pursued by their Presbyteries, besieged in their manses, and at length evicted from church and manse; Macdonald was even relieved of the pitiable sum collected for the building of a new meeting-house at Annat. These were old men by the standards of that time, the meek sons of North Uist: Macdonald was sixty-eight, and Macfarlane almost sixty. They, and their people, were cast into extreme hardship.

Macdonald had come to Shieldaig to pastor a congregation still denied sites for buildings by a ghastly landlord: for five years, he had been forced to conduct services in the open air. On the brink of his threescore-and-ten, he and his flock were back on the hills. And they still tell of him in Torridon, the old man preaching in hail and rain, shivering, sometimes brushing snowflakes off the Bible as he read. In Raasay, proprietrix Mrs Wood — widow of the unlovely Herbert — also withheld sites for a new church and manse. Macfarlane could not even stay on the island; he lodged in Broadford, and sailed out in an open boat to take services. A nervous man, he was terrified of the sea. A rower once smiled at the minister trembling in the stern. "Why, Mr Macfarlane, hasn't the Lord promised to save you?" "Oh, yes," came quavering the reply, "but He didn't promise not to drown me!"

There seemed little earthly hope for the long-term survival of this new body. Yet it held on, and slowly amassed funds and erected buildings, and ordained ministers. Through all its vicissitudes and failings, the Free Presbyterian Church has survived, and indeed till very recently it was the only statistically growing church in Scotland.

The fruits of Rainy's dream must be quickly related, as they have some bearing on what was to follow. Union negotiations with the United Presbyterians proceeded apace after 1893, and in October 1900 the nuptials took place. The Free Church and United Presbyterian Assemblies marched joyously forth from their Edinburgh halls to meet at Waverley Market and proclaim the new United Free Church of Scotland. But a clutch of Free Church ministers and elders, the battered rump of 1893 "constitutionalists" who had ignored Macfarlane's call, were now of sterner stuff. They did not go to Waverley Market. Barred from the Assembly Hall they had left, they met elsewhere and announced themselves to be the true and continuing Free Church of Scotland, with no part nor interest in the union. Rather than pursue another union with the Free Presbyterians (for some had been foremost in the persecution of Macfarlane and Macdonald) they launched a legal action against the United Free Church for the name, funds and entire assets of the Free Church.

This famous lawsuit was a step more worldly than wise; it did more damage than good to the Free Church cause. They were now mocked and derided as the Free Presbyterians before, and despicably treated by the United Free majority — driven from manses and churches, stripped of pensions, even stormed by mobs during worship. But the twenty-seven ministers who adhered to the Free Church pressed doggedly on. Their case was thrown out by the Outer House of the Court of Session, and then the Inner House. But they appealed to the House of Lords. A judgement was imminent when one of the Lordships suddenly died, and the case had to be heard through again. In 1904, to the frenzied consternation of the United Frees and Principal Rainy, the House of Lords pronounced the minority to be indeed the true and only Free Church of Scotland, alone faithful to the constitution and principles of that Church, and hence alone the rightful owner of all churches, manses, colleges, schools, mission-huts, libraries, equipages, and the many thousands of pounds in the banks.

Even his enemies had to admire the reeling Rainy, now past his eightieth birthday, for his resilience at this point. He orchestrated a public outcry, and called in favours from every political contact he had; it was a time of rising tension between Lords and Commons (the great Parliamentary Act battle would come in 1910), and Members of Parliament were only too delighted to embarrass the Upper House. In a case without precedent before or since, the legislature intervened in the course of law. A Parliamentary Commission met, took charge of all properties, and divided them between Free Church and United Free in very rough proportion to their respective numbers. The minority were denied a single college or library, and many of its congregations again made homeless.

The Churches (Scotland) Act is still remembered with bitterness today. The Established Church took advantage of the confusion, quietly arranging for clauses to be inserted into the legislation that transferred from Parliament to General Assembly almost complete sovereignty in doctrine. The United Free Church owed deliverance to the very Establishment she professed to deplore. And the endeavours of Rainy the unionist, who had locked the Free Church into marriage with an almost entirely Lowland denomination, put four churches throughout Highland districts where there had previously been but two. He did not live to see the merger of the greater part of his super-church with the Established Church in 1929, to form the modern Church of Scotland. At his death in 1906, tributes were paid to him in Parliament, thousands attended his funeral, and Rainy was described — in all seriousness — as the "greatest Scotsman of his day". He is now completely forgotten.

The Free Church of Scotland — indelibly dubbed the "Wee Frees" — had emerged with just enough money and property for her needs. She (belatedly) repealed the Declaratory Act and, restored to Calvinist purity in faith and worship, began to court the Free Presbyterians.

The continuing division of these two denominations, so alike in all important respects — traditional Reformed worship, evangelical theology, Calvinist doctrine — is one of the great tragedies of Highland history. Yet, even in 1904, it was too late. The divide was set in concrete. Many Free Presbyterians recalled with justifiable bitterness the events of 1893. And the two bodies could not agree on the import of the Declaratory Act. The Free Church insisted that, being *ultra vires*, it had never truly entered the constitution. But this made nonsense of Macfarlane's stand in 1893; and that the Free Presbyterians would not have.

Macfarlane was now minister at Dingwall and much beloved; he died in 1926 at the grand old age of ninety-two. But it was the Glasgow minister — Neil Cameron — who became the dominant voice in the Free Presbyterian Church. Born in Argyllshire in 1854, Cameron came to the ministry late in life after decades as a hill-shepherd, and was in 1893 one of the senior divinity-students. He was not a university graduate and in no sense an intellectual, though he had a sharp theological mind and was a most effective preacher. Yet Cameron was more than a match for those highly gifted Free Presbyterian ministers that urged for union with the repentant Free Church minority — men who had come out with him as students, men like John Macleod and Alexander Stewart and John R. Mackay. For he was a man of tall and handsome bearing, possessed of great charisma and with the most terrifying eyes — eyes that seemed to penetrate your soul, recalled those who knew him. And he was a natural politician, much more skilled at rousing Free Presbyterian sentiment than bookish colleagues, able to argue in terms that old and unschooled elders understood.

More than any other man, Neil Cameron shaped the Free Presbyterian Church. And he undoubtedly destroyed any chance of union with the Free Church. In 1905 and again in 1917, pro-union colleagues came to Synod urging a return from the wilderness. Each time Cameron led Synod to reject such calls by a large margin. And the pro-union men — eight ministers in all, and many divinity-students — obligingly left the Church, further strengthening his position.

The Free Church has survived, always perhaps two or three times bigger than her Free Presbyterian sister, supporting more than a hundred ministers, mildly conservative and predominantly — but not overwhelmingly — Highland. This reality has long haunted the Free Presbyterian consciousness. Constitutionally, apart from the legal niceties of precisely the impact of the Declaratory Act, there was no difference between the denominations. And early this century there was virtually no difference in practice. Without real distinctions, Neil Cameron — perhaps unconsciously — set out to manufacture them.

Almost all the matters of policy that are advanced by Free Presbyterians today to justify separation from the Free Church, originated under Cameron's leadership. Free Presbyterians prohibit Freemasons from church-privileges; the Free Church does not. Free Presbyterians are not allowed to use public transport on Sundays even to go to church; members of the Free Church are. Only the Authorised Version of the Bible (and its Gaelic or overseas equivalents) are allowed in Free Presbyterian pulpits, and they regard it as the only sound and perfect version; the Free Church has never held this view, and modern translations sit on many lecterns. The Free Presbyterians are much stricter on dispensing baptism, and impose rigid rules on their communicants. Free Presbyterians prize uniformity throughout the Church, and the identikit nature of services from Assynt to Auckland is one of their remarkable features; the Free Church values diversity.

In almost every regard the Free Presbyterian Church is more conservative, more decided, and more intensely Highland. Unlike the Free Church, there has never been a Lowland counterweight, drawing on the traditions of the south, to balance the supreme court. Though there are areas of the Free Church — principally Lewis — where her discipline is quite equal to Free Presbyterian rigour, their judgements can always be overturned in the higher courts of the Church.

But the achievement of the Free Presbyterian Church has been astonishing. She has always managed to train and maintain just enough ministers to survive. By 1910 she had established a foreign mission in South Africa — a young black Christian from Rhodesia by chance bumped into a Free Presbyterian in the centre of Edinburgh, and soon the Rev John Radasi was back in his native land to propagate the Gospel. By the Great War the Free Presbyterian Church had established three home Presbyteries, and was sending deputies to preach in Canada, New Zealand and Australia. By the Second World War there were schools, churches and medical services supported by the Free Presbyterians in Rhodesia; there was a huge congregation in London, and several others in Australia and Canada. The *Free Presbyterian Magazine* first appeared in April 1896, and every month subsequently; a complete set paints a fascinating picture of world and social change in the last century.

By the autumn of 1988 the Free Presbyterian Church of Scotland had thirty-eight ministers in total, including one in London, one in Northern Ireland, one in Australia, one in New Zealand, four in Rhodesia and two in Canada. She had five home Presbyteries and three overseas Presbyteries. She maintained two old people's homes in the Highlands, a magazine for children, a flourishing publishing outfit, a good bookshop, and the extensive Zimbabwe mission — a hospital, a superb secondary school, many primary schools, and congregations that attracted crowds of two or three thousand at a time. Already this work was extending into Kenya and Malawi; indeed, most Free Presbyterians alive today are black Africans. She is the only mainstream church in Britain to have had a black man as her titular leader — African ministers were Moderators of Synod in 1963 and 1988 — and was amongst the first to condemn apartheid, in 1961.

The Free Presbyterian Church is often deplored as highly negative. Certainly her pronouncements are forthright and, by modern standards, extreme. Synod has repeatedly condemned Communism, socialism, homosexuality, unscriptural divorce, pornography, Scottish nationalism, *in vitro* fertilisation, artificial insemination by donor, and Sabbath-robbing British Summer Time; she has advocated capital and corporal punishment. Always, always, fighting for the Sabbath; and always condemning the doctrines and practices of the Church of Rome.

Rules enforced by discipline in the Church condemn cremation, going to the cinema, going to the theatre, going to concerts, using church premises for sales of work

In June 1965, to the outrage of the great majority of islanders, a Sunday ferry service began to Skye. A large and angry crowd watched the first boat berth

or sports-clubs or *soirées*, using public transport on the Lord's Day, attending services of other denominations (a thorny one, as we shall see) and the celebration of Christmas and Easter. Contrary to popular myth, however, the Free Presbyterian Synod has never forbidden church-members to own or watch television-sets, nor has the Church ever banned (nor even discussed) the use of artificial contraception in marriage.

But the Church, both in Synod resolutions and in its magazine, has often spoken up for the beleaguered and oppressed. Though its rules for women are derided — they are not allowed to preach or hold office, nor wear trousers, and must always have their heads covered during public worship — women form the bulk of communicants, and some — such as the wonderful Jean Nicolson — have taken posts of high responsibility in the mission-field. And the Church's appalling image for blackness, darkness and repression is not borne out by the facts. To be sure, Free Presbyterian ministers are invariably clad in clerical best; elders and deacons go to church in sober garb, and women wear long flowing high-necked garments of studied modesty.

Yet, when I think of Free Presbyterians, I think not of sullenness but of laughter:

voices quick to chuckle, faces to which smiles come readily. The most beautiful women of all ages, of serene expression and queenly bearing, exquisitely courteous; large and happy families (though the famous Campbells of Struan, all twenty-one plus parents, are not typical) in homes of fun and hospitality; old men, almost illiterate, who had in the world aspired to nothing more than road-making or crofting, but who knew the Bible literally word for word, and outdid many a minister in the finest points of theological understanding. Many an evening I have spent in a Free Presbyterian church or meeting-house, watching an attentive audience of young and old hanging on every word of a lengthy (usually forty-five minutes to an hour) and closely argued sermon, and joined my voice with theirs in the full high vibrant strains of psalmody, the old tune beautifully decorated with grace-notes and appogiaturi, and sometimes a precentor giving out each line in the Gaelic fashion.

I have sat at table in many Free Presbyterian homes, and joined in devouring a groaning spread; I have bent my knee with them in family worship, and been asked to take part myself for all my Free Churchness; I have, to this day, many Free Presbyterian friends, and of all the clergymen I have known the only one who has given me consistent encouragement and understanding is a Free Presbyterian minister.

It was, and is, a family church, with many degrees of inter-relatedness, and a kirk of tribes and dynasties; a family, compact and close, all knowing each other, and like all families prone to moments of the most acute and bitter division. And the intermeshing of Free Presbyterian clans in 1988 was astonishing.

The aged minister in Wick, R. R. Sinclair, was by then the most senior serving minister: his father James had been another 1893 student. His sister, Annie, had married the Church's first Scottish missionary in Rhodesia, John Tallach. He was a son of Raasay missionary Andrew Tallach; the family came from Dornoch, and the name was most interesting — it is said that these Tallachs had been Jacobite refugees from Wester Ross, and that the name was only of eighteenth-century origin, corruption of the Gaelic adjective translated "Kintail-ite". John's brother, James, was minister at Kames. John's son, Ian, became himself a minister in 1972 at Perth. And John's nephews at Kames were equally devout. Fraser Tallach was by 1988 minister at Kinlochbervie; his brother James a doctor now resident as minister on Raasay; brother Cameron a medical missionary in Hong Kong with the Reformation Translation Fellowship; and brother John, the youngest, minister at Aberdeen.

And more. Ian's brother, yet another James Tallach, also returned to the African mission as a builder. Ian himself married Anne Macleod, his second cousin — her grand-mother, and R. R. and Annie Sinclair's mother, had been sisters. Anne Macleod's brother, Donald B. Macleod, was a rising Free Presbyterian minister and, from 1970, editor of the *Free Presbyterian Magazine*. And Ian and James Tallach had twin sisters, one of whom married into the Macaskill family of Inverness. One Macaskill cousin was minister in Assynt till his death in 1982; two others, also twins, were ministers in Dundee and Dumbarton.

Dundee minister, Donald Macaskill, was married to Margot Ross. Her brother Edward was an elder in Lochcarron. Another brother, Jackie, was Lochcarron minister. Brother Donald was minister at Laide; brother Neil minister at Ullapool, and brother John minister at Tain and Fearn. Sister Sheena was married to the nephew of a late minister at Halkirk. Another sister's husband was Malcolm Macinnes, minister at Toronto. Malcolm Macinnes himself had two sisters. One was married to Fearn elder Roderick Mackenzie, whose three brothers were also Free Presbyterian elders — and more of them anon. Another sister of Macinnes was the wife of Gairloch minister Alfred Macdonald. His brother, Fraser, was minister at Portree. And their brother Iain . . . but why continue with this tangle? I have said quite enough here to demonstrate the intertwined genealogies of Free Presbyterianism.

The Church has survived many troubles: union disputes in 1905 and 1917, controversy over Prohibition and Sabbath bussing, and other spectacular rows. In 1936 she was rent asunder by the "Dornoch dance case", when the kirk-session in that town suspended an elder — and him the Provost — after permitting a dance in his home; the sensation was deemed worthy of coverage by the *Times Of India*. In 1938 a most popular minister, the Rev Ewen MacQueen of Inverness, tabled a Protest and quit the Church after the Synod overturned one of his discipline judgements. Hundreds flocked out with him.

A row broke out on the precise nature of a Protest in the Supreme Court — did it *invariably* and *automatically* separate one from the Church? The question was critical: if Macfarlane's Protest in 1893 had not immediately separated him and his adherents from the Declaratory Act Free Church, then the historical link with the pure pre-Declaratory Act Free Church had been broken. But some Free Presbyterians held the right of Protest to be an essential Christian liberty. And every Free Presbyterian thought their side of the question the only possible and reasonable position.

In 1945, after an almighty row at Synod in Glasgow, three Free Presbyterian ministers left for pastures new over the issue. One, Roderick Mackenzie, who had succeeded Cameron at St Jude's, followed MacQueen's example at Inverness and began keeping separate services in the name of the "Free Presbyterian Relief Congregation" at Renfrew Street. Mackenzie had been best man to James Mackay at the Lord Chancellor's father's wedding; in the late Sixties, when Free Presbyterian leaders met secretly to consider negotiating a truce, the young advocate was despatched to Glasgow as an emissary. He went once to Mackenzie's manse, knocked on the door, obtained no answer (the old fellow was probably out), and did not trouble to call again.

"And give *them* the satisfaction?" chortled Mackenzie in old age, when someone asked if he planned to join the Free Church. He died in 1972. Not until 1980 did the last MacQueenites in Inverness cease separate services; not until 1984 did Mackenzie's surviving adherents abandon the Glasgow meetings. Their little church was subsequently bought (through subterfuge) by the Society of St Pius X, who consecrated the building for the celebration of traditional Latin Mass.

FRIDAY, 10TH NOVEMBER 1988

On this autumn evening the Free Presbyterian congregation in Aberdeen held the opening-service for a new place of worship on Alford Place. Coach-loads and car-loads made their way to the city from the north and west of Scotland. An elder sat in the back of a minibus carrying him and other brethren to the jollification; months later, he recalled the shock that came. "The driver had his radio on . . . the Scottish news . . . and at six o'clock there was the headline: 'The Lord Chancellor, Lord Mackay of Clashfern, has been suspended as an elder of the Free Presbyterian Church for attending a Catholic funeral . . .' Well — just a total hush. No-one said anything, but the driver swung his head round, and grinned, and stared, as if thinking, 'My, what sort of weird people are you?' "

And there were the television pictures, on every bulletin: the announcement in grave tones by dispassionate newsreaders, and a backdrop-picture of the spire of St Jude's; and the moving images, the shabbiness of Woodlands, and the sleekness of the limousine, and the shy ministers walking up the path and pretending not to see the cameras. The harassed Moderator of Presbytery, in a light grey stock, reading a statement and promising photocopies, his sharp Inverness vowels brittle with nerves; and Lord Mackay himself, standing tall on the steps in the television lights, hands clasped like a martyr at the stake, explaining what the suspension meant, and what sealing-ordinances were, and no, he considered what he had done was perfectly appropriate, and he had no regrets.

Religious journalist Stewart Lamont, beaming before the cameras, explaining who the Free Presbyterians were — "they've produced some incredibly talented people — once an FP, always an FP" — buttons popping with pride at the secret knowledge. Television, and more television. A look at the next day's papers with *Newsnight*, and there was *The Times* with the headline "Free Church suspends Lord Chancellor", and you rang them indignantly to point out the error and explain the difference, and this bored southern voice said that the people in Scotland must be very stupid not to know what they meant. (Later, a reporter from *The Scotsman* would ask my father, "What is the Church of Scotland?")

Mackay on television, leaving his car and going into the church and then leaving the church and speaking and going away, and pictures too of his minister, Angus Morrison, and of other ministers and elders — and a beautiful shot of two shutting and chaining the mighty gates behind them. But there was one whom no camera caught; someone of great talent and force of personality, the architect of this hour. Lord Mackay indeed was a wonderful man, but even more remarkable was the Rev Donald MacLean.

CHAPTER SIX

A Decade of Disaster

The suspension of Lord Mackay by the Free Presbyterian Church for hearing Requiem Mass did not flow inevitably from the Church's testimony. Though a vigorous Protestantism was part of Free Presbyterian witness, no-one in the entire history of the Church had ever been dealt with for such conduct. The Free Presbyterian brand of Protestantism flowed from a positive understanding of the Christian Gospel that offers salvation in Christ alone, and thence a detestation for many aspects of Roman theology; it was not a Protestantism of simple anti-Catholicism, far less the stupid bigotry of the Orange Lodge. (Membership of which, incidentally, is proscribed by Church rules.) Many Free Presbyterians in the cities worked with Roman Catholics, and got along just fine. The Free Presbyterian Church of Scotland is far removed from the Gospel-hall bigotry of the Free Presbyterian Church of Ulster, with which it is utterly unconnected, and predates by many years. The young Ian Paisley did apply as a private student for Free Presbyterian divinity training in the 1940s; he was shrewdly turned down.

No: the Mackay trial was a matter born in the cold tangle of church politics, and the Lord Chancellor himself — unbelievably — became a helpless pawn in a struggle between two Free Presbyterian camps. In earlier and happier days the case would have quietly foundered. But, by 1988, there were men fighting to direct the Free Presbyterian Church along a certain path; and also men fighting equally desperately to stop them. Each camp saw in Lord Mackay, and in the case that surrounded him, a last chance to settle the struggle, to deal a shattering and final blow for control of the Free Presbyterian Church of Scotland. They had not the breadth of vision, not an understanding of the forces with which they toyed. So the stage was set for a tragedy in which the Antichrist could wrest the script from their hands.

Over nine decades the Free Presbyterians had, unconsciously or otherwise, held their separate identity by imposing a rigorous uniformity of order, and by stressing at every turn their distinctiveness from the continuing Free Church of Scotland. They were not like the Exclusive Brethren, living literally apart from the world; Free Presbyterians prized education and progress, and bred very competent businessmen. But the Church strove always to make itself "pure" — in its standards, in its practice. And such a goal is not attainable. You begin by outlawing a certain thing, and then to outlaw a further thing, and then many things; hence you pile up more and more rules, until your very structure groans beneath their weight, and people become reluctant to submit themselves to such minute authority.

Hence the Free Presbyterian Church had very few actual communicants; congregations were composed largely of uncommitted but loyal adherents, often converted, but yet mere spectators at the solemn bi-annual Communion seasons. The Staffin church, for instance, had in the mid-Eighties a reported attendance of sixty — of whom precisely two were communicants. Such a phenomenon (reflected to a degree in the other Presbyterian churches of the Highlands) owed something to the solemn Gaelic understanding of salvation: that it was in a sense presumptive to profess redemption. But it also followed from the rigid demands made on the lives of professing Free Presbyterian Christians.

The more laws you have, the more difficult it becomes to enforce them. Inevitably, some offenders escape. Discipline becomes therefore partial, inconsistent. Others, duly chastised, resign and leave. You end, after a succession of little defections on each new decree, in a body stressed and suffocating. And in one which, though made up of the most humble individuals, is rotten with collective pride.

The Most High withdraws his favour. Demoralisation sets in, and bitterness, and backbiting. In this reality, men are driven to further extremes. Thus it always is, and was: party-lines will form, and duly formed, and by the autumn of 1988 the Free Presbyterian Church was split from top to bottom. No-one understood this better than that great individual, the most powerful minister of the Church, who would now stake his all on the humbling of the Lord High Chancellor — Glasgow pastor, Clerk of Synod, and the man who had trained most serving Free Presbyterian clergy, Donald MacLean.

Donald MacLean was born in the Gorbals in June 1915. His childhood is surrounded in mystery, for he did not care to talk about it, but his mother had Raasay connections and his father hailed from the Coigach district, west of Ullapool. I am told that his father served as a local councillor, and was a born politician; I am also told — by MacLean's enemies — that he ran a public house, though why MacLean should be blamed for that I do not know. At any rate, though not communicants of the Church, the parents were good Free Presbyterians; and from childhood the boy walked to St Jude's on Pitt Street, there and back, twice each Sabbath — a distance, he would recall proudly in old age, of sixteen miles. And he never forgot the preaching of old Neil Cameron, that hard but faithful shepherd; immaculate in top-hat and frock-coat as he marched from his manse, and those blazing eyes.

MacLean came to a personal understanding of Christ in his youth, going to the Lord's Table at the age of nineteen; he seems to have been converted through the preaching of the new minister, Roderick Mackenzie, that clever and stubborn son of Lewis. By then MacLean was studying for chartered accountancy. He qualified and obtained a good position, and then the Second World War broke out. He had a good war, and could be justly proud; enlisting as a seaman, he quit in 1945 as a lieutenant-commander, having specialised in submarine warfare. He had aroused affectionate comment by, on leave, always attending church in uniform. In later life, like many veterans, he was apt to portray himself as a vital agent in Hitler's downfall.

Even by that summer of 1945, when MacLean was formally received by the Southern Presbytery as a student for the ministry, he already stood high in Free Presbyterian counsels. Senior ministers consulted the young man on the case of Roderick Mackenzie and his "Protest" campaign. After completing his studies, Donald MacLean was ordained and inducted to the pastoral charge of the large Portree congregation in the autumn of 1947. His career thereafter was swift and upward. He became editor of the Church's *Young People's Magazine*. He was made Assistant Clerk of Synod: a post more administrative than powerful, but important. In 1956 he accompanied R. R. Sinclair to the Rhodesian mission, where there had been very serious troubles; they had a wonderful time trekking across country and probing drains and preparing reports, and the difficulties were duly resolved. In 1958 MacLean became theological tutor, teaching doctrine to a generation of new Free Presbyterian ministers: at the 1989 Synod, twenty-six of the ministers present would be MacLean graduates. And in 1960 he was called to pastor the biggest Free Presbyterian congregation of them all, St Jude's in Glasgow.

Now I am going to say harsh things about the Rev Donald MacLean, and it is important therefore to early stress his virtues. (I shall write only nice things about him when he is dead.) He was probably the best all-round minister the Free Presbyterian Church has had in recent years, and certainly the ablest leader it has ever seen. MacLean was a man of vigour, intelligence and vision. He was an outstanding preacher: others might excel him on occasion, but none could so hold one's attention, and unlike some of these he was a solid expositor of the Word, not given to mysticism nor rambling anecdote. He was also a very evangelistic preacher — again unlike some of the brethren — and he appealed regularly and powerfully to the unconverted, offering Christ to them freely in the Gospel, and many responded. He was not that hyper-Calvinist of popular fiction, who will not preach the Gospel "because the Lord has His elect".

He spent much of his time in study, as a good minister should do. But he was an assiduous and jocular visitor of the ill and the housebound. Old women adored him — MacLean's photograph, in all his clerical finery, adorned many a mantelpiece — and young people were very fond of him. He liked them and courted them, holding most useful meetings for students in his Glasgow charge, and his manse was often open for them. (He owed a great deal to his wife, the warm Grace MacQueen from Daviot, who bore him five children.)

But MacLean was also a leader of overwhelming and mesmeric charisma. He was extremely handsome — strong features, tall and elegant bearing — and retained a remarkable youthfulness into very old age; in his late seventies, hair still dark and figure still trim, he could yet pass for a good-looking fifty. And he had an astonishingly, powerful and compelling voice, grating and nasal, and almost unpleasant: a curious blend of west-end whine and Royal Navy gung-ho and Gaelic lilt and clerical chant, but a voice that ranged from ferocious snarl to gentle rhapsody to avuncular chuckle. In the pulpit, he could be truly frightening, commanding it like the captain on the bridge of a destroyer, pacing about as he warmed to his theme, and his hands chopping and floating in a range of expressive gesture. But the roar would subside, and he would melt a little, and gently argue some fine point, and perhaps tell an apt story.

He dressed well and expensively. He was, I think, acutely self-conscious at many levels, and he took care of his image. He wore coats and suits and shoes of the finest quality. He always wore a frock-coat when addressing a congregation, even at the prayer-meeting — this was not Free Presbyterian custom. He always wore a hat: a roundish Homburg. He disliked the round dog-collar, preferring the traditional Scottish garb — a stiff, white, starched bow-tie, worn under the points of a good turned down white collar, with gold stud in the white and starched front, the whole forming a white V in the black of jacket and wasitcoat. This rig is now confined to the Free Presbyterian Church, though still popular with her ministers; you cannot buy these ties today — they are squared and flat, a special design — and making or laundering them is a problem. When Glasgow's men's-linen launderer — Anniesland Collars — closed some years ago, to MacLean's dismal regret, he had to confine the "white front" to his Sabbaths and the Highlands, and thereafter wore the standard washable dog-collar midweek, unless it was Communion or the Synod. But details like this mattered to him.

He was a man of awesome physical presence. He had a crusher of a handshake, and he liked to stand very close to you, almost intimidating. He had a stare that petrified and a look that could kill. (More irreverent observers, seeing him out in best togs, said he reminded them of Lugosi's Count Dracula.) His face was strong and expressive, though marred a little by very bad teeth — still, he had bright gold fillings. He was not as brave as he looked; if you stood up to him, he would often concede the point, and certainly respect you for it, and he was quite capable of admitting he was wrong, and taking good counsel. But such was his usual bluster and self-confidence, and so chaffing was his humour and so prone was he to self-glorifying anecdote, that he acquired an unenviable reputation for arrogance. Most Free Presbyterians admired him; many feared him. But some, all their lives, utterly detested him.

This was not fair. MacLean was not, I think, the proud tyrant that many held him to be. He was a self-made, self-invented man, and in all such men there is a fundamental insecurity. He did not grow up in this mighty mould, nor with that wonderful accent, and in this lay his barely perceptible self-consciousness — streams of banter interspersed with nervy cackle, facial twitches. But he was a man of enormous force and drive — not an egotism at all, but an almost Nietzschian will-to-power; a will that would, in any walk of life, have carried him to the very top. Such was the strength of Donald MacLean's persona that he had an alarming way of imprinting his tones and carriage on all who knew him well. Many of his students grew to speak, dress and even walk like the great man; even your own voice could take on these crushed and surging vowels after hearing him.

MacLean was propelled through his career by that will; by childhood memories of the noble Cameron (on whom he certainly modelled himself) and by consuming zeal for the greater glory and advancement of the Free Presbyterian Church of Scotland. To him her truths, in a phrase he was fond of using, were as "clear as the noonday sun"; he would say, in another phrase he was fond of using, that "I can only have liberty of conscience in the one Church where my conscience is at peace, in the Free Presbyterian Church of Scotland". In all endeavours he was truly sincere. But the weapons he deployed in the crusade — that acidulous sniping wit, Cameron's old trick of swinging the elder-pack against the clergy, his vicious jibes against colleagues, and the ceaseless hunt for enemies within — these showed the worst side of Donald MacLean.

Why, in human terms, he confined his ambitions to the Free Presbyterian Church might tempt some psychologist's thesis. It is just possible, even subconsciously, that MacLean in his little sphere harboured envy against Lord Mackay. But I am certain too of other things, that some people of certain piety and discernment held him in high regard; that his grumpy charm appealed to even the smallest children, and that when he was relaxed by the fireside in scuffed slippers and with a vessel of something warm in his hand, the anecdotes and wisdom would begin to flow, and he could be the most enthralling company.

A powerful man, of glorious talent, heading for the heights. And it was MacLean's calamity, and his brethren's, that there is no place in the Presbyterian universe for such people. One is our master, even Christ; and a Presbyterian church has no place for bishops and princes, but must run on the consensus (too often a mediocre consensus) of equals. The only way the Free Presbyterian Church could accommodate a man like MacLean was to have others of similar ability and stature to keep such energy in check and maintain a balance of order.

There were such men: old warriors of Free Presbyterianism. But, as the years went by, death took them away. Others abdicated. Some, fully MacLean's equal in one or other of his fields, were compromised by their own weaknesses of sense or personality, or were simply too good to appreciate the danger, as well as the blessing, such a man as MacLean can pose to the cause of Christ.

The year 1967 saw the death of the last male communicant of the pre-Declaratory Act Free Church. The old generation had gone, those who remembered the battles of 1893; a new generation faced what was perhaps the greatest decade in Free Presbyterian history, a brief time of confidence and expansion.

The Church had opened an eventide-home in Inverness, Ballifeary House, a most useful and beneficial institution. From 1970 there were annual theological conferences, attended by all ministers and male members. Youth-conferences began; these were all innovations MacLean heartily endorsed. He also encouraged some youth divinity-students — there was a remarkable crop of thirteen at study in 1968 — to form an organisation for evangelising Scotland and the nations. The Blythswood Tract Society — it was named after the district bordering the old St Jude's — opened a Christian bookshop and printed tracts; later, in the Seventies, there were more bookshops, and a Bible-study correspondence-course that attracted thousands from all over the world. Active in this movement were two of the brightest students, Jackie Ross and Ian Tallach.

Here MacLean made a rare political slip. The boys of Blythswood began to preach in the streets of Glasgow to passing crowds, with his blessing, and this attracted the ire of colleagues. Was this not most disorderly? Did it not tend to Billy Graham-style emotionalism? The matter was raised at Synod: MacLean bravely defended his students, and pled their cause, but lost the issue. The practice was banned. The Glasgow minister smarted. Thereafter, he strove to be ever the darling of the orthodox.

But further glories lay ahead, many on MacLean's initiative. The new Church Extension Committee started services in Perth and Stirling: in 1972 the towns were made an Extension Charge, together with Dundee, and Ian Tallach — an able man — appointed as its first minister. He worked hard, and the congregation rapidly grew; he visited schools and factories and Perth prison, and worked harder, too hard.

In 1974 two congregations in Canada, which had quit the Free Presbyterian Church in 1929 over the issue of Sabbath transport, returned to the fold. The African mission continued to expand, and another black minister was ordained. Meanwhile, a succession of districts received ministers for the first time. New preaching-stations appeared in Australia and New Zealand; a Presbytery was formed in these lands, supporting three ministers.

The Church seemed suddenly to explode with talented young people. Many applied for the ministry. A comprehensive history of the Church was published. There was a degree of revival in Scotland at this time; many came to Christ, and further afield in the English-speaking world there awoke interest in traditional Reformed theology. The Banner of Truth Trust had begun to reprint books unavailable for decades or even centuries; many people from England and beyond began to show interest in Free Presbyterian values. In 1977 a little group at Barnoldswick in Lancashire, who had come together from various church backgrounds and none, were received by Synod into the Free Presbyterian Church.

The Church had long attracted a certain kind of proselyte; often English, and usually from a background of liberal theology but sonorous and dignified worship — people who, though persuaded of evangelical truth, disliked the chaotic liturgy of tambourine-bangin' charismatics. Two such converts might be mentioned: one was the curious Edward Greene, a schoolboy at Eton, who came to Christ by a chance attendance at Free Presbyterian worship while camping in Applecross. Greene became a passionate Free Presbyterian, falling in love with Gaelic Psalmody and the practice of giving out the line; he became a competent precentor himself.

At Oxford, Greene fell in with another convert, a German youth called Christian Puritz, and the two students actually formed a Free Presbyterian Society at the university. Word of this came back to MacLean, who dashed off a typically imperious letter. "How dare you take the name of our Church for this association! Kindly forward copy of your constitution for our immediate perusal." A few days later, he received said constitution — folio upon folio of flawless Latin. Nothing more was heard of the matter.

Greene applied for the Free Presbyterian ministry. The Southern Presbytery turned him down. He appealed to Synod, and lost by but a single vote. (He held such odd views: he wanted the Church to legislate only for Psalm singing with giving out of the line, and to make its members disconnect all services — electricity, water — on the Sabbath.) To his credit, Greene later admitted the Synod decision was most wise. He grew up to take over and run a private tutorial college at Oxford, which made him rich; he lived with his mother in an ancient and characterful building at the heart of the town, and trained the servants to sing Psalms before meals. Free Presbyterians still talk about his spectacular descent on Harris in February 1988 with his mother and an old lady-friend from Edinburgh, to attend the opening of a new church and eventide-home in Leverburgh; an epic journey north, with Greene imperiously hiring limousines and planes and finally a small ferry, to arrive at the service just precisely late enough for a sensational entrance.

Christian Puritz immersed himself in the work of the Blythswood Tract Society, though he never actually joined the Free Presbyterian Church. He began to be seen as rather a nuisance, capping various indiscretions by rising from his pew in St Jude's to challenge MacLean's sermon — an interesting new experience for the minister. Puritz later settled in England and got himself a wife, which did him a power of good.

In 1977, MacLean succeeded Sinclair as Clerk of Synod. 1978 brought a wondrous Providence. In the last years of his life an eccentric millionaire, R. W. Forsyth — proprietor of a celebrated Edinburgh department store — began to show interest in the Free Presbyterian Church and in Gaelic. He approached them, poor fellow, to suggest that he bequeath the Church a substantial sum to promote the Gaelic language through ceilidhs and concerts. They tactfully explained why this would not be appropriate.

He was hugely impressed by their honesty. And when Forsyth died — such a recluse that the kirk minister at the funeral had to ask, "Can you tell me something about the man I'm burying?" — he left a fortune to the Free Presbyterian Church of Scotland, some six hundred thousand pounds, for the promotion of Gaelic and all causes pertaining thereto, as well as to benefit the elderly and the young. The Forsyth Fund — by 1988 it was worth nearly three million pounds — cannot be used to support the ministry, nor for work overseas, but it has been put to excellent use in subsidising the youth-conferences and the *Young People's Magazine*, financing a Gaelic quarterly supplement for the *Free Presbyterian Magazine*, funding a new eventide-home, and in maintaining and even building churches throughout Scotland — as well as equipping them with hearing-aids for the deaf.

In this MacLean exulted: was it not a sign of clear favour from the Most High? And the Church's cup did finally overflow when, in May 1979, James Mackay was ennobled and made Lord Advocate. Naturally, he now had to renounce his position as Assistant Clerk of Synod, which he had attained in 1970: Mackay was made the Church's legal advisor in 1963, and had gone regularly to Synod since 1957. Wonderful were the motions and resolutions he endorsed, countersigned and on occasion drew up: resolutions on hanging, and divorce, and sodomy, and artificial insemination, and Europe, and Rome — enough to keep the *New Statesman* in knocking-copy for a month, should I be malicious enough to reproduce them.

The Assistant Clerk and his colleagues had dealt with some difficult cases in the Seventies. In 1971 a troubled Synod had considered the case of Rev Alexander Murray, who had won election as a County Councillor for Applecross. Though he had stood with the consent of his Presbytery, and they could appreciate the pressures of the situation (the only other candidate was an atheist), it contravened an earlier Synod resolution forbidding ministers to stand for political office. Murray had wrought great good for the Applecross community (like the construction, at long last, of a coastal road from Shieldaig) and so Synod left him *in situ*. But Murray was not granted permission to run for re-election.

In 1973 MacLean brought a most authoritarian resolution to Synod, one that would authorise the courts of the Church to discipline Free Presbyterians who attended the services of other denominations — even evangelical services, even (especially) Free Church services. This had long been occasional Free Presbyterian practice — Neil Cameron once bustled north to, quite improperly, take charge of such a case in another minister's congregation — but never before had it been enshrined in canon law. Now MacLean filled the gap. "The Synod expresses its strong disapproval of ministers, office-bearers, communicants and adherents of this church taking part in meetings arranged by other churches in this land, and instructs the relevant church courts to keep a watchful eye on this matter . . ." MacLean said, "I would expect that any kirk-session in the Free Presbyterian Church who discovers those belonging to that congregation, who already had the privileges, attending the services of other churches, to deal with them according to the discipline of the Church."

This was the most wonderful debate; it lasted to the Synod of 1974, and MacLean's motion was further modified in 1975, but it was passed substantially intact. In vain did a wiser minority protest: Sinclair himself leading the opposition and crying, "It is contrary to Scripture and Moncrieff" — he being the author of the Church's manual of procedure. For this was a new departure. This was the church of Christ threatening members with discipline for something that was scarcely self-evidently sinful. And it was a branch of the cause of Christ effectively proclaiming itself to be not merely the best, nor purest, nor most faithful, but the *only* church of Christ that Christians could rightly attend.

Some, years after, remembered early evidence of MacLean's obsession with the issue: in the early Sixties, London Baptist minister Dr Martyn Lloyd-Jones — the finest preacher of our century — held services in Dingwall Free Church, and young Free Presbyterians had gone to hear him. Shortly afterwards, their minister — Donald A. Macfarlane, a saintly old man — had a call from MacLean, urging him to discipline the pack of them. Macfarlane, deeply upset, refused. But he remarked to his wife, with horrid prescience, "That spirit will one day split our Church."

In 1976 there were two violent Synod debates. An elder of the Wick congregation was pursued for having spoken at the "Six O'Clock Club" in the town, a Christian youth club that played records, showed films and sang choruses. The Scottish press seized eagerly on the affair early in the year, trumpeting the changed days in the Free Presbyterian Church — a red flag to the bull if there ever was one. Fortunately for the elder, this Sodom and Gomorrah of an organisation was wound up before Synod met, and there the case had to take end. A Glasgow member was so carried away that he tabled a Protest. Panic-stricken brethren managed to talk him out of it.

There followed the next ordeal by Synod, triggered by Malcolm Macinnes, the young minister of London, who had upset his people by coming to the mind that it was wrong to wear distinctive ministerial dress. Macinnes argued, quite correctly, that the New Testament advocated no such garb, and that what applied to worship in the Church (nothing to be done save what Scripture directly commanded) applied too in this instance. The Southern Presbytery did not agree, and he had appealed.

The discussion still makes wonderful reading, with Iain Tallach and Malcolm Macinnes presenting abstruse theological argument, various sages discussing the impact of weather conditions in Manitoba or Rhodesia, and older ministers almost weeping with passion — one trying to make a frock-coat of Christ's seamless garment, another saying that these were dark days when students for the ministry went about hatless and in bright ties, and that they would go to pot like the Free Church, and some of their ministers in sneakers. "What are sneakers?" asked a puzzled Moderator.

The debate was not as comic as it might appear. Macinnes was technically correct, but he ignored excellent reasons of expediency for the clerical collar, and made trouble out of something that had never been an issue before. All ended in chaos. Three motions were put to Synod; that backing Macinnes and Tallach lost, and the supreme court tied on two against them which — as James Mackay pointed out — were in essence identical. The Moderator cast his vote blindly, and the Free Presbyterian Church importantly confirmed that ". . . Since 1893, ministerial dress in the United Kingdom has had as its distinguishing feature the clerical collar, either in the shape of a white collar and bow-tie or the round collar. Ministers belonging to this Church in other lands have worn the round collar or, in cases where climatic conditions made this inappropriate, a white collar and black tie . . . the Presbytery see no reason why this useful custom should be changed . . . In these days of lowering standards . . . the Presbytery expect that its ministerial members will conform to the practice which has prevailed among us hitherto."

Roma locuta erat. Another dangerous precedent had been set. Contrary to its principles of 1893, the Free Presbyterian Synod had allowed itself to be manoeuvred into the foolish stance of commanding the extra-Scriptural. And the rising revisionists were not slow to point this out. Four clergy asked for their dissent to be minuted, and spoke of liberty of conscience. They would be prominent in the 1989 rebellion.

In 1978, Fraser Tallach — then Broadford minister — was arraigned at Synod. He was a most clever man, immensely scholarly, though chronically unable to discipline his talents. He lacked concentration, and one must say that this owed something to dreadful ill-health — he had been one of Scotland's first kidney-transplant patients, in November 1969, and has been for some years the senior transplant-survivor in Scotland; perhaps, now, in Britain. But he yet had liver trouble, heart trouble and a host of other troubles. When I last heard of Fraser Tallach, he had just broken his heel.

At any event, he foolishly chose to immerse himself in the Charybdis of the Protest controversy. It is a feature of this recurring disease that victims come to consider the canon-law issue the most important facing Christendom; and each is certain he understands it perfectly as none other before. Tallach started tracting and arguing on the subject, reduced Skye to a tizzy, and arrived at Synod with such wads of material to document his speech that the writer of the public record simply omitted it altogether.

Things looked bad for Tallach; many wanted him disciplined for good and all. But James Mackay stepped in, suggesting a masterly compromise resolution — laying out the dangerous Protest matter in terms a child could follow, rapping Tallach well on the knuckles, commanding him to desist — but letting him off without penalty. "But avoid foolish questions, and genealogies, and contentions, and striving about the law; for they are unprofitable and vain," concluded Mackay sagely, quoting the Apostle Paul. So Tallach escaped the lynch-mob with a promise of silence. Alas, he was thereafter a marked man: and one of the keenest minds in the Free Presbyterian Church was thus locked out of its counsels and thinking.

All most unpleasant. Still, Lord Mackay was now out of it. The Forsyth bounty had come. Heaven smiled. Donald MacLean and his friends looked to the Eighties with sunny confidence. But it would prove a decade of disaster.

The year 1979 was a year of omens. In April, Ian Tallach collapsed and died at Heathrow Airport, as he waited for a flight to Holland with Jackie Ross on Blythswood Tract Society business. Though one of the Church's most industrious ministers, Tallach has never been honoured with an obituary in the *Free Presbyterian Magazine* — and one pathetically stupid lay-preacher actually described his removal as "the mercy of God." Other ministers too died off, some most pious and wise; had these lived to take part in the 1989 Synod — men who combined Free Presbyterian principle with much common sense — our tale might have a different ending.

In August, a new young minister — Angus Morrison — was ordained to the charge of the Oban congregation, a most winsome and gifted man. He came of South Harris stock, and during the summer that Hebridean parish had been struck by the most fearful woe. The South Harris minister, Angus Cattanach, was — in terms of sheer intellect — the most brilliant of Free Presbyterian ministers, and a preacher of such majesty and enthusiasm that he seemed to open the very gates of Heaven. He was now suspended by the Outer Isles Presbytery in the most chaotic and secret circumstances, following some marital sensation; his congregation, who adored him, were told scarcely anything — perhaps from a misguided aim of protecting the Cattanach family.

There was well known to be a horrendous domestic problem in the Cattanach manse, which need not be described here. Hence there was widespread sympathy for the minister throughout the Church: he was held in great esteem as a preacher, and so incompetently did the Presbytery now deal with him — hounding Cattanach to the brink of breakdown — that the whole Church soon seethed over the affair. More than anything else, it poisoned Free Presbyterian fellowship. Scarcely anyone could be found who took a sober and balanced view. Pro or anti-Cattanach advocates were found in both traditional and revisionist camps. Some said darkly that a bad end would come to the ministers who had silenced such a voice, and this rapidly gained credence — for one Outer Isles minister died, three developed serious health problems, and two were later suspended themselves.

There now broke out a rash of turbulent priests. In 1980 the Dumbarton pastor, Rev John Brentnall, allied himself with the Church's missionary to Glasgow Jews — Rev Moshe Radcliff — and dared to revive the Protest controversy. Yet again the wretched Synod heard a debate on the subject, with the two clerics — neither Free Presbyterian by birth; Radcliff was an Austrian — insisting that one could table a Protest without separating. Their overture received a derisory three votes. They then, with fantastic arrogance, tabled a Protest of their own. The Southern Presbytery met after Synod to suspend them for a year, and declared the Dumbarton pulpit vacant. In 1981, unrepentant, Brentnall and Radcliff were suspended *sine die*. (Spies had observed them preaching to the Mackenzie remnant at Renfrew Street.) So Brentnall and Radcliff took the Southern Presbytery to court.

By this stage, Free Presbyterians counted such episodes in political arithmetic.

Some Presbyteries were clearly more "liberal" than others, and the filling of vacancies became the stuff of plotting — would a particular majority in a particular Presbytery retain its control? The Outer Isles Presbytery was the most conservative. The Northern Presbytery — it covered a vast area, from Aberdeen to Scourie — was the most liberal. A pattern began. A beleaguered conservative in that court pursued an issue or personality. Even if the kirk-session took action, the accused then appealed to the Northern Presbytery. It invariably took the liberal view, and reversed the kirk-session finding. The conservatives, undaunted, brought it to Synod: and the Synod always overturned the Presbytery — because they, the main "revisionist" group in the Church, could not vote on a case concerning them. The only way the liberals could carry Synod was if the Outer Isles vote was similarly removed — for all its Presbyters supported the old paths.

Thus, in 1981, the Inverness kirk-session refused to let an elder, William Mackenzie, address the local YMCA, because it was — well, the YMCA. The Northern Presbytery said he could. The Synod said he couldn't. Thus, in 1984, conservatives tried to stop the Aberdeen church hosting a group called "Friends at Ten" — a ladies' circle, for flower-arranging and so on. The Northern Presbytery upheld Friends at Ten. The Synod banned them from the sacred precincts. Thus, in 1985, the Northern Presbytery did not call Fraser Tallach to order for publishing a pamphlet on (help) Protest, entitled *The Ides of May* — the Synod did. Thus, in 1987, an Inverness adherent — Alasdair Fraser — applied for admission to Communion. The kirk-session said he could not go, because he was a member of the Culcabock Golf Club which allowed play on the Sabbath. The Presbytery said he could. The Synod said he couldn't.

And, through all this time, heads rolled. In 1982 a most unfortunate character, the Rev Donald Alick MacLean of Halkirk, was proposed for Moderator of Synod. His ecclesiastical career was paved with mishap. Ordained in 1954, he was despatched to the mission-field in Rhodesia; within a year the Government of that land had ordered his recall to Scotland by the Church. MacLean had behaved with great foolishness, playing the grand white leader: he had quarrelled with native elders and deliberately destroyed kirk-session minutes; ordered a black maidservant to go down on her knees to apologise to him, and flung her to the floor; beaten schoolboys with a stick as thick as his arm, and in one unfathomable spell of idiocy ordered an entire school to copy out by hand (as a punishment for not showing rapt attention to his Sabbath sermon) a chapter of the Book of Joshua, five times — then refused to supply them with the necessary paper. The children went on strike: the authorities intervened. "It would appear that Mr MacLean will not tolerate an African who is not completely subservient to his will," wrote a distressed Government official to the Synod.

The 1955 Synod berated MacLean in private, and tried to hush things up; there had been much trouble on the field, and a young Angus Cattanach had been similarly recalled for some error of judgement. But MacLean then went about Scotland to spread such tales of the Church in Africa that a furious 1956 Synod made the entire saga public (it is all printed, as I have related it, in the *Proceedings*). Incredibly, he was not suspended. MacLean later ministered in Skye, and then took a call to Halkirk. There he began teaching part-time at Thurso Academy — religious education — and the 1967 Synod, perhaps unjustly, ordered commensurate docking of his salary. MacLean dramatically resigned, and later un-resigned. By 1982 the Church harboured many who could not stand him.

It is the custom that the post of Moderator of Synod, largely honorific, is not contested. But this candidate Synod refused to accept. The London minister Alexander McPherson was also nominated, and won by 28 to 22 votes. MacLean was profoundly hurt. Later that year he resigned the Halkirk charge — permanently — and quit the Free Presbyterian ministry, being received in 1983 as a minister of the Church of Scotland. He pastored briefly in Lewis, and then took a charge in Tomintoul, where he pursued his favourite hobbies — litigation, and the tending of prodigious flocks of sheep.

In 1985, Cattanach's successor in South Harris, Duncan MacLean, was suspended *sine die* after a farcical episode in Lochcarron. In Skye, Staffin minister Donald MacLennan — formerly of Uig, in Lewis — was caught up in some frightful family conflict. It came to Presbytery, and he too was suspended; he left for the Church of Scotland, and is back ministering in Lewis. The minister of the North Harris congregation, Angus Mackay, retired. That parish was shortly convulsed in conflict and scandal.

The impact of all this on Free Presbyterian morale may readily be imagined. Amidst this frenzy of demons, two camps now fought for control of the Church. A bitter division set in. There were ministers who would not speak to each other. There were ministers invited to the biannual Communion weekends of one camp, but not of another. John Tallach, now in Aberdeen, did not ask certain conservative ministers — John Macleod of Stornoway, Donald Boyd of Daviot, Mr MacLean of Glasgow — to his Communions; but he, and his brother Fraser, were not asked to theirs. It was a disgraceful state of affairs in a Christian body.

It would be quite unwarranted to blame Donald MacLean of Glasgow for all this. (As far as Cattanach was concerned, MacLean's intervention at a critical point saved him from certain — and practically irreversible — deposal.) But the Glasgow minister's impassioned leadership was a major cause of the crisis. He pursued what can only be described as witch-hunts. He conceived intense dislike for certain personalities — and, I am afraid, they were principally preachers rivalling himself in popularity. He did not hesitate to publicly denounce his enemies. Indeed, during the Brentnall and Radcliff fiasco, an irate Dumbarton member — George Macleod — wrote and circulated a document listing some of MacLean's choicer judgements on colleagues. All sound fearfully plausible. An old minister in Oban — "he's as much use in Synod as the man in the moon". The North Tolsta parish in Lewis — "like a congregation in the African bush". A Wester Ross minister — "he makes a lot of noise, but it's never about anything important". Roderick Mackenzie — "doing Satan's work while some of us were fighting

Hitler". A Lowland minister — "nothing between his ears, but his vote is useful". A Skye minister — "oh, that fool. He is *low*."

Yet MacLean was unassailable. He was Clerk of Synod, a court he politically and physically dominated; he was Convener of the important Finance Committee, and senior tutor, and minister of the great power-base at St Jude's. Ill-health struck him down briefly — there was heart surgery, and he resigned as tutor and Finance Convener in 1986 — but he bounced back, mighty as ever, set on the path of glory. Though many were restive, there was none to stand against him. Few matched him for courage and none for stature. R. R. Sinclair was a veteran of the Great War, son of a Church founder, former *Magazine* editor, former Clerk of Synod — he alone came nearest to MacLean in prestige, but was essentially a quitter.

Most of the older ministers admired MacLean greatly. The few who did not lacked guts. And most of the younger pastors — clever, likeable, revisionist — simply abdicated.

Jackie Ross immersed himself obsessively in the expanding Blythswood empire. John Tallach studied for a higher degree. So did Angus Morrison. Fraser Tallach dedicated his time to arcane researches, painted a spectacular mural on the manse-gable, and recorded tapes of spiritual songs to raise money for kidney patients. And Alex Murray, now minister of a mighty consolidated charge in Sutherland — Lairg and Bonar and Dornoch and Rogart and Helmsdale, a district requiring the full labour of six Free Church ministers — saw fit to return to politics. In 1986 he was elected to Highland Regional Council, to whose affairs he devoted the bulk of his time.

The Church fermented, and MacLean rolled on apprehensively watching for further crisis.

Another observation on that Dumbarton memorandum. "Lord Mackay was very good on technicalities. We're much better off without him."

CHAPTER SEVEN

Black November

In June 1986, Angus Morrison became minister of the Free Presbyterian Church in Edinburgh. That July, Lord Mackay — still an obscure judge in the Lords — attended a memorial service for the late Lord Russell of Killowen. A small report of the proceedings was buried in the *Daily Telegraph*: it noted the presence of Lord Mackay and other eminences, and described the ceremony — which included a Requiem Mass.

Someone brought this to the attention of Roy Middleton, Free Presbyterian elder of the convert-group at Barnoldswick. Middleton was a pleasant little man of curious appearance: very sparse and lanky fair hair, and an ingratiating face that abounded in tics. Though he toiled by day at some dull deskbound job, he was self-consciously intellectual: he studied ancient Puritan theology and possessed a complete set of the *Free Presbyterian Magazine*. He dressed invariably in black.

Middleton was most bothered by this news-item. He harboured no malice against the Lord Chancellor, and would say insistently that he feared for his brother's walk with God; but in truth his driving motive was fearsome devotion to Free Presbyterian purity. Church discipline is a most valuable and necessary institution, and a church without it is no church at all; but when the good standing of a church becomes the fuel of disciplinary action, and not the good of the brother, that discipline becomes perverted and lethal.

With all the zeal of the convert, Middleton and some close friends — including Tom Maton, a genial New Zealander who was an elder in Gairloch — began to circulate this cutting. People began to talk. Most alarming. Lovely man, Lord Mackay, but really . . . something must be done . . .

In October 1987, Lord Mackay became Lord High Chancellor. Mrs Thatcher twitted him gently, being fond of him. "Oh, James," she said, "you'll have to do something to get yourself *better known*." The *Guardian* cartoonist, Steve Bell, pulled out the caricature-stops. Scene of a nervous Thatcher introducing Mackay to Cabinet colleagues: "Apparently James belongs to some *strict* Scottish sect . . ." "*Wumman*," thundered a lumpy new Lord Chancellor, "wull ye no' cover yer *laigs* in mah *presence*?"

The strict Scottish sect, and its Clerk of Synod, were having a bad year. To be sure, the Northern Presbytery had been routinely squashed at Synod in May. But the same Synod finally lifted the suspension on Angus Cattanach, if only by a handful of votes: Alex Murray's campaign had swept the opposition. The Outer Isles Presbytery could not participate, and its ministers could only feebly protest: one of Cattanach's most virulent foes had been literally (if briefly) silenced by a stroke, and the Stornoway minister — John MacLeod — was off ill, and the North Tolsta minister could scarcely speak in public, his memory ravaged by successive thromboses. These three poor men were now the only ministers in a Presbytery of seven pastoral charges.

Cattanach's reinstatement sent them reeling with shock. By this time the Church wallowed in such cynicism that the rights and wrongs of the case hardly mattered. Rattling off a pungent list of the hapless Cattanach's faults and failings to some acquaintance, one young minister concluded by hissing, "All the same, I'm still going to vote for him — to spite that lot in the Outer Isles!" Worse followed. Some months previously, a few of MacLean's pet ministers were despatched to Canada to ascertain that brothers in that land still walked in the path of the just. To Vancouver and Toronto had fled in the Seventies Douglas Beattie and Malcolm Macinnes — more quitters against MacLean — and the deputation assessed them sternly. This, and this, and that, and that, was wrong: and they ticked off ministers and sessions and filed a dark report, and then proceeded to another charge at Chesley. Here ministered a Lewisman, Donald M. Campbell, most fervent in the faith. Why, in taking to do with farm-girls who wore trousers to drive tractors, he had at length persuaded them to wear skirts over the male attire.

The thought-police returned to Scotland to deplore Beattie and Macinnes and heap praise on Campbell. But in August 1987 a bleak minute appeared in the "Church Notes" section of the *Free Presbyterian Magazine*: "At a *pro re nata* Meeting of the Canadian Presbytery on 31st March 1987 the Rev D. M. Campbell (Chesley) was deposed from the office of the ministry for adultery. The Chesley congregation was declared vacant from that date. Rev Malcolm Macinnes, Clerk of Presbytery."

From this squalor, the Free Presbyterian leadership crashed into further rebuff. For several years, John Brentnall and Moshe Radcliff had pursued the Southern Presbytery in the courts. In 1984 the Court of Session dismissed the action, agreeing with the Southern Presbytery (who had suspended them) that they were indeed guilty of contumacy. But they, flush with legal aid, appealed.

In December 1985 the appeal was heard by the Inner House. The Lord Justice-Clerk and three worthy wigs were rapidly bogged down in the case; though they, like their predecessors, would not enter into the virtues of Protest (wise men), they concluded that the suspension of Brentnall and Radcliff could only be justified if they had been indeed contumacious. Which, by a very fine definition of contumacy, their Lordships concluded they had not. An aghast Southern Presbytery appealed themselves to the

Moshe Radcliff and John Brentnall — obsessive, litigious and successful

House of Lords. On learning that success there only met yet another reference of the case to the Court of Session — where success was plainly a lottery — the Church sensibly, but reluctantly, conceded victory to the vagabonds.

Brentnall and Radcliff looked for remunerative settlement: Brentnall sought £45,000 and Radcliff £90,000. The negotiations were protracted and unpleasant: they settled, at length, for £17,000 and £30,000 respectively. I might add that such awards come with interest — 15%, applied retrospectively from the date of commencing the action. MacLean, as Clerk of Synod, had to prepare a humiliating public statement for the October issue of the *Free Presbyterian Magazine*, detailing the legal misery and outlining the hugely expensive payments in conclusion of the case (if not the horrendous legal fees), which he quaintly described as *ex gratia*. MacLean can have never more lacked *gratia* than at this moment. The Church could ill afford this outlay of precious non-entailed funds.

In fact, the Church that had seemed so vibrant in the late Seventies was now a failing force. The Forsyth Fund had depressed givings from members. The endemic march of suspension, deposition, resignation and death created more and more vacancies that the Church could not fill. By October 1988 there were fifty-five sanctioned charges, and seventeen vacancies: of the thirty-eight serving ministers, nine were over sixty and four were over seventy. There were only two divinity students.

Even settled congregations were shrinking. Highland depopulation continued: MacLean had had the vision to follow settlers to urban districts and plant new churches, but back home church attendances seemed no longer *de rigeur* in any district. People were having smaller families. Many Free Presbyterians simply defected, young folk forsaking its discipline for pastures brighter — the Baptists, the Church of Scotland, the Brethren, the Pentecostals, the charismatic fellowships, and even (it was whispered) the Free Church. In 1970 St Jude's boasted a congregation of nearly a thousand, and perhaps seven thousand five hundred people attended the Church each Sabbath across Scotland. Though MacLean would repeat and repeat this optimistic figure to outsiders, by 1988 the total attendance in Scotland — from all observation — was barely three thousand.

MacLean could take perhaps some dark satisfaction from the Synod of 1988. Alex Murray, politicking on, had come a fine cropper: when chairing a committee meeting in Highland Regional Council, he had called on a Catholic priest from Arisaig — Father Thomas Wynn — to pray. This the two surviving loyalists on the Northern Presbytery, D. B. Macleod and Donald Boyd, could scarcely believe. Murray was unrepentant. They took it to Presbytery. Presbytery found for Murray. They appealed. And the Synod, in a most bitter and personalised debate, agreed with them. Murray was suspended for three months and his stipend for that period sharply cut.

In July 1988 the grand old minister at Wick, R. R. Sinclair, still serving, still fit and active, turned ninety. But there was a smell of death about his brethren. Never had the Church been so divided: Murray, vast and gentle, had many friends, but equally critical opponents. His congregations, and others, diverted their church-givings to his manse to make up for the shortfall in pay. In August, he resumed his duties in the far-flung charge. (This, as we shall see, was savagely disputed.) And on the Lord High Chancellor, the hounds of heaven were closing fast.

We must now narrate the process against Lord Mackay in the Free Presbyterian Church. And, as the years go by and I look back, it seems more and more a script of inevitability: a fore-ordained pattern of events, in which all became puppets trapped by events and the failings of their own psyches, and yet responsible and accountable agents for the calamity that came.

Angus Morrison, minister at Edinburgh, was one of the finest men I have ever known. He was a stocky little man with a big clever head, on which black hair with a mere kiss of grey at each sideburn curled back, and had always a serene and warming smile. He was a stirring preacher, one whose sermons seemed acts of adoration and joy — "the joy of the Lord is your strength" was a favourite text — and spoke with bubbling, happy warmth, and yet earnestly. He was a devoted pastor and a wise counsellor. He had a strong mind. He frequented Rutherford House, an evangelical think-tank in Edinburgh. He had a beautiful and vivacious wife, Marion Matheson, and two delightful toddlers. His manse was a haven of laughter and warmth; and even now, in the night, I recall its warmth with nostalgia. There was only one weakness to this paragon. He lacked bottle.

"Angus Morrison sits on the fence," snapped MacLean once, "but he's fallen on the wrong side." Morrison had little interest in church politics. He was scrupulously careful to invite ministers of all opinion and faction in the Church to his pulpit. He was also, as I say, timid; and though perhaps in this, like Samuel Rutherford, "e'en his faults erred on virtue's side", it was to have sad consequences.

For there is little doubt that, if Angus Morrison had taken seriously the rising tide of criticism about Mackay and the Mass, he could have acted then — quietly, but firmly, without even raising the matter in his kirk-session — to warn Lord Mackay and extract from him an assurance that he would not, in future, attend a Mass. Back to Middleton and friends with this promise, and all would have ended there: no publicity, no sensation and no division. In saying that, of course, I have the blessed advantage of hindsight.

But what was wrong with the Mass? Two things: it conflicted with Scripture, so the Free Presbyterians believed; and since almost the foundation of the Church both its courts and *Magazine* had frequently berated public officials — ranging from King Edward VII to Winston Churchill to our present Prince of Wales — who attended Roman Catholic worship. For the Roman Catholic Mass is not the same thing as Protestant Communion. In the Protestant liturgy, the wafer or bread is merely symbolic of the body of Christ; to eat it is not to receive Christ, but to remember the breaking of His body as He Himself symbolised it prophetically at the Last Supper. The sacrament is to obey His command — "this do in memory of Me", to strengthen our faith, to remind us of His work of atonement, and to show before an unbelieving world that we are for Christ and not for another.

The Roman Mass, however, centres on the doctrine of transubstantiation. Catholics hold that the wafer is indeed the very and literal body of Christ, transformed by the power of the priest. And it is to them a sacrifice, which is why they have an altar and not a table — though it be an altar without fire and a sacrifice without blood — and, in celebrating Mass, the atonement of Christ — the Crucifixion — is mystically re-presented (and, in a real sense, re-enacted). The wafer, though with the attributes of bread, is in its essence transformed to the substance and being of God. And the priest raises this wafer — do they not call it the Host? — and the people bow down and worship it, and when they eat it they believe they are truly receiving Christ Himself.

Vatican II changed the liturgy in important respects — the Mass is now celebrated in the vernacular and not in Latin, and the priest faces the congregation throughout. Nevertheless, unbiblical features of the rite remain: the wine, for instance, is usually drunk by the priest alone, though Christ Himself said, "Drink ye all of it." And the dogma of the Mass — the dogma of transubstantiation — is dogma still. In short, the Mass is sacrifice; it is pure idolatry, the worship of an image, prohibited by the Second Commandment (or First, by Catholic reckoning), and a re-enactment of Christ's once-and-forever death on Calvary hill — and a Requiem Mass is nothing less than a sacrifice for the dead.

And I must here make plain that, for all I am about to relate, there is now no doubt in my mind that no-one professing the tenets of the Free Presbyterian Church could properly be present at the celebration of Mass, far less an elder; and, though they handled it so uncharitably and foolishly, in pursuing Lord Mackay the Free Presbyterians were absolutely right. "Oh, come on," recalled a minister wearily when it was all too late, who had himself supported Mackay at Synod but at last remained with the Church, "he'd been a Synod Clerk for years. He'd signed the protests . . . I mean, he *must* have known the score . . ."

Lord Mackay — and by that time he was surely aware of the scandal boiling in the Church — defiantly attended another Requiem Mass, at the funeral of Lord Wheatley in Edinburgh. The looming process against him never referred to this visit; still, there were photographs and TV pictures of the service, and Mackay's attendance, which thereafter were lavishly produced.

The whispering became a clamour. Angus Morrison dismissed all suggestion that he take action. So Roy Middleton and Perth and Stirling minister Donald J. MacDonald prepared a formal petition to the Edinburgh kirk-session. Many said afterwards that they should have directly approached Mackay himself; it is, however, debatable if this was necessary in a matter of public knowledge. MacDonald, by the way, was not a born Free Presbyterian either, hailing from a Church of Scotland background in Lewis; he was a gifted man, and a good preacher on occasion, though wild pre-conversion days had left him with a countenance not so much lived-in as positively derelict.

I have this petition by me as I write. It is drafted by the criteria of Church procedure, and its argument is simple, citing repeated instances of *Free Presbyterian Magazine* protests against public figures hearing Mass — Woodrow Wilson, Lord Halifax, the Duke of Windsor (as Prince of Wales), Winston Churchill — and Presbyterian ordination-vows (for all office-bearers) in which they "disown all Popish, Arian, Socinian, Arminian, Erastian and other docrines . . . contrary to and inconsistent with the . . . Confession of Faith" — and cite Mackay's attendance at Requiem Mass as alleged in the *Daily Telegraph* of 17th July 1986. (The petition does not quote a single text of Scripture: had the kirk-session been sharper, they could have dismissed it as therefore improper and invalid.) Middleton and MacDonald humbly crave that the kirk-session duly investigate the *fama* — allegation, rumour — on Lord Mackay; that they check the truth of the *Telegraph* report, and that if it prove false they advertise the fact in the *Magazine* "to vindicate both Lord Mackay and the courts of the Free Presbyterian Church of Scotland"; and that if indeed it is correct that the kirk-session will review Lord Mackay's conduct and proceed to deal with him.

Session met at the Gilmore Place Church Hall on 11th June 1988. Angus Morrison and all his elders were present — Lord Mackay, perky Iain Mackenzie of Assynt, mild John Scoales of Berwickshire (a convert through marriage, and later grace), big Desmond Biggerstaff of Ulster, and the session-clerk, the gentle Murdo Nicolson of Raasay. The petition was read. MacDonald and Middleton spoke, sweetly and respectfully.

Lord Mackay spoke. He said, amongst much else, that he had never seen the *Telegraph* report, and no-one had told him the matter was to be raised in any Church court, though it had already been raised (improperly) at the Southern Presbytery. Synod had even sent him warm congratulations on becoming Lord Chancellor. Middleton and MacDonald had never approached him personally, though they had dissented in Presbytery when similar congratulations were sent to Mackay.

They replied. Lord Mackay had, perhaps, not been directly approached for simple temerity. The kirk-session agreed to receive the petition. The merits of the petition were discussed. MacDonald said that to attend Mass in any circumstances was sinful conduct. If the report was accurate, the court should deal with Mackay in a spirit of Christian love, admonish him, and secure an undertaking that he would never go to Mass again. Middleton agreed. It was the duty of all office-bearers to vindicate the courts of their Church.

Lord Mackay replied. He had attended the Requiem Mass for Lord Russell of Killowen, and after much thought. He had taken a professional oath to "do right to all manner of persons". Lord Russell had been his friend and a much respected judge. It was well known where Lord Mackay stood on Roman doctrine. He repudiated all its errors. But, in our culture, funerals provide the only public opportunity to condole with a bereaved family and show respect for the dead. He made a distinction between watching a Mass and going forward to receive the Host. Those who merely watched had no part in it. Lord Hailsham had been at this service too, and given the address, and actually discussed the Mass: he had never agreed with Lord Russell on it, Hailsham had said, and therefore never shared the sacrament with him.

Mackay said it would be quite wrong of him in public office to make a distinction between the faiths of any it was his duty to honour. He had considered the petition very seriously indeed. No fair person, said he, could infer from his presence at Mass that he approved of it. He could not give the undertaking sought. "To do so would make it impossible for me to continue as Lord Chancellor."

The petitioners replied. Mackay's view, they wailed, was quite different from that of the Reformers and the fathers of the Church. It was not, said Middleton, a matter of private judgement. It was wrong for Free Presbyterian elders to take this view. "I did not go to my own grandmother's funeral, because it was a cremation!"

Mackay, Middleton and MacDonald now left the hall as procedure required. There was a short discussion. A lengthy resolution was unanimously adopted by the kirk-session. It dismissed the crave of the petition, agreed with all Mackay had said, and called on brethren to strengthen his hands in seeking to bring Christian influence to bear on the affairs of Britain: in essence, the petitioners should buzz off. Had the kirk-session reprimanded Mackay, or at least besought him to give some assurance for the sake of peace in the Church, the thing might have ended there. But Middleton and MacDonald were recalled. The finding was read to them. Did they acquiesce? They did not. They asked leave to appeal to the Southern Presbytery. This was granted, along with the necessary extract of minutes.

And at this stage Mackay made a terrible error of judgement. Slowly, this case was gathering pace; it was brought now to a court controlled by a man who disliked him intensely and had all the votes he needed to find against him. Even if these votes were not forthcoming, Mackay's pursuers were so set on the matter that they would surely bring it to Synod. By that stage, whatever measures were taken for secrecy, the affair would certainly become public knowledge. The media would descend. The Free Presbyterian Church, and Mackay himself, would be held up to mockery and ridicule. In such an arena determination would only grow to vindicate the Church's honour. And, whoever won, the Church would almost certainly split.

Again, hindsight. But Mackay, at this stage or even after the Presbytery finding, should have resigned — walked out — stepped away from the whole matter. He was actually advised to do so by an association of Christian lawyers, and warned that he would split the Church if he did not: I have this on excellent authority, but he ignored it. For it must be said that Mackay loved his Church and its fellowship. He did not want to leave it. Perhaps, naively, he did not realise the ferocity of his enemies. He certainly did not appreciate the intensity of the hatreds and passions that built up over the years: passions, unleashed, that would make havoc of all.

Presbytery met, as we have seen, on 4th November. And in these minutes we see Donald MacLean at perhaps his greatest, and most typical, and most destructive hour.

Present was he, and Greenock minister Lachlan MacLeod, and Presbytery Clerk Donald J. MacDonald, and Angus Morrison: also the young stern minister at Oban, Hamish Iain Mackinnon. There were the Macaskill twins, Donald of Dundee and George of Dumbarton: identical as jellies from a mould, unless you knew them very well, former Scottish doubles badminton champions, who had together run a printing firm in Inverness until both (together, but not knowing of the other's mind initially) had felt the call to the ministry. Donald and George were most attractive men, and George was Moderator of Presbytery.

There was another minister, George Hutton of Larne in Ireland. He and his "Bible

Presbyterian Church" had been received into the Free Presbyterian communion only in May; they had been formerly with Ian Paisley's curious outfit. Hutton was a plump and genial fellow. His elder was with him, and representative elders from congregations in the Presbytery bounds — Fort William, Stirling, London and so on. There were seventeen present altogether; only London minister Alex McPherson was absent.

MacLean took charge, and all fell before. He moved that the case be heard in private because of media attention: Hamish Mackinnon moved for a public hearing. MacLean won, ten votes to six. (The Moderator has only a casting vote in Presbyterian courts.) Mackinnon moved that Fraser Tallach — he had come to give moral support to Mackay, an old friend — be associated with Presbytery, and thus allowed to speak if not vote; MacLean, ignoring a standard courtesy to visiting ministers, moved against, and won.

Even from the printed page one can imagine him that afternoon: proud and confident, eyes glittering, all present quailing as that icy glance fell upon them. The Clerk, MacDonald, had to leave his post for the discussion as he was a party in the case. MacLean moved that he be replaced by Mackinnon *pro tem*. MacLean moved that a burly St Jude's elder present, Kenneth Gillies, be appointed officer of court. And MacLean was again obeyed.

By his motion the documents were taken as read. Parties were called to the bar. The arguments were trotted out once more: MacDonald and Middleton urging the necessity of vindicating the Church's witness, etc, and Angus Morrison adamantly insisting that presence at Mass did not necessarily associate one with its blasphemy, etc. Mackay spoke, an address on the matter that shows the might of that intellect, and in reading betrays great tension and sadness. There were questions put to all, and they were then removed from the hall.

The Presbytery debated. MacLean argued forcefully for Middleton and MacDonald. George MacAskill, Moderator, interrupted to say that Free Presbyterians had gone to Roman Catholic funerals in the past, and the Clerk of Synod — MacLean — had known of this. The Clerk of Synod denied all knowledge of such instances. (But the tale would persist.) He did not see how, giving the desired undertaking, MacKay would have to quit office. He would be more useful as a Protestant Lord Chancellor. Donald Macaskill spoke of Christ and the Pharisees. George Hutton said darkly that Rome always worked forty years ahead in her plans. Mackinnon said that, if a Christian Church brought down a Christian Lord Chancellor, it would empower those who sought a Roman Catholic Lord Chancellor. Fort William elder Murdo Matheson said it was not a question of the Mass but of the death of fellow men; he read a piece by Spurgeon on the evils of strife — especially in small churches. "We are talking about a Mass, but we ought to be concerned about a mass-exodus from the Free Presbyterian Church!"

The debate concluded. MacLean read a motion of terse and brutal judgement. It called on Presbytery to proclaim its disapproval of Lord Mackay's conduct in attending

Requiem Mass in July 1986, as inconsistent with his position as an elder of the Church, which held the Mass to be idolatry and the Pope to be AntiChrist, that man of sin and son of perdition; such disapproval of said conduct being the consistent witness of the Church for over ninety years; and to note that Mackay expressed no regret, and refused to undertake not to attend similar in the future; therefore Presbytery sustained the appeal, and reversed the judgement of the Edinburgh kirk-session, substituting the judgement that Lord Mackay of Clashfern be suspended from the exercise of the functions of an elder and the sealing ordinances of the Church (baptism and Communion) for a period of six months from this date.

Donald Macaskill moved a counter-motion: that Presbytery dismiss the appeal and sustain the finding of the Edinburgh kirk-session. The vote took place. For Mr MacLean's motion there voted the said Donald MacLean, and the Revs Lachlan Macleod and George Hutton, and four ruling elders. For Mr Macaskill's counter-motion there voted the said Revs Donald Macaskill and Rev Hamish Iain Mackinnon, and three ruling elders. MacLean won by seven votes to five: the Moderator declared the motion carried.

Hamish Mackinnon dissented with reasons, and sought leave to complain to the Synod. Macaskill, Matheson and MacRae adhered to this dissent and complaint. Parties were called back into the hall, and the decision read to them, and asked if they acquiesced. Lord Mackay said he did not acquiesce. Thus spoke too Angus Morrison and the other Edinburgh elders. (But Murdo Nicolson, got at, later abandoned the Mackay camp.) MacDonald and Middleton thanked the court. It was then announced that, the matter being under appeal and now in the province of Synod, the suspension of Mackay could not take effect. MacDonald challenged this, in vain. Oh, what an inquisitor went there!

The Presbytery agreed on the barest of statements to the Press: the appeal had been sustained, but there had been a further appeal against that finding to Synod. The matter was therefore *sub judice* and no further comment was possible. Lachlan MacLeod briefly took the Moderatorial chair, as Macaskill bustled forth to announce the judgement to an incredulous world. Macaskill returned to the chair. The Clerk resumed his duties. The meeting closed with prayer.

Historically, the discipline of the Free Presbyterian Church was always tight. But it was never, until MacLean made it so, divisive and confrontational. Free Presbyterian courts operated by consensus, hating to put such matters to a vote, and in the old days the brethren worked together to reach a mutually agreed solution. It is striking how even the most significant turning-points in Free Presbyterian history — rejection of Free Church union, Sunday bussing, Protest — passed Synod with unanimous or near-unanimous majorities. Furthermore, the Church wielded other tools of discipline besides simple suspension or deposition. Crushing censures, public rebuke before the

Girl at *clarsach*: National Mod, Oban, October 1992

About-turn at Tarbert: ferry *Hebridean Isles* heads for Skye, but never on a Sunday

Fishing boats at Stornoway harbour, about 1985. Little of the industry now survives in the West Highlands

Restless natives – youngsters in Stornoway, 1990

Mr John Macleod: half the permanent population of Calbost, Park, Isle of Lewis

Gaelic placenames, Gaelic activist, and much tourist confusion: by Parkend, Isle of Lewis

Girls at the Mod: they sing it, but do they speak it?

Enterprising incomer, Isle of Raasay

Island skipper, Scalpay, Harris

Assynt landscape, Sutherland

Time out: National Mod, Oban, October 1992

Calum's Road, Isle of Raasay. Built single-handedly by crofter Calum Macleod, over a period of ten years

Mackay meets the press to explain his suspension by the Southern Presbytery, 10th November 1988

congregation; these were both effective and relatively safe penalties for misconduct, MacLean had brought things to a new pass.

Suspension — and especially suspension *sine die* — was now the only disciplinary device, and enthusiastically applied. To be suspended from privileges is a soul-destroying, heartrending blow for any Christian worthy of the name; it is, rightly, only applied in the most fearful cases of sin — that which is seen as sin by the world, drunkenness or crime or sexual misconduct — and even then only if the member is quite unrepentant. (Suspension from office is a different matter: repentance is little defence.) But by 1988 MacLean and his cronies used suspension as a political weapon; and he was quite prepared to do so by the barest of voting margins. MacLean had a warrior's temperament, and in his own eyes his strength was as the strength of ten, because his heart was pure.

And, indeed, it probably was. But such a view inflicted repeated trauma on his Church and fellowship. And the suspension of Lord Mackay was a gross political mistake.

There was widespread concern amongst Free Presbyterians at Lord Mackay's conduct in attending Mass; many felt the Church would be compromised by inaction. All MacLean and his Presbytery needed to do was to pass a censure-vote couched in strong but merciful terms. They did not even have to seek an assurance from Mackay that he would not do it again. They merely had to tell him that, though he had done it, he shouldn't have done it; that the Church would not tolerate its repetition, and that if he heard Mass again in defiance of this ruling he would be dealt with decisively.

Lord Mackay would not then have been forced to make a humiliating public promise. Yet he would have been amply warned. If he had gone to Mass again, despite it, there would have been little sympathy for him even amongst his friends. He could then have been suitably punished with little division. Such a resolution by Southern Presbytery would have ended the crisis there: Mackay would have left chastened but spared, and everyone else happy, and that would have been the end of the thing with Donald MacLean coming out of it all rather well.

And the draconian suspension-ruling first stunned Free Presbyterians and then aroused them to fury — on behalf of Lord Mackay. Never mind his indiscreet conduct, or his lack of basic savvy as an elder of the Church: he was a brother beloved for his sweet nature and humility, one who had never in all the years of greatness put on airs; a Lord High Chancellor who was unselfconsciously happy to have as brother-elders simple crofters, joiners, labourers, and clock-repairers. Almost all who knew him loved him; many felt, in the shock of the moment, that they and their Church had been made to look bestial and ridiculous.

There can be little doubt that, in that immediacy of suspension, the advantage flooded to the Mackay party. Had Synod met that November to hear the appeal, it would certainly have overturned the Presbytery decision, and Mackay would have been vindicated and restored. And such an emergency Synod could have met — and nearly did meet — and Lord Mackay himself was the man who stopped it.

For at this point the Lord High Chancellor simply abdicated. Alone of the defendants, he did not appeal. He would not direct the efforts of those who toiled to save him. In the end, he declined even to attend the Synod in May. Perhaps he genuinely did not believe that the Synod would really sustain this suspension, and thought the battle was already won. Perhaps he feared for his public and political credibility. At any rate, he soon sank into a strange fatalism about the matter. "He's withdrawing already," said a despairing supporter, "he's written us off."

If not he to lead, then who? Angus Morrison certainly had the brains and the motivation, but lacked the confidence to control the Mackay campaign. The Macaskills were too straightforward to manage a tough campaign for hearts and minds. Hamish Mackinnon was too brittle. So into this vacuum of leadership there stepped someone who, for all his virtues, was quite ill-suited for a Highland ecclesiastical battle to save Lord Mackay of Clashfern.

William Hugh MacAngus Mackenzie, elder of the Inverness congregation, was that elder who in 1981 had been prevented from addressing a meeting in the YMCA — by the authority of the Synod itself. But he was a most loyal Free Presbyterian, at least in adherence, and was the second of four brothers in a marvellous — and rather typical — Free Presbyterian family. Their roots were in Ullapool, their inheritance in Fearn. And to understand much of what follows I must tell you at once that the Mackenzies were extremely rich.

The combined personal wealth of the four brothers — in property, land, share-holdings, and cash in the bank — can have been little less than twenty million pounds. They owned some of the best farmland in Scotland, around their Fearn stamping-ground. They also held the Highland News Group, a bloc of northern papers including the *Highland News*, the *Lochaber News*, the *Northern Star*, the *Caithness Courier*, the *John O'Groats Journal* and the *Ross-shire Journal*. (This publishing empire was sold in 1990 for a sum approaching nine million pounds.) And they had an Aberdeen-based company called Seaboard, which built supply-vessels for the North Sea oil-rigs. They also had a little Christian publishing company, Christian Focus Publications; it produced good books, but was more a hobby than a business.

All the brothers were elders of the Free Presbyterian Church. Roderick and Hugh belonged to the Tain and Fearn congregation; Roderick was the oldest, of warm personality and a voice deep as a gravel-pit, rather tubby. He owned the spectacular Geanies House: a fine old mansion by Portmahomack, from which most of the Mackenzie empire was run. He was lovable, but could be insufferably patronising.

Hugh was the shyest; he did little more than farm. Kenneth was the baby of the family, under forty: he lived in Aberdeen, was an elder in the congregation there and looked after Seaboard. He wore beautiful double-breasted suits and silk ties and colourful braces; he had the most exquisite leather briefcase, and — naturally — a portable telephone, on which he talked grandly at the oddest occasions. He also had several expensive cars, and a palatial home by Banchory — with swimming-pool, sauna and full-size snooker table. His children went to private schools.

But William was the boss. And if you wanted to see him and his clan in ecclesiastical action, you had to pay frequent visits to meetings of the Church's Northern Presbytery. It was, as I said, the most liberal court of the Free Presbyterian Church: the domain of the "revisionists". They were those Free Presbyterians who sought a softer, more socially acceptable identity for the Church. They were, almost without exception, the younger and wealthier and least Highland Free Presbyterians. They had little time for traditions like clerical dress or giving out the line — too ethnic — and resented too such policy views as the Church had on capital punishment, the European Community and Rome. They were very ecumenically minded, cultivating friendships in other churches. They disliked what they saw and interpreted as the eccentricities of current Church discipline.

In the summer of 1988 the Northern Presbytery refused to prevent the Rev Alex Murray from returning to his pastoral duties, despite demands from a minority that no suspension could be lifted until repentance was ascertained. (The minority's appeal to Synod was frustrated, for Murray — Presbytery Clerk — refused to furnish the necessary extracts of minutes. But they found a way past him.) When D. B. Macleod left for a trip to the African mission, he vacated his post as interim-moderator of the large and vacant charge at Inverness. The delighted Northern Presbytery promptly conferred the important job on John Ross of Tain and Fearn. When Macleod returned in the New Year, Presbytery refused to reinstate him.

The Inverness vacancy was a key battlefield between revisionist and conservative factions of the Church. The congregation was huge — nearly four hundred regular attenders — and had fallen vacant in 1987: it was now badly split. A bare majority wanted to call Malcolm Macinnes. Almost as many bitterly opposed him, disliking his stand on clerical dress and his turbulent personality; they wanted someone more orthodox. By May 1989, the congregation was in such deadlock that there was serious talk of dividing it into two new charges. At the centre of this conflict, and many others, was Willie Mackenzie.

Willie lived in the pleasant Crown suburb of Inverness, in an elegant villa called Dee Bank. His wife, Carine, was a highly intelligent woman who wrote Christian books for children; they had three gorgeous daughters, and a hairy dog called Moss. There were gadgets, for which Willie had a harmless fad: a hot-air blower to light the fire, a CB radio-set to contact him on the ranch, the standard tools of the Eighties — portable 'phone, computer, VCR — and a hi-tech kitchen. But it was a hospitable home, famed for its fellowship and parties: and many a night, midweek or at a Communion, the house rang with singing and laughter. For Willie and Carine were warm and kindly people.

He was a tall man, with thinning hair and impish smile and dark inscrutable eyes. Willie called himself a farmer, and dressed rustically, favouring tweed jackets and woolly jerseys and porridge-coloured suits. Women adored him. But he operated like a poker-player: terse, canny, mysterious. He slipped information to you titbit by titbit, one at a time — "Keep this under your hat, but . . ." — and knowing you would do no such thing. When you rattled him, which was seldom, he grew snappy — "I'm not ashamed of anything I have done!" — and those eyes hinted excommunication if you persisted.

He liked the media, and for that reason he liked you: but if a story from William Mackenzie landed you in trouble, his memory could become very foggy. He rang you a great deal, early and late in the day; but if you rang him, he was never quite available, and called back in his own sweet time. When he wanted to cut you down a little, he would let slip something cruel or critical a mutual acquaintance had said of you. Confronted on the telephone, he fell coldly silent, and you rambled on into an ingratiating jabber. In person, he might beam and pat your knee and say, "Oh, this is what I love about you, your intensity . . ."

It was on one of those occasions in Dee Bank, late in November 1989, after a happy lunch in his home, that we were talking about the troubles of the Church. Willie spoke sorrowfully about MacLean: an able man, but he got into people's minds and brainwashed them. This was the way with all his acolytes, like Donald Boyd in Daviot. "D'you know what they call Dr Boyd? Donald MacClone . . . ! Oh, very mild, yes — but he's a dangerous man, Dr Boyd."

MacLean knew fine of Free Presbyterians who had gone to Mass, said Willie. Did I know Duncan MacLean, lately minister of South Harris? Well, his wife had been a converted Catholic, and her mother had died, and — well, Requiem Mass, boy, so Duncan promptly rang wise Mr MacLean in Glasgow. "And he said it was quite all right! Aye, boy, Mr MacLean said that . . ."

Carine came in with the girls. She passed out chocolates from a box. Willie reached to the fire and switched off the hot-air blower.

But the Church would never split, would it?

"I believe the Church may very well split. I hope it doesn't, but if it does, I believe it would be good for the Church." An emergency *pro re nata* Synod, he thought, might be a very good idea. There was talk of it about the Church.

Early in December, I decided to probe this possibility. I was then working at Radio Highland in Inverness. I rang Alex Murray to see if anything had been raised at the recent Northern Presbytery meeting. He would only speak off the record. He suggested I ring the Moderator. I rang first the last Moderator, Fraser Tallach in Kinlochbervie. "Ah, yes!" he said, and confirmed that moves were afoot to invite Ndebele to convene an emergency Synod to decide the appeal for Lord Mackay. But, said Fraser Tallach, he rather doubted if it would help the Lord Chancellor. "We need time for the dust to settle, for folk to face up to the implications of what's happening . . ." Did Mr Tallach fear a split?

"What, a new denomination? *Ridiculous.*" He suggested I ask the Clerk of Synod. I settled for the Assistant Clerk of Synod, Alfred MacDonald of Gairloch. Mrs

MacDonald put the 'phone down as soon as she heard "BBC". I pursued his brother, Fraser MacDonald, a former Assistant Clerk. He was most nervous. He referred me to the grand old man, Sinclair in Wick. He was helpful, but irascible. "Such a Synod can only be called by the Moderator. And only if *he* thinks it's an emergency — see? That's the law! That's the law!"

I rang Angus Morrison, my friend. No: he would not speak on the record, but he would be very happy if I flew a kite. I thought grimly that I could hardly fly anything so full of "coulds"and "mights" and "sources close". I rang Willie Mackenzie. "I don't want to comment on that," he said, without warmth. So there was nothing for it but to pursue Ndebele. I dialled Africa. After an appalling struggle with telecommunications, tangling with a thick Glaswegian at one end and a puzzled Ndebele operator at the other (his English, in fairness, being better than my Sindebele), I ran down the Moderator *emeritus* of the Free Presbyterian Synod. Aaron Ndebele was a stout African of great personality and humour: I had met him before. But there was a fearful echo on the line.

"If it became an emergency, yes," he roared at length, "yes, I would call an emergency Synod." So at last I had the magic words, and with them a news-item broadcast by Radio Scotland that night; I also taped a report for the Radio Highland news.

That was Friday. On Monday morning — 5th December — I chased the story again, ringing Angus Morrison. "No go," said he dismally, "Lord Mackay is against it — he wants to let the thing go quiet, leave it till May. He's very upset by the publicity . . . He thinks, by May, it'll all have run out of steam, and the public interest died down." And that was that: even with "sources close to the Lord Chancellor", the story was dead in the water.

Yet, looking back, it seems almost certain that an emergency Synod that winter would have saved Lord Mackay from suspension. And to spike such a move, on the risible grounds that "it'll all have run out of steam", was an appalling error. For it gave time to his enemies, and time was all they needed to lock up hearts and minds. Over that winter, and into 1989, that year of revolutions, the Free Presbyterian Church of Scotland lurched towards destruction.

CHAPTER EIGHT

The Ides of May

The year 1989 dawned in the north. Inverness simpered in a pleasant Indian summer until February, when the elements assembled in the glens and decided to unleash their furies. The month swept in; there were gales, and then ferocious rain — torrential, unceasing — and, on a morning, Inverness awoke to find its fine old railway-viaduct over the river had been swept away in the small hours, only minutes after an early train had rumbled over to the west. For a day or two the town faced catastrophic flooding; the waters rose, and flowed into some basements and parkland, and then abated. We were told that the rains had coincided with a high spring tide, and later that the Hydro had foolishly opened sluices above the Great Glen. The bridge was demolished and rebuilt; and some sages recalled that Kenneth Mackenzie, the Brahan Seer, had foretold that "when there are nine bridges over the Ness, the streets will be full of ministers without grace and women without shame". A ninth bridge had been completed in 1986.

Ministers of the Free Presbyterian Church had, I dare say, grace abounding; but some proved shameless enough in that wild spring. The Mackay case was under appeal to the Synod: it was therefore, as the Southern Presbytery had announced, *sub judice*, and not to be further discussed until May. But this presumed too much of human nature. Donald MacLean spoke to the papers — the *Daily Telegraph*, the *Daily Record* — and corresponded in the *Glasgow Herald*. In February 1989 he was interviewed at length on a BBC Scotland *Focal Point* documentary, and even posed in his pulpit for the cameras. Alex Murray also appeared, and Middleton, and the St Jude's youth-fellowship. This *Focal Point* programme was typical of most coverage of the Church at this time: bigoted, gullible and patronising.

Scottish Television spent that spring preparing a profile of Lord Mackay for Channel 4, entitled "Make Way for the Lord Chancellor": Mackay promised lengthy interviews, but — after one aggressive session — stopped all co-operation. A panicky researcher, desperate for background information, rang William Mackenzie. He was most genial. "You know the story about Lord Mackay's birth, don't you?" "No — what's that?" "Ah!" said Willie, and nothing more, and promised faithfully to help. He then rang all around the Free Presbyterian Church warning all on no account to speak to Scottish Television.

But I directed the poor soul to R. R. Sinclair and John Tallach. The three of us met at Scottish Television in Glasgow that March, where both were filmed. R. R., in his ninety-first year, spoke powerfully, bewailing those men "leading the Church away from the ways of our fathers". Afterwards, John Tallach and I shared a compartment on the northern train. He was an interesting fellow, younger than Fraser — James was in the middle — laid-back and baby-faced, with a Stornowegian drawl; John preached with his hands folded, his head tilted and his eyes shut, addressing a spot on the floor some ten feet forward and slightly to his right. He had written some very good children's books; according to Willie, he wrote a novel every summer-holiday — for fun — and destroyed it on return.

We talked of this and that: the call to the ministry, writing, preaching. I remarked jocularly that it was as well I had not joined the Free Presbyterian Church. John Tallach smiled, and gazed out of the window, "You might," he murmured, "have leapt aboard a train about to explode!"

An abashed girl from Scottish Television rang some weeks later. The camera had malfunctioned and the interviews were unbroadcastable.

The Free Presbyterian bookshop, entirely by coincidence, acquired stacks of a book by the Puritan John Bradford — *Hurt of Hearing Mass* — and advertised it widely in the Christian Press. D. B. Macleod's *Free Presbyterian Magazine*, also entirely by coincidence, began to publish a string of topical articles — "The Sacrifice of the Mass", "The Church's Authority and Liberty of Conscience", "The Discipline of the Church". Public worship across Scotland degenerated into a theatre of political statement. Revisionist clergy prayed pointedly and at length for the Lord High Chancellor, Conservative ministers prayed, equally pointedly and no less lengthily, for deliverance from Popery.

Early in March, Willie invited me to do some work for Christian Focus Publications, and asked me round for tea to discuss the project. When I dropped by he produced something interesting — pages of typescript. "This is our next little book at Christian Focus," he said, "by John Tallach . . . It's called *A Plea Against Extremism*." He saw my face. "Yes, John, I know it's *sub judice*, but we need something to counteract the *Magazine*."

I leafed through the typescript. It was a chaotic job. I remarked that it needed some editing. "Aye," he said, not really listening, "and there's a petition on the go too, on the Mackay business. Willie Fraser's organising it — you know, wee Willie, that's General Treasurer of the Church? A petition to the Synod."

"I don't know if that's a very good idea," I said. "If you remember the 1945 Synod . . ."

"Aye, aye," said Willie benignly, "but it's not *really* to influence the Synod —

just to give people a focus for their feelings. This way, they can sign it and let off steam — much better than having folk writing to the papers and putting a bad name on the Church. We're getting a lot of signatures, you know. Mrs MacKay's signed it — you know, the wife of our retired minister . . . ? He said there was no problem at all . . ."

The weeks went by: and through the whispers around me, I learned something of the gathering struggle. People said confidently that MacLean was worried, that he thought he might lose at Synod — so he was pulling out all the stops. Lachlan MacLeod was to be Moderator, because he would take MacLean's orders. It was to be a very large Synod. In theory, every member of Presbytery in the Free Presbyterian Church is a member of Synod: in practice, due to travel costs, the overseas Presbyteries are scarcely represented. The 1987 Synod met with one Canadian minister and two elders, and nobody at all from the Zimbabwe or Australia and New Zealand Presbyteries.

But the Synod of May 1989 would be the biggest ever. Every minister of the church was to come, except for two of the four Africans, and — it was hissed — these foreign boys would do what they were told. Besides, some men had been nobbled. It was Dr Gillies' turn to go to Synod as elder for Stornoway, but he was for Lord Mackay and — lo! — he was dumped; it would be Dr Robert Dickie instead. Donald MacCuish, representative elder for Inverness, was also a man of revisionist mind and — pop! — he was replaced by one Eleneth Sutherland.

So the revisionists claimed. But it was nonsense. Representative elders had been fixed back in June 1988, when the Mackay case was but a twinkle in Middleton's eye. And the Church Interests' Committee had proposed Lachlan MacLeod for Moderator in the autumn; he was due the honour, and as a member of the Southern Presbytery would not be able to sit over or even in the Lord Mackay hearing. Still, paranoia fuels a virtuous glow of martyrdom.

Yet there was no doubting the anger in Willie's voice when I 'phoned him from Wick, on 22nd March: I was in the shivering town fulfilling some commission. "Heard the latest?" hissed Willie. "Those people have put out a pamphlet!"

"What people?" I asked, mystified.

"Middleton, and D. J. and Donald Boyd. *Free Presbyterians and the Requiem Mass* — pictures of Neil Cameron and Donald Macfarlane on the cover. I mean, it's just blown the *sub judice* thing apart . . . They're putting it out to bookshops across the Highlands. Boy, I think every newsagent in Inverness has a pile of the things — do you know that they're *paying* shopkeepers to give it out? And that they've been told to ring the Free Presbyterian Bookroom in Glasgow if they want more copies?"

Didn't Mackenzie spies do well? I said, "This is high-risk stuff for the Right. If they lose at Synod . . . But you're putting out a pamphlet yourself, aren't you?"

"That's different." Doubtless. It was a week or two before I saw the accursed work for myself. It was very readable, well produced, with good print and a glossy blue cover. Alexander McPherson had written the foreword, MacDonald a theological disquisition on the Mass, Middleton a history of Free Presbyterian protests against Mass attendance (heavily sourced), and Boyd an essay on the essential sinfulness of a believer's presence at such idolatry. If you accepted their premises, it was all very persuasive.

Willie, at Lord Mackay's suggestion — so he said — hired me to deconstruct it, checking all references to the *Free Presbyterian Magazine*, on which Middleton had drawn heavily. So I was paid £4 an hour for this arduous research, and furnished with a splendid set of bound volumes of *Free Presbyterian Magazine*, rustled up by Willie from Tallach in Aberdeen. I think I found a dozen minor mistakes, of which only one was important, and earned in all £44. It was years before they asked for the books back.

The "Three Pamphleteers" were the prime focus of effort against Mackay; Donald Boyd of Daviot, whom I had already met, was probably the cleverest. He was tall and handsome and earnest, still young at thirty-four, insistently logical, a little pedantic. I was rather afraid of him. But above the trio was another, of three senior conservative ministers — Alfred MacDonald, D. B. Macleod and John MacLeod. These three were the Church's divinity tutors, and held between them many important posts. Alfred was the Gairloch minister and Lord Mackay's successor as Assistant Clerk: a curious man, very severe and unpredictable, but often charm personified, and capable of great kindness. D. B. — cruel youngsters dubbed him "Deadly Boring" — was tall, wraith-like and courteous, *Magazine* editor and minister of Dingwall. Everyone told me that John MacLeod had an appalling temper. I must say that I always found him very sweet and personable.

Whatever their limitations, all these men grasped the psychology of Free Presbyterians. They had a coldly tight analysis of the situation. The Synod was the battlefield: there they would concentrate, and if they secured the majority, the rest of the world could go hang. They cared nothing for public opinion. Why, see how MacLean had been badly burned by the *Focal Point* episode: in St Jude's, some people were asking aloud what sort of minister they had who went play-acting in the house of God for worldly television. So there was no more courting of the media. The loyalists cut reporters dead. The Free Presbyterian leaders dug in and awaited the Ides of May.

Willie began to hold regular meetings of his northern cadre. His brothers came, naturally; and two Aberdeen elders very much of Kenneth Mackenzie's stamp — David Laing, lawyer, and Dugald McPherson, estranged son of the London minister. There were but two ministers, John Tallach and John Ross. John Tallach sat in their midst like a benign and absent Buddha, a little too holy for Presbyterian power-politics: Ross, a nervy little chap, tended towards the Mackenzies' viewpoint. There were two tough and aging businessmen lately retired to Inverness, Bill Byers and Willie Fraser. In the hands of this cell rested the ecclesiastical future of the Lord High Chancellor. And he, and his minister, could do little more than ring with humble suggestions.

Such men had in truth left the Church a long time ago. They no longer spoke of Free Presbyterian principles, because they no longer believed them. They were acutely conscious of the quaintness of their kirk in the eyes of the world. And it was of that world they increasingly thought: they cultivated the media, and flattered naive young men like myself, and laid contingency plans. By May, I think, they had already drawn up steps for separation should the Mackay case be lost: I have no proof, but too much worked too conveniently at the end of the Synod. Yet they had no strategy or sense for victory at that court.

John Tallach's *A Plea Against Extremism* appeared, full of misprints. It did not really deal with Mass attendance at all, but with a separate issue — was the Roman Catholic Church in any sense a Christian church, however apostate? — and this was not really relevant to the case. In the south, morale faded. One night I rang an unhappy Lowland minister. "Oh, John, I'll be next. They'll get Lord Mackay: I know all these guys at Synod, and we're going to lose this thing by five votes. And then they'll come for me . . . They want us *all* out. They don't want Lord Mackay to repent . . ."

But there were other calls. "I'm hearing, John, that Middleton and friends have drawn up a Deed of Separation — aye, all ready in case they lose at Synod . . . och, I can't remember where I heard it, but can you not make something of it?" Another day, I was asked to make something of petition statistics. "Over a thousand signatures, now — and I'm pretty certain that's more than half the Church in Scotland. I'll bring the details round to you — attendance-figures . . . "

The Synod papers were sent out, and I asked Willie to wangle me a copy. He also gave me the latest pamphlet — *One Is Your Master*, by Fraser Tallach. It had a bright yellow colour, and was much better than John's: racy, and highly relevant to the Mackay farrago, but too late to make any difference. I began pumping out stories on the case to the *Press and Journal*, and had my first by-line; *The Scotsman* rang for a big feature. So did the *Glasgow Herald*. I gave the *Herald* a piece the *Press and Journal* had turned down, and it was splashed on 25th May as a headline-exclusive — a glorious hatchet-job on Donald MacLean, and for sheer style and virulence perhaps the finest piece I have ever written: unfortunately, it was not true. For these extraordinary days of Synod, I was briefly the most important and sought-after journalist in Britain. And yet, looking back, I would now have forgone my petty triumphs, if it could have averted the tragedy that was about to unfold.

Synod gathered in the Inverness church, at Chapel Street, on the night of Tuesday, 24th May. (The best record of speeches and discussion is in the *Inverness Courier* coverage: the account given in the *Free Presbyterian Magazine* of July 1989 is disgracefully inadequate.) It was a bonnie church, large and bright with soft decor and red carpet and varnished woodwork; a congregation of perhaps six hundred people, the Synod members fenced off before by lengths of white tape. R. R. Sinclair was missing, but would come the following morning. But the Skye ministers, and the Ross-shire ministers, and the Outer Isles ministers, and the Lowland ministers, and the Tallachs, and the Rosses, and the Canadian ministers, and the Africans, and the Antipodeans: Donald MacLean at the Clerk's table, frock-coated, iron-grey hair sleekly combed, mouth set stern. The Assistant Clerk, Alfred MacDonald, with his cross little eyebrows. And the Moderator climbed to the pulpit, Ndebele dark and burly, and read out verses from Psalm 38, and we sang these first six stanzas, to the tune *St Kilda* — "In thy great indignation, Oh Lord rebuke me not . . ." — and it was the most powerful singing I have ever heard, strong and dark, and very terrible. So we sang these six stanzas, myself and the children and the women and the adherents and the members, and the Moderator and Clerks and members of Synod, the Synod of the Free Presbyterian Church of Scotland, and not an open mind amongst them.

Of that first night I remember only the oppressive heat of the building, for it had been a close and sweltering day: Ndebele announcing another Psalm, and forgetting to read the verses out, and sitting down, and the wild-eyed precentor looking about, until I signalled to stand and sing. (I sat boldly at the bar of Synod — beside the pulpit.) Ndebele preaching, and those thick African consonants, heavy and earnest; and it was terrible too, and majestic. The Synod electing the new Moderator. Alfred MacDonald calling the roll, like the schoolmaster he had been, at great speed, and each member chanting "Here!" or "Present!" like little boys; Roy Middleton only gasped and nodded, and Alfred knew fine he was there, but barked his name again — "R. MIDDLETON!", and Middleton croaked reply. "Well, speak up, can't you?" said Alfred, with a cruel smile. (At later roll-calls, Donald Boyd called "Here!" for Middleton.)

The Moderator was elected. Lachlan MacLeod took the chair, blushing and diffident. Alfred tried, and failed, to move for the hearing of the Mackay case in private. The Synod rose. Angus Morrison and Donald Boyd shaking hands, as if they were the best of friends, and not in armies at war.

The following morning, Pastor Jack Glass turned up from Glasgow and leapt from a car with several lackeys, and they lined up in front of the church with their banners and started singing some Orange rant. To a man the reporters and photographers scurried over, to give him his fix of publicity: I have never so despaired of my profession. I remember the banners. They said "LORD MACKAY — FAILED PROTESTANT". We went into the church. There was a lawyer, one David Williamson, small and mustachioed: this fellow was given a seat beside the Clerks, so that anyone suspended this week would be suspended good and well according to the Court of Session. And, as the week went on, those eyes scanned us in the body of the kirk and the Synod assembled, and shone in mirth and incredulity.

The fathers and brethren considered the case of Rev Alex Murray, and the petitions brought before them from Macleod and Boyd, and the discussion sank in the mire of competing canon laws. "Now, where are we?" said a bewildered Moderator at one point, and the Court dissolved in nervous laughter. Later he rose again, but MacLean had risen too, and threw him a glance of stone, and the Moderator of the Free Presbyterian Synod sank back into his chair without a word. Boyd spoke, and Macleod spoke. The Synod divided, and voted by a majority to receive the petitions. The Synod divided again, and voted to consider them as Dissents and Complaints against the Northern Presbytery. Parties went to the bar. Dugald McPherson and John Tallach spoke for the Presbytery. There were questions. Parties were put out. There was a long, griping debate.

There was a darkness in the Synod: a darkness in this Church, like the heaviness of the day. Even to myself — and, I fear, most of the Synod — the debate and issues became quite incomprehensible. I remember Alfred moving for the Synod to do something, and then withdrawing his motion. The lawyer gave counsel. The Synod at length sustained the Dissent and Appeal, instructing the Northern Presbytery to meet as soon as possible to consider the restoration of Rev Alex Murray. The lawyer then announced that Synod had just returned matters to the *status quo*, of pre-16th August 1988 — and that the Rev Alex Murray was now, as he had always been, suspended. This appeared to be news to half the court. Parties were brought in. The bare resolution was read to them. Murray looked shocked, but not unduly so; he was walking back to his seat when someone rose and shouted, "Does Mr Murray realise that he is no longer a member of this Synod?"

Murray froze. He looked at the elder. The elder looked at the Moderator. The Moderator looked at MacLean, and MacLean looked at the lawyer, and Murray looked at the lawyer, and asked, "Is that correct?", and the lawyer nodded, and smiled and shrugged. And I remember that Murray seemed almost to crumple; but he went back to his seat and picked up some documents, and turned to face the congregation, and walked very slowly out of the Synod ranks to sit by myself, and I think there were tears in his eyes. Angus Morrison rose to shout, "Mr Moderator, this is an outrageous decision!", and was called to order; Morrison withdrew the remark, and said, "Then, I will say it is manifestly unjust." Various members of Synod joined him in dissent.

"We must now consider the case of Lord Mackay," said the Rev Donald MacLean, and we did: mighty he was that week, tall and handsome, immaculately dressed. The petition was brought before Synod, the petition signed by over a thousand persons. Its sponsors were aggressively questioned. Harsh things were said. The Synod divided, and voted not to receive it. In this they were technically correct: a petition is irrelevant to any discipline case, which is decided on its merits and not on popular feeling, and — besides — a petition is only valid in Presbyterian procedure if it is the only means to bring something to a court, and the Mackay case had already come up by appeal, dissent and complaint. But the fact of one thousand signatures should have been heeded.

MacLean read aloud a letter from Lord Mackay, briskly. It was not the most sensible of letters. Though courteous, it defiantly argued the case Mackay had put before; and yet — in his absence — there was a pathos about the little sheet of notepaper to which the Lord Chancellor was now reduced. Parties went to the bar. Ndebele took the chair.

Angus Morrison spoke, a mild and clever speech, long, but already defeated. Hamish Mackinnon spoke: aggressive, clever-dicky. Donald MacLean spoke for the Presbytery majority, and he stood at the bar of Synod with hand on hip and eyes like lightning. "The Lord Chancellor of a *Protestant* country, with a *Protestant* Queen on a *Protestant* throne, is under *no* obligation to attend a *Popish Mass!*" He spoke of Calvin, and of the essential witness of the Church. Alasdair Gillies, a likeable Glasgow elder, spoke too against Mackay. Someone called, "What about Dr John Kennedy?" (That great Highland minister, touring Rome, had slipped into a church to observe Mass for the dead Pope Pius IX — and his recollections were reprinted uncritically in the *Free Presbyterian Magazine* two decades after.) "Dr Kennedy was on holiday," said Alasdair Gillies, rather feebly.

Parties at the bar were questioned. All knew by now of the *fama* against MacLean — that he had told Duncan MacLean it was quite all right to go to Mass, for I had repeated it in the *Glasgow Herald* — but, oddly, no-one, not even Roderick Mackenzie, asked him point-blank while he was at the bar of Synod. Absurdly, and improperly, questioning of parties at the bar was concluded when many members of Synod still had questions to ask. Great confusion broke out: voices were raised in anger, and Ndebele bellowed, "Members of Synod, keep cool! The debate will continue tomorrow for as long as you like." But North Uist minister Alex Morrison, a cousin of mine, moved successfully that questioning take end.

I remember the Synod adjourning for the night, and we filed out, and old Elizabeth Tallach — mother of the ministers — nearly weeping for the events of the day, saying that this was a dark time for the Church, and I said to her, "We have to look up", and a young man behind us hissed rudely, "Yes, you look up, because God will judge you for the lies you have written." I remember MacLean shouting to me in the car-park, and storming up, right up till his buttons pressed my chest, roaring that the Duncan MacLean story was not true, and my bones melted in fear, but I withstood him insolently. I now fear he was right.

I remember going to Dee Bank, where the Mackenzies and their friends were: John Ross, Bill Byers, John Tallach, Dugald McPherson, Roddy Mackenzie, a dismal Alex Murray, and David Laing. I was offered a drink: I took a whisky. Roderick Mackenzie asked me, "Now what did you think of the Synod? Don't tell us what you think we want to hear, tell us the truth." And I said what I felt: it was darkness, plain darkness, it was demonic, and I think it was, though not in the sense I meant at the time. But there was a murmur of agreement about me. Willie said, to cheer me up,

"You know what Alex said about you when we came out? He said, 'I thought I would go and sit beside wee John. He's the only person in there as unpopular as I am!'" I looked at Murray, and his craggy face beamed with black humour.

We talked of Donald MacLean. Roderick said, "These men — MacLean, Middleton, Boyd — if they are the Lord's, the Lord will deal with them; and if they are not, we should be sorry for them and pray for them." Rather shaken, I protested that many Christians were fed by their preaching. Roderick Mackenzie shrugged. "Indeed. And the ravens fed Elijah."

ENDGAME

The morning sunny and smiling. The crowd poured into Synod, and the Synod poured into Synod: Boyd and Middleton had come at the crack of dawn, long before the press, because Middleton had a horror of being photographed. (Reporters went begging to Willie: and he found a video of the *Focal Point* programme and freeze-framed Middleton's face, and they photographed that.) The Southern Presbytery were not recalled to the bar of Synod, and so waited in the car-park outside, in two separate huddles, casting one another uneasy glances. The church was next door to an undertaker, and in mid-morning a huge lorry rumbled into the car-park to decant a load of coffins: the photographers were beside themselves with joy.

Inside, debate continued. R. R. Sinclair gave his speech, waving away the proferred microphone — "I don't need that!" — and he did not, for his voice was clear and strong, and his pink old face scarlet with passion, and he stood on his toes and punched his fists, and doughtily defended the Lord High Chancellor. "My father was a founder of the Church, see?" he cried. "And this Church could *split* today. That's the reality, Mr Moderator!" Ian Matheson of Laide, former sheriff at Fort William, announced that he too had once attended Requiem Mass, and *his* conscience was clear. I remember that he spoke with his eyes shut, swaying, and the microphone in his hand bobbing erratically, so that his voice ebbed and boomed. The Rev Petros Mzamo, minister at Mbuma, compared the hearing of Mass with attendance at tribal ancestor-worship. The Rev Archie McPhail of Assynt, whose wife was Angus Morrison's sister, pointed out that Morrison and John Tallach went regularly to a Protestant mission in Italy: none could doubt their sincerity against Rome. "By suspending the Lord Chancellor, we have handed to Rome on a platter a propaganda victory of a most notable kind."

Roderick Mackenzie said, "I remember being at Synod ten years ago, standing at that door, and Mr MacLean said to me, 'We're managing just fine without James Mackay here.'" He was shouted down, and told to withdraw: Mr MacLean was not there to defend himself. John Ross spoke for Lord Mackay. "If we suspend him, the name of the Free Presbyterian Church will stink." His brother, Rev Donald Ross of Laide, spoke against Lord Mackay. Jackie Ross spoke for Lord Mackay, and Neil Ross against him: four brothers, two opinions, one divide. The Rev John MacLeod said, "If you love Christ, you won't go to a Mass."

I left to go outside and soothe the excluded brethren. Angus Morrison looked thin and tired; he had visibly aged in six months. Desmond Biggerstaff and John Scoales ambled over to hand me a scribbled Protest, a sad little thing on a torn jotter-page. The Rev D. J. MacDonald came to talk to me, concerned and kindly: how could I write such things, when he understood I was a professing Christian? He was, in truth, a good man. Dear Lord of Heaven, they were all good men.

Back in Synod, Dr Boyd said, "We are to flee from idola-*try*!", hitting the last syllable with an indeterminate Kelvinside vowel. Alex Morrison, craned back to look at the audience: he caught my eye, and beamed, and winked. Aaron Ndebele briefly left the chair to speak against Mackay. "He is my friend, but can I allow him to go near fire?" — and we collectively imagined those pink chubby hands clawing the Lord High Chancellor from the flames, and there were muffled giggles. Dugald McPherson rose and, for reasons best known to himself, read I Corinthians 13 — the Apostle Paul's hymn of love — a stunt, not a speech. My cousin Alex gave the best address: he was a small dark man of sixty-two, with a deliberate way of speaking; he swivelled as he spoke, slowly, stern blue eyes searching us out. "I loved Lord Mackay as much as any man. But when the Antichrist of Rome kissed the ground on his visit to Scotland, he claimed this land for his own. We as a Church must make a stand for the truth."

Malcolm Macinnes hectored the Synod on liberty of conscience. Members of Synod raised hands, waved papers, even stood — James Tallach especially was desperate to speak — but no more were called. Ndebele pronounced the discussion closed. Synod would meet after lunch to hear motions and then vote.

We met again at three. John Tallach moved a motion to reverse the Southern Presbytery decision; it was enormously long, and hard to follow. He was seconded by Ian Matheson, who went into great detail about his own Mass visits (this speech is completely omitted from the official *Proceedings*). D. B. Macleod moved a counter-motion, that the Presbytery decision be sustained, and further that Lord Mackay be not restored until he had professed repentance. "I move this counter-motion . . . in a spirit of love and charity towards Lord Mackay." Alex Morrison seconded. "I refute absolutely the notions of malice and prejudice in this case." John Tallach had the right of reply. He said something about extremism.

The suspension of Lord Mackay of Clashfern, Lord High Chancellor of Great Britain and Northern Ireland, was confirmed by the Synod of the Free Presbyterian Church of Scotland by thirty-three votes to twenty-seven; of the ministers, eleven voted for Mackay and thirteen against. Fraser MacDonald of Portree buried his head in his arms on the pew-ledge and abstained. Perhaps he was praying.

The Southern Presbytery were called in and told of the decision. Ndebele read it to them, and asked each man solemnly if he did acquiesce. Angus Morrison said, "No, Mr Moderator, I do not acquiesce: I appeal to the Head of the Church, the Lord Jesus Christ." He was close to tears. Behind me, several women were weeping. Willie Mackenzie was chewing his lip. Reporters strained for a better view.

Macaskill and Macaskill stood with Angus, repeating his formula; so did Biggerstaff. When Hamish Mackinnon said too, "I appeal to the Head of the Church, the Lord Jesus Christ", Alfred MacDonald lost his head. He bounced to his feet to say indignantly, "Mr Moderator, this isn't really regular: there has been ample debate —", and Hamish Mackinnon, at his finest hour, turned and roared, "I have appealed to Christ! The Assistance Clerk of this Synod cannot interfere with my appeal to Christ!" — and there was uproar: suddenly the church was filled with cheering, and applause, and a furious stamping of approving feet. An old minister wailed, "Silence! Silence in the house of God!" The Rev Donald MacLean said, "Well, Mr Moderator, this decision is indeed an answer to the prayers of many within this Church and to those of many of the Lord's people beyond."

A great many members now asked for their dissent to be recorded. James Tallach appended reasons of his own, that he had been given no opportunity to put questions to parties at the bar, and was further denied the opportunity to speak. Ndebele looked at him unhappily.

Malcolm Macinnes now left his seat and marched to the front, clutching a piece of paper. "Mr Moderator, I wish to make this statement . . . " Alfred rose to cut him down. He moved that Macinnes be not allowed to speak. Macinnes stood rather foolishly as the Synod voted with the Assistant Clerk. Then he shouted, "This is a Protest, and I am tabling it, and I am separating from this Church", and he dropped the paper on the Clerks' table, and spun about, and stormed out of the church with a face like flint. There was a dreadful silence, and MacLean stood to snap uneasily, "Well, Mr Moderator, I move that this Protest is incompetent and be not received." The Synod voted, and agreed. It emerged later John Tallach, Douglas Beattie and several elders had appended their names to this Protest, and it was in fact held *in retentis* by the Synod — physically held, but not officially recorded.

The Church was truly, legally split. And now Synod went hastily into private, and we surged out into the waiting cameras and reporters, and the shining sunlight of the day, R. R. Sinclair shouting, "I went through the Great War: I'm not afraid of those boys in there!", and Hamish Mackinnon giving an interview, and Angus Morrison sitting in Kenneth Mackenzie's Jaguar and dialling the Lord Chancellor on a portable 'phone. Outside, I met Malcolm Macinnes for the first time: he shook my hand eagerly, very excited, and then the TV cameras crowded in on him, and he rapped out some statement. Willie Mackenzie asked me to hurry off and make photocopies of the Protest: he handed me a copy, and I have it here. Word-processed, off the Dee Bank Amstrad, in canon-law formulese, modelled on Macfarlane's plea of 1893.

Suspension of belief — reporters surround Rev Angus Morrison outside the Free
Presbyterian Synod

When I came back I collided with someone younger: Andrew Grant, a tall blond seventeen-year-old, whose mother was yet another of the Ross family, who had spent the day watching his family fall apart. Andrew was a friend of mine, and very distressed: he said, "Oh, I know you need to report this, but you're making it all worse — you're putting wedges in, driving us apart . . . " A woman ran by, sobbing into her hands, chased by several TV crews; a photographer ran backwards before, snapping her.

A t Dee Bank that night, while excited churchmen gabbled in the lounge, I was shut into a room by myself with a gargantuan supper. On the sideboard I found a document which I still have — a photocopied manuscript by David Laing, outlining requirements for a Deed of Separation, clearly written some time in advance of the Synod. It is long and very technical, but it set forth the argument to which the seceders would resort — that the Free Presbyterian Church had repudiated the rights of private judgement and liberty of conscience, and thus vitiated her constitution, and was in truth no longer the Free Presbyterian Church: the seceders now were, and they laid claim to all rights and property. It was nonsense, of course — there had been no Declaratory Act, no alteration to any Church documents or principles, merely a discipline case which they had lost — but it was powerful nonsense. Anyway, it took me in at the time.

On the morning of the 26th May, the day after Lord Mackay's suspension, Hamish Mackinnon confirmed to reporters outside Synod — myself, and a man from *The Times* — that a new body was to be set up, and that it was to be called the "Reformed Presbytery of the Free Presbyterian Church of Scotland". Lord Mackay now issued a statement, finally repudiating the Free Presbyterian Church; and no wonder, for the morning papers as one expressed amazement that so senior a figure had belonged to such a loopy sect. This came up the wire from London, and I made copies and took it to Dee Bank. Angus Morrison had asked me for it: Willie would not let me near him, standing and blocking the door into the lounge, but I could see past him. Apart from an old and innocently lunching Skye minister — staying with Willie for the week — the room contained a great gaggle of plotting clergymen. Malcolm Macinnes, Douglas Beattie, John Tallach, Fraser Tallach, John Ross, Jackie Ross, Archie MacPhail, the Applecross minister Lloyd Roberts, Angus Morrison (waving shyly at me), Donald and George Macaskill — all ministers, and the rest of the Mackenzie gang with them. They were lunching on beef salad, at the table or perched on chairs; there were bottles of fizzy drink and great bowls of crisps, and an air of general jollity.

"We all like you, but it would be better if you weren't here," said Willie firmly, and I was steered into another room with some salad and crisps and lemonade of my own. Presently Lloyd Roberts, a dark little Englishman, ambled in to use the telephone. He said to me, "It's for the young folk we're doing it — it's for them we're separating."

Back on Chapel Street, the Synod proceeded unhappily with business. The

Revisionists had cleverly tabled an overture to Synod, signed by several senior ministers, demanding that Synod affirm liberty of conscience as put forth in the Westminster Confession. MacLean led the Synod in its rejection, giving the secession movement a major propaganda coup. There was great tension. Members eyed the empty seats about them. Even MacLean looked rather subdued.

I found Roderick Mackenzie and Hamish Mackinnon still about: Roddy looked at my piece for Saturday's papers. "No, you can't say we were all 'having a wonderful party' — put 'a wonderful time'. We mustn't hurt Lord Mackay, you know." Nothing much would happen, he thought, for a few days. "We'll take a week or two — to wind down — have some public meetings. There's no great hurry." I waited outside Synod till very late at night, munching sandwiches: it dissolved after midnight, and Angus Morrison came out — he had returned in the afternoon — and was immediately swept off in a fast car to Dee Bank. I followed him, but was turned away.

On Saturday morning I phoned Willie for the latest news. He sounded tired but exultant. "John, we formed a Presbytery last night, and we've signed a Deed of Separation."

"A new *church*? Already?"

"Several. We've called it the Associated Presbyterian Churches. Yes — *churches*. Plural. Look, it's biblical. I know we've moved very fast, boy, but things have moved on."

Apparently Malcolm Macinnes had been booked to preach in Inverness that Sunday, but the Synod late last night had taken over. Donald Boyd was the new interim-moderator — the departure of John Ross being taken as read — and he had booked Neil Ross (John Ross's brother! Macinnes' brother-in-law!) to preach instead. So Willie and company had launched an immediate split and the first separate services would be on Sunday. "Besides, people are so angry, John — if we didn't do something, they'd all be away to the Free Church this weekend." That, I solemnly agreed, would be too awful for words. I said I would pop over. Willie concurred.

The scene at Dee Bank was like the aftermath — well, of a wonderful party. They were all in the lounge, with empty pop-bottles, and trays of cake and biscuits, and bowls of crisps and nuts. Alex Murray sat on the sofa, jacket discarded, wearing incongruous bright-red braces. Douglas Beattie and Malcolm Macinnes were slumped in armchairs. Fraser Tallach paced the room, nervous, excited. Peter MacAulay, a Gaelic radio-reporter, was taking notes. "A glorious sense of freedom," said Fraser Tallach, stretching exultantly. Malcolm Macinnes said drily that the freedom was just dandy: for himself, he hoped to go mountaineering next week. "Have you heard the name? What do you think of the name?" asked Douglas Beattie.

I said it sounded like United Biscuits. Macinnes smiled. "Well, United Biscuits do rather well, don't they?" "It's ridiculous," snorted Fraser, "they should put *plc* on the end." I asked about the Deed. Willie said it had been signed around three in the morning,

Angus Morrison the first to put his hand. Had they taken a photograph of this great moment in church history? "I think we tried," said Carine, bringing in tea, "at least, Willie went for the camera, but the flash wasn't working."

"And what about Free Presbyterian principles?" I asked. "You know — Sunday buses, the Authorised Version — you'll be carrying those on?" There was a strange silence. Everyone looked at the floor and out of the windows, and no-one answered: I realised I had been tactless, and turned to the piano to cover my confusion. I sat at the beast, and played some old Highland tunes, and a couple of Psalms, and a hymn, and Fraser stood behind me and sang: he had a beautiful voice. People left, and people came: Donald MacCuish, some Inverness friends, Angus and Marion Morrison with their two children. Willie shepherded us all outside to take a photograph. Angus put his arm round my shoulder and hugged and said, "John, John, my friend." Willie took the photograph. Somebody accidentally jostled somebody on the steps. "Schism! Schism!" we all cried.

Willie's girls flapped about, excited, printing things off the Amstrad — Deed of Separation, first Presbytery minutes — and ran off to toil over a hot photo-copier. Catherine, the oldest, stuffed envelopes — a mailing to Free Presbyterians, stating APC principles and what the new body aimed to do. The envelopes were already labelled, hundreds of them, with names and addresses. They had made good use of the petition.

The first APC service was held the following day, in the big echoing assembly-hall of Millburn High School in Inverness. About one hundred and eighty attended. Malcolm Macinnes preached from John 20: 20 — "Then were the disciples glad, when they saw the Lord." About a hundred and sixty met in Chapel Street that morning, I learned much later — wild APC sources claimed at the time that there were only forty-five people at the Free Presbyterian service. An APC Presbytery met on Tuesday, 30th May, at Dee Bank, and excited ministers and elders and reporters and a television-crew packed the dining-room. Macinnes presided as Moderator. He gave a short speech, announcing that the new denomination hoped to begin a campaign of global evangelisation. There was public discussion on the need for some APC publication. "Something as unlike the *Free Presbyterian Magazine* as possible," said Douglas Beattie grimly.

The meeting went into private: Roderick Mackenzie accidentally handed me an agenda, but I had to give it back and leave the room. I just had time to glimpse that an early item was the case of Alex Murray — still technically suspended — and that the list of prospective congregations and ministers included several who had not yet quit the Free Presbyterian Church — like James Tallach and Angus Cattanach. In the event, none of them did.

The Presbytery broke off for tea after a couple of hours, Murray duly restored. (His congregation had gone to the Lairg manse that Sabbath, to hear him take "family worship".) The house became very confused, because kirk-sessions started meeting in every room — Aberdeen in the study, Inverness in the lounge. I remember something else: of all the ministers there, only two wore a clerical collar.

Had the senior Free Presbyterian ministers shown an ounce of leadership over that crucial weekend, and acted rapidly to reassure their people, the secession movement would have been a good deal smaller. But none — not MacLean, not D. B. Macleod, not Boyd — had a clue of what was going on, nor did they think to telephone me to find out. The Church Interests' Committee met at Dingwall on Saturday 27th, to issue the most ill-considered and triumphalist statement — "The witness of the Free Presbyterian Church has never shone more brightly than this week." My landlord, hearing of this, said acidly that it was either a very small witness or a very big telescope.

Fourteen ministers eventually signed the Deed of Separation and joined the APC. The greatest shock was the departure of R. R. Sinclair: he called a lawyer and signed a minute of adherence on Monday 29th, and that was that; the news stunned the Church, and many left on his account. Douglas Beattie left, of course: and John Ross, and Jackie Ross, and Alex Murray, and John Tallach, and Fraser Tallach and all the Southern Presbytery minority — Morrison, Mackinnon, the Macaskills — save Dundee elder Alasdair MacRae. They all took with them the bulk of their congregations, though the Macaskills had none of their elders, and lost their church-buildings. None of the Skye ministers, however, left the Free Presbyterian Church. Willie claimed on 30th May that Cattanach had turned up at Dee Bank, very agitated, wanting to sign the Deed, but he had nobly sent him home. Cattanach evidently thought better of it: he was now minister at Staffin, and very happy, and I heard him later say with feeling that if it were not for the Staffin people he would yet be tramping Scotland with his suitcase.

Archie MacPhail and Lloyd Roberts might after all have stayed in the Free Presbyterian Church if it had not been for Alfred MacDonald. At a meeting of the Western Presbytery in June he demanded insolently that they make plain where they stood: against such hostility, loyalty evaporated. But their congregations were split from top to bottom. In the autumn of 1992, MacPhail sensibly merged his APC rump in Assynt with the small Free Church congregation, and pastored the united body. A retired minister of Kames, Donald A. MacDonald, also adhered to the APC cause: he was denied a seat on Presbytery, and died in 1990.

Perhaps seven hundred people — between a quarter and a third of Free Presbyterians in Scotland — came out with the APC. The secession movement was strongest in the Lowland towns, Caithness and Sutherland, and weakest in the Outer Isles: it did not touch Africa, but wrecked some parishes in New Zealand, and of course Toronto and Vancouver. Many deserters later came to their senses, and returned, but the picture is complicated by the arrival of previous refugees — Free Presbyterians who had left years before for other churches, and now flocked to the APC — and also by new recruits who had never been Free Presbyterians at all. Furthermore, a good many took advantage of the general confusion to quit the Church for her traditional rivals — Church of Scotland, like many folk in Harris, or Free Church, like John Scoales in Edinburgh. So perhaps the Free Presbyterian Church lost a good third of her people in Scotland. There was one district, however, where the APC did not dare to form a congregation — Glasgow! And two members of Synod behaved most eccentrically. A Lewis elder, Kenneth Morrison, had voted against Lord Mackay; he now chose to repent, and joined the Free Church. Tain elder Kenneth Robertson actually signed the Deed of Separation in Dee Bank, on that crazy night, and attended the Presbytery four nights later — but he, too, then quit for the Free Church.

Not a family was spared division and heartbreak. The split put brother against brother, father against child, man against wife. The suffering of the Ross clan can be imagined. Old Mrs Ross, a delightful lady, followed most of her family into the APC. But Edward Ross at Lochcarron remained in the Free Presbyterian Church and faced the awkward task of scrubbing his brother's name from the church notice-board: Jackie sensibly scrubbed it for him. Several Free Presbyterian ministers — indeed, MacLean himself — saw offspring turn APC. James Tallach was in a most difficult position. Only one Raasay elder supported the Synod stand, and everything within James must have called him to go forth with his mother and brothers, but he was the island's only minister and its sole medical cover: the congregation would have been rent in twain if he had turned APC, and there would never have been a minister on Raasay again. He did not, and they fell in behind him, and Dr James was perhaps the only Free Presbyterian minister in Scotland to emerge from the whole mess with his reputation enhanced.

Several vacant charges went APC, like Fort William. Congregations whose ministers had remained loyal now split: there were old scores to settle, and old resentments, and so Laide and Stornoway and South Harris and Gairloch and Dingwall gave birth to APC groups. As the summer wore on the APC became actively schismatic. They moved into Portree, and began services there — though Fraser MacDonald was no extremist, and had not voted against Lord Mackay — and forced Angus Morrison to take the inaugural service. He said to me about this time, "I am profoundly uneasy", for he now realised this was a new denomination and no mere holding-group: but it was too late. He obediently preached: and afterwards, when I began at last to examine APC claims in print, our friendship cooled.

The APC ministers lost some church-buildings — Dundee, Dumbarton, Lochcarron — but held on to others: Edinburgh, Oban, Fort William, Wick, Aberdeen, Lairg, Tain and Fearn. (Angus Morrison honourably vacated the Gilmore Place church in 1991: he and his people went to share a Church of Scotland building.) No APC minister, however, chose to vacate his manse. Macfarlane and MacDonald might have preached on the hillside and taken lodgings, but none of these modern heroes deemed liberty of conscience worth such sacrifice. They talked grandly of taking the Free Presbyterian

Church to law, for all its property and funds, but of course they did not, for they had no case to argue. The Free Presbyterians held, at last, a *pro re nata* Synod late in June, and issued a dignified and clever statement. It repudiated APC claims and put on hold the prospect of legal action to recover the manses. The next Synod, in May 1990, put off a law-suit permanently. The Bible, the Synod observed, forbade Christians to go to law with each other: they would suffer joyfully the despoiling of their goods. So, in the end, the Free Presbyterians came out of it rather better.

As the APC brethren hung on to all they could, public sympathy for their cause dwindled. The first issue of the *APC News* did great damage: a breezy tabloid of syrupy spirituality and personalised invective, ridiculing Donald Boyd (alone, for some obscure reason) in three separate articles. Any prospects for union between the Free Church and the APC melted away. Some like myself asked hard questions. Why had they taken such a dramatic and irreversible step in such secrecy, disorder and haste? Why would they not give up their buildings? Did they plan to repay loans from the Forsyth Fund? Why had they felt it necessary to establish yet another Presbyterian denomination? Why would they never, never consider mending fences with the Church they had left?

Now I must stress that some of those who joined the APC were as near to saints as I ever knew: Elizabeth Tallach, and R. R.'s sister Annie Tallach, and Annie Ross, and others, and I could never call such people wicked or impious. But the APC majority — predominantly young, wealthy, southernised, and uppish — were beyond understanding such questions. We waited for answers. And we are waiting yet.

What remains to say? Time has passed, and the dust has settled. It is hard now, looking back, to face these old furies and divisions. I think Lord Mackay was wrong, and foolish, to have gone to Requiem Mass, and I think the Free Presbyterians were entitled to take to do with him; but he should not have been suspended for it, and that blunder — and the ensuing collision of personalities and power-factions, and the badly handled case of Alexander Murray — drove him away and blew the Church apart.

The split came in a moment of blind passion: a group of exhaused emotional men, meeting late at night, properly shocked by the turn of events. But "he that believeth shall not make haste"; and it is a solemn thing, especially for ministers, to rend the church of God in a moment of rage. "Some have suggested that the Protest and Deed of Separation were drawn up before the Synod even met. These suggestions are without foundation," wrote John Tallach in the first *APC News*. But it would be a fearful thing indeed, if Tallach really admitted to leaping into such irreversible action without consideration or forethought.

No real comparison can be made between 1989 and 1893, except that the APC purposefully lifted some of Macfarlane's rhetoric. But Macfarlane took weeks, even months, and took time to relax and ponder, before launching his separation-movement. And his cause was the headship of Christ over church and nation, and the purity of the Gospel; liberty of conscience is merely one link of Christian truth, and dangerously fashionable to the unconverted world. The APC has many virtues — it lays important stress on evangelism and revival — but has not proved a successful agent for these. The body that once orated of "global evangelisation" can barely keep services at Broadford; and some who naively thought their churches would fill once cleansed of Free Presbyterian taboos have found a harder reality. By the summer of 1992, the APC had a mounting financial deficit. Most congregations were smaller. Alex Murray and John Tallach publicly squabbled as to whether women had to wear hats in church.

As we approach the centenary of 1893, the Free Presbyterian Church is united and stable, though much reduced. There are still serious problems: the Church is short of men, and has been forced to merge many congregations, and several charges presently pastored — Greenock, North Uist — are so small that they are most unlikely to be granted new ministers when the present incumbents retire. Yet the Church is solvent, peaceful and remarkably happy. There are some encouraging signs of growth overseas.

Donald MacLean retired as Clerk of Synod in 1990 — he was succeeded by D. R. Macleod — but remains minister at St Jude's, and is still uncannily ageless and forceful. He has mellowed rather, and I fancy the disaster taught him something. MacLean was Moderator of the 1992 Synod in Glasgow, presiding with humour and benevolence: he will also preside, and preach, at the Free Presbyterian centenary-celebrations in May 1993. The Church of Scotland Assembly Hall — the very place, with the very table, where Macfarlane made his stand a century ago — is to be hired for the day.

Lord Mackay of Clashfern is still Lord Chancellor. He has never joined the APC, though he worships in the Edinburgh congregation on occasion; and he has shown little regard for those who walked into the wilderness on his behalf. Late in 1989 he held a prayer-breakfast in Edinburgh, inviting Roman Catholic clergy to participate; he managed to abstain on a Bill authorising human embryo-research, and has, by word and action over these last years, done much to vindicate the Synod that suspended him. His entry in the current *Who's Who In Scotland* mentions no ecclesiastical past or commitment; it does, however, list the Lord Chancellor's eleven honorary degrees.

I have little contact now with the APC: I have, however, many Free Presbyterian friends, and homes in that Church where the door is always open. Much is forgiven and forgotten, but sometimes, in the night, my subconscious opens graves, and up they rise — Angus Morrison, Willie Mackenzie, Andrew Grant, R. R. Sinclair, and more. Just once after all these things, hastening from a service in Edinburgh in May 1990, I was stopped by a certain outstretched hand. A soft voice enquired for my welfare, and sad eyes glowed beneath the quizzical brows and a cloud of white hair; I squeezed the hand, and wished peace to the Lord High Chancellor, and left him with my phantoms of a fellowship destroyed, of friendships that can never be rebuilt.

Raebhat

"You betrayed them," said the Cousin.

"Uh?" say I, jerking out of my thoughts, and looking about the room. It is late at night, in the guesthouse, and I have the television on with the sound turned down, for a cosy flicker in the absence of a fire, and — besides — there are only two channels still broadcasting, and the programmes are very boring, and I have put off the sound with the light.

"Them. The APC. Willie Mackenzie . . . or maybe all of them, the FPs as well," says the Cousin, and I see him now sitting in the other armchair, looking at me. There seems an edge to his voice.

"Maybe I did," I say wearily, "but I have gone through all that many, many times, in the watches of the night, for many nights these past three years, and I can't make head or tale of my own motives and reasoning in those days — never mind anyone else's . . ."

"Well, stuff the motives. Look at the facts. These were your own people — our people, as you're always telling me — and you set them up. You visited them, you gossiped with them. You sat in their homes and shared their tables and enjoyed their hospitality. And then you went right out with your pals in the media rat-pack and helped stitch them all up."

"You may be right," I say, and nothing more, and that throws him. He sits uncomfortably in the chair for a little while, and I gaze out of the window. There is not much to see, except the wet tar of the car-park beyond, and the white gable of the off-licence that has put the Shawbost people into such a fankle, and — beyond — the glint and twinkle of distant houses, in Carnan, Baile Stigh, South Shawbost. That, and the gentle thrum of raindrops spraying on the window, in which the lights blurr.

"I think," I say at length, "that there were two mistakes. The conservative lot — the anti-Mackay boys — didn't have the sense with the media that Mackenzie and his cronies did, and certainly never cultivated me to the extent that he did — or any journalist. My, only Boyd would talk to me, and even he watched his words — the rest, oh, their wives said they weren't in, or put the 'phone down, or barked that it was *sub judice* and they couldn't say a word. That was their mistake — and the second was mine, to get too close to the story, and start rooting for the Mackay faction, and end up being well and truly brainwashed by Willie. But I'll tell you this. I threw far, far more muck at MacLean and the Free Presbyterian loyalists than I've ever thrown at the APC. Screeds of untruth and invective — and yet, the reality is that it's the Free Presbyterians who are good to me now, and them I visit happily, and who send me cards at New Year. And it's the APCs who cut me dead, and there's only one minister would give me the time of day if I asked for it."

The Cousin grunts. "The APCs are more progressive. Realistic. Not extreme . . . and they're very loving."

"If you want to find how loving they are," I say with feeling, "just you start criticising them!"

"The Free Presbyterians have only seventeen ministers in Scotland, several of those geriatrics and only one the right side of forty. They have less than two thousand regular worshippers, umpteen vacancies, and less than a hundred and ten male members — out of whom must come all their ministers, elders, deacons and precentors. They're a hard-right group of Bible-bashing fundamentalists, they repudiate almost every aspect of the modern world, they live in monastic seclusion from every other Christian body in the United Kingdom, and they're probably less significant in modern Scotland than our Sunni Muslims and Jehovah's Witnesses!"

"You, my lad, have been doing your homework," I say, smiling, "but many have prophesied the end of the Free Presbyterians before, and they have a nasty habit of confounding 'em. As for your hard-right nonsense — well, wasn't that just their problem with public relations in 1989? The television boys told us plenty about trousered women, praying priests and banned Christmas trees. I don't recall a single reporter, save myself, pointing out that they were the only Church in Britain with a black Moderator! You can function in the modern world perfectly well as a Wee Free, or a Wee Wee Free; you'd have to adapt your ways much less than if you were a Muslim or a Jew. But if they'd had a third of the vitriolic nonsense poured on them by the media that the Free Presbyterians had to endure in 1989, there'd have been an awful lot of reporting luvvies locked up by the Racial Equality boys."

Now there is a long, long silence. There seemed nothing more to be said on Presbyterians, Free or otherwise. Just the sad soughing of the wind about the corners and walls of the house, and the rain, and the flish-flash of images on the television.

The Cousin stretches, and smiles. "So," he says, more amiably, "you'll be heading into the modern world with the rest of the book? All that wonderful hi-tech social-realism *West Highland Free Press* stuff of Highland renaissance? Highland Board grants to somebody setting up a factory for frog-flavour crisps on the shores of Loch Duich. Fishing quotas — lots of stuff about 'pelagic' and 'nephrops'. Gaelic jargon? An Commun Gaidhealach? Commun na Gaidheal? Comataidh Telebhisein Gaidhealach? Going out be-bopping with the boys of RunRig? Bumping about the Uists with waxed-jacket naturalists, panting for a sight of the red-necked phalarope?"

"Keep your phalaropes to yourself. No, nothing so fancy or as dutiful as all that. I'm interested in culture and people — real people, Highland people, struggling to survive assorted élites and self-appointed leader-figures determined to drown us all in a sea of good intentions."

"Survive? You mean, just stay on living here — that there's a danger of total, utter clear-out?"

"No, I don't really mean that, though there are many very small communities right on the edge of things that could disappear — tiny hamlets, where once there were fifty families, and now just one or two elderly people. The real danger is to tradition and values. After all, the Highland population has actually risen, because of those wretched white settlers pouring in, searching for the good life with a view."

"And the misguided policy of the Highland developers," says the Cousin, who is having a good night of it. "It was urbanised, wasn't it? Let me put it to you — dearie me, this sounds really formal — that the Highlands and Islands Development Board, born in the Sixties, was loaded with Sixties naivete. Technology! Huge ambitious schemes for the space age! Mighty multi-million plants employing hundreds of people! So they built those things — that pulp-mill at Corpach, the smelter at Invergordon, and floated them on *humungous* amounts of grant and subsidy, and when the cash dried up the moguls ran off with the loot, but *not* before," and the Cousin's eyes glint with hard anger, "Hundreds of people had flocked to those areas, imported as labour, and swamped the original communities, brought lots of problems with them, and then — of course — were left high and dry. Wasn't that it?"

"I'm impressed," say I, sincerely, "and I remember Corpach myself, because I was born there the year the pulp-mill came — and I remember the building-sites, all the ticky-tacky housing going up, and the place losing all its old charm and identity, and the mill went in 1980, and Corpach and Caol and that whole area is a depressed and miserable dump. But I'm not going to go into that, because it's been better told by other people, and it would need a lot of boring research on my part, and it'd be very boring at the last to my readers."

The Cousin arches his brows. "So . . . ?"

"Ordinary people, small and ordinary communities. And the survival of this culture, the Highland culture, even at the end of our old world. How it's suffering. But how it's coping. And how it can survive."

"John," says the Cousin, "it's over. It's dead already, or nearly dead. Gaelic is *doomed*. Do I speak it? Do you speak it? Look at the figures. What'll it be when the new census comes out — 70,000? What's that? There are football-stadiums holding bigger crowds than that. And if Gaelic disappears, dies, then Highland culture'll die with it."

"Not necessarily," say I, lighting a cigarette, feeling the soft certain catch in my lungs. "Oh, but yes, I agree – Gaelic is dying. Indeed, I think you could say it is dead already. But our ways — the old ways — must they logically vanish with a mere language?"

The Cousin is staring at me. I realise, with some satisfaction, that he can scarcely believe his ears.

"I don't speak Gaelic," say I, "and I don't see any reason to feel guilty about that, because that is my reality, and the greater reality is that Gaelic is doomed quite certainly to die as a living language, because deaths every year of native speakers far outweigh the births of Gaelic-speaking babies — and if those wee ones reach school with Gaelic, even fluent Gaelic, they'll be knocked out of it by their friends, by television, by rock music, by RunRig no less. And if they aren't, then the present cloud of virtue over the whole thing — that they *must* speak Gaelic, because An Comunn and Teacher and sweet old Donnie Munro say they should — will provoke reaction. They'll rebel. And they'll abandon it. Do you realise that the last true Gaelic monoglot — adult monoglot, not a toddler — died in January 1992? That almost all Gaelic speakers can read and write in English better than Gaelic? That more and more Gaelic speakers are more fluent in English? And that a Gaelic learner — even the best learner of all — does not really read or hear Gaelic; he translates in his head, and the understanding his head gives him is an English understanding, not a Gaelic one?

"But," I say, "the *important* things of our culture, the things that are facts, not squiggles or bleeps of communication — these can survive . . . if we choose to keep them. Not to go away, and to turn our back on them — like yourself!"

"Now, wait a minute . . . "

"That is what you are," I say, seizing an insight, "a literary device of a most unique variety . . . You're a moral illustration, my Cousin: you are the road not taken. You despised the past. And you turned your back on the past, because you could not face that pain of your people, lest it awaken your own pain that you have suppressed, which you hate, and you fear. And you have gone to southern people, and adopted all their southern ways — all their foolish, temporal, worldly, godless ways — and you've spat on the heritage of your fathers, and repudiated your own identity. You think that you are sophisticated, and myself so quaint, but you are a renegade, and you are contemptible."

We stare at each other for a very long time, and neither of us moves. We are stitting very still, with a silly commercial now miming on the television, and the noise outside of wind and wet in the April night.

"All the same," say I, not wanting to crush him utterly, "you are not without wisdom."

"You get wisdom," said the Cousin, "when you go where I am going."

"And where is that? You still haven't told me."

The question hangs forlornly with the smoke. He looks at me, still, very angry. The words come with forced carelessness. "You annoy me. You irritate me exceedingly.

You come at me with this foolish, fatuous, utterly *inane* psychobabble, and — believe me, pal, much more of this, and I'll kick your feet so far up your nostrils you can tickle your brain with your toes."

It is, I have to grant, an original and striking metaphor. "Well. That'd be an interesting new experience."

CHAPTER NINE

A Hapless Land

A thinned and scattered people, we Gaels, we seed of the west and north, in the districts and counties that comprise the modern Highlands and Islands. The area now covered by Highland Enterprise — as the former Highlands and Islands Development Board is restyled — includes the island authorities, all of Highland Region, part of Grampian's Moray district, the Argyll and Bute district of Strathclyde, and the other Clyde islands of Arran and Cumbrae. All this is 14,934 square miles, some seventeen per cent of Great Britain, over half the landmass of Scotland; the total coastline of peninsulae, islands and sea-lochs is over five thousand miles, and of the hundreds of islands and islets, ninety are inhabited.

But those inhabiting this half of Scotland, as calculated by the HIDB in 1986, number only 370,000, or about eight per cent of the Scottish census. It is scarcely surprising to find the population-density calculated at twenty-three to the square mile — 169 to the mile in Scotland as a whole, 233 in the United Kingdom. The largest community, Inverness, has perhaps fifty thousand people: there is nothing in the region deserving the name of city. In all the Hebrides, only one community (Stornoway, population almost eleven thousand) is truly a town. And many would no longer regard the Highland Enterprise mainland areas as truly Highland at all. Orkney and Shetland, and the north-east extremity of Caithness, were never part of the Gaidhealtachd; their culture has much more in common with Buchan, Aberdeen and the East Neuk. Gaelic, as we shall see, has retreated rapidly northwards and westwards even in my own quarter-century of life. Nevertheless the 1991 census figures, just released, indicate that nearly half of all Gaelic speakers now live outwith the Highlands and Islands — dispersed through Glasgow and central Scotland.

The population of the Highlands has, in my own lifetime, actually risen; in 1966 only 299,000 people lived in the HIDB area. But this reflects partly the high-scale follies of Sixties regeneration — to man the huge new industrial plants the HIDB had to import labour from the Lowlands — and partly the tide of incomers, like the professionals who now descended on Inverness to run the new departments and quangos of Highland revivalism. Or, more significantly, the flood of rat-race refugees, the detested "white settlers" who have poured into Mull, Skye and the west over the last fifteen years.

There are committees for this and government bodies for that; there are grants and subsidies for almost every economic or productive activity that can be imagined. Entry to the Common Market was the last and finishing blow for the west-coast fishing industry; but the authorities have encouraged prawnfishing, and aquaculture, and the European Community poured much valued aid into the Outer Isles. Highland transport, at least for vehicles, has improved beyond recognition since 1966. Almost all the inhabited Hebrides now have good reliable car-ferries. Traditional fjord-ferries — at Ballachulish, Strome, Kylescu, Kessock — have been replaced by mighty bridges or road-loops. With the spectacular exception of the Fort William to Mallaig highway — the last single-track trunk-road in western Europe — all the main Highland roads have been modernised to a high standard.

Tourists continue to head for the Highlands and Islands, in jerkily increasing numbers; stories from the area feature regularly in the Scottish and London press, and Scotland has long appropriated Highland things — Gaelic, bagpipes, tartan — for totems of her own national identity. The Highlander "is the man on Scotland's conscience", said William Ross in 1965, speaking in the House of Commons as Secretary of State for Scotland, as he unveiled the legislation that established the HIDB. And, indeed, there has long been an interest in Highland affairs far beyond the scale of the area's economic importance, and sympathy in our needs and troubles that goes furth of the Highland line and indeed furth of the Border. There are votes far and wide for statesmen good to the Teuchters; and they know it.

The ancient Highland world, the one that died at Culloden and was dying even before that, is but distant legend. The dark era of the Clearances is now a myth, potent and real, imperfectly understood, but a most useful weapon for aspiring politicians and demagogues, for launching a pop-group in record-plugging fervour, for bugging the authorities, for making Brian Wilson great. What has only lately vanished is the early-modern Highland world, from the end of the last war to about 1970, when the Gaels enjoyed new prosperity and electricity and a much higher standard of living than hitherto, yet before the mass-media had accessed the glens and islands to debauch the culture, and before the corrupting lucre of mass-tourism, and before the frightening tide of southern immigration.

Four-channel television, bed-and-breakfast pandemic, white settlers — these have come now with a vengeance.

Hardy and intrepid race . . .

The exploitation goes on.

In the last three years, I have toured and re-toured Skye, Raasay and the Western Isles, and the collage of my memory frames a hundred scenes and vignettes. I have climbed Dun Caan on Raasay, and it a hot and hazy day, and looked over the seas and sounds to Skye, and Lewis, and Gairloch, and Applecross, and Kyle, and the Cuillin; and looked down, over the green-clad ruins of lost Raasay villages, Screapadal and Hallaig. I have, in high June, crossed on the little ferry from Barra to South Uist on an evening, and cycled to Daliburgh, over a bright and sunlit landscape, quite still, with brown cattle grazing and high larks singing; and, the next day, gone up the great golden strand that is the entire western coast of South Uist, to Howmore, where there are still inhabited thatched houses, and the machair a cloak of green that bobs with a million flowers.

I have spent two nights on the streets of Stornoway, talking to teenagers who flock to these narrows in the small hours after partying, some drunk and some high, a few violent, the great number affable, the lot of them a lost bewildered generation. And I have gone to the Butt, to the land of my father's people, to see old uncles and old aunts, and marvel at the blast and swirl of ocean about the Butt itself; and I have returned, many times, to Shawbost and my people there.

I have stayed in the squalor of Broadford, that Oxgangs-on-Sea, where the views are magnificent and the near reality depressing; a soulless, sprawling place, where the white settlers have set up camp with their ludicrous crafts and silly businesses — beauticians, herbalists, weavers of this and carvers of that, a bookbinder — and old men, retired from Sussex and Essex and Norfolk, far from children and colleagues and the friendships of decades, sit alone drinking in the bar of the friendless hotel.

But also, a January or two ago, I have gone to Braes to pay homage to the men that made battle.

To be honest, I had planned to go to Braes to see Sorley MacLean, that great Gael, and called him to ask if I might interview him for my paper, on the religious climate and values of his childhood world and how these moulded his poetry. I met him before, and he was most friendly, but at the mention of *interview* there was a great hollow groan. "Oh, John," he sighed, "I am just sick to death of interviews . . . and, besides, I have many most dear friends, of the Free Church and the Free Presbyterians, to whom I would not want to give offence — you'll understand me . . . ?" I said, thinking on my feet, that I understood perfectly — he had given so many interviews — there were so many demands on his time — I had pious friends too — but, seeing I hoped to come to Braes anyway, and would be at Peinchorran where he lived, would he be so kind as to receive me and tell me something of the battle? And to this, brightening, the old man was happy to agree.

I had the problem of reaching Peinchorran, for then I was not driving and had no car. Only the school-bus goes in winter, there and back from Portree, early morning and late afternoon, and I could hardly drop in on Sorley MacLean for breakfast. Peinchorran is at the very end of the Braes, across the mouth of Loch Sligachan and separated by a mere three hundred yards of sea from the main Kyleakin-Portree road and the terminal of the Raasay ferry. But to reach Peinchorran from the Sconser slip, you must look longingly at the village and then drive all the way along Loch Sligachan, and up Glen Varragil, away beyond Ben Tianavaig, almost to Portree, and join the Braes road there as it meets the highway, and so double back south down the coast through the Braes townships, until you reach Peinchorran, within shouting distance of the Sconser slip you left some thirteen miles ago.

It was January, but wonderfully mild weather: Portree, tourist-free, lay snug, and a low canopy of cloud hung over the island like a cloche over cucumbers. All was warm, still, and softly bright. I decided to take the main bus to Kyleakin, alight at Sligachan, and walk up the north shore of the loch — where there is no vehicular road, but a definite if winding path for the walker. This is known as the *Leitir*, and I should point out at once that — though no mishap came to me — this path is in fact highly dangerous in winter; sudden rain can bring ferocious spates of water down the gullies without warning, and the odd life has been lost over the years. I did not know this then, and not a drop of rain came down those four winter days I had in Skye, but I should have been troubled by the drowned and bloated sheep I kept finding about the lochside.

But no, not a drop fell: and I crossed the deserted camp-site at the head of the loch, and bounced from tuft to tuft through bog, and paused for a cigarette at the tumbled stones of a long abandoned cottage, most ancient, and reached the shore, and found the path, and it went up, and down, and through gullies, and I had to hop over the odd rivulet, and the cloud hung low and the light was soft, and the great kiss of Glamaig sat over the road on the southern shore, and the peaks of Sgurr nan Gillean gnawed at the sky beyond Sligachan hotel. Perhaps it took me an hour to reach Peinchorran. It was a steady, demanding but not laborious tramp, and I remember watching the Raasay ferry sail out of the Sconser slip as the green sickle-curve of Peinchorran came in sight, and then I crested some outcrop, and the houses stood in line below.

I clambered down, on to the road, and there was I in Braes. I was wondering which house was Sorley MacLean's, when I saw him padding about the garden in a waterproof, and I called to him, and he recognised me, and came stumping to take me in. Sorley was in his eightieth year: a short, sturdy old man, with large round head and bristly moustache and a poet's hard watchful eyes. Number 5 Peinchorran was his home, the croft of his great-great-grandfather Angus Stewart, that had been a leader of the people in 1882, and the first crofter to give testimony to the Napier Commission. It was today a modern, comfortable double-cottage, bright and carpeted; there was a log-fire burning in the grate, and the walls of the lounge lined with books and pictures.

Renee greeted me, his wife, of Inverness: tall, merry, oozing capability, and quite unperturbed at my descent, as if every day she had journalists coming in and them soaked to the knee with half of Ben Lee in their boots. In no time at all I was being fed coffee and gingerbread, and Sorley MacLean was in the opposite armchair, most excited at my approach. "So you came over the *Leitir*?" he boomed, and chuckled, and slapped his knee, and when I said that I hoped to walk back to Portree by the road he snorted, and said, "A man who has come over the *Leitir* is not walking to the battle monument, never mind Portree." "We are going into town anyway," said Renee, with an authoritative glint in her eye, "and the *bodach* can tell you all about the battle as we drive, and we will stop at the monument."

And so I was left by the fire to dry off, and the poet sat and talked to me; and though he indeed looked younger than his years, there was something most ancient about Sorley MacLean. He had the attitude and presence of a *seannachie*, a teller of old old tales, bearer of oral tradition. He had the voice, precise and strong, drawling and at times singing, of a bard; it lingered lovingly on a concluding *s*, and chewed over the polysyllables, and punched some strange hard vowels, in a manner that reminded me of another MacLean in another place. But mostly, of that day, I remember Sorley's face: the soft, moist mouth of mischief and wisdom, the eyes that were veiled and hard: not of a hard heart, but of a mind that missed nothing and forgot no-one.

He besought my genealogy, and I talked of the four lines of my grandparents, and especially of my mother's MacLeans: even today in the islands, and even if it is not a poet you meet, this is how they wish to know you first, by blood-line and clan, and who you are in the tribal sense, for it is all in the blood. "MacLeans?" he said, and worked his hands for a while. "There was a MacLean, *Alasdair Dubh*, of Mull, and he went to Lewis — yes, he fled to Lewis, after the Battle of Killiecrankie in 1689. Now he was not the progenitor of *all* the Lewis MacLeans, but he was the father of some of them."

"But he must be of our people," I said eagerly, "for there is a tradition that my mother's people, when they came to Uig, came from Mull."

"Perhaps, then, that is whose you are," said Sorley, "*Alasdair Dubh*", and we sat and talked more, of poets and writers from Lewis, and of the many versions of an ancient Raasay song, the Lament for Iain Garbh MacLeod — "witches, in one of them, in the form of cats, sitting in the rigging of his boat when it broke up and sank" — and of other genealogies. "There is a man on Raasay," said Sorley, "at Oskaig, whom I believe is the true chief of the MacLeods of Lewis, though not recognised as that, and the chief of the MacLeods of Raasay is in Australia."

We prepared to go. Outside it was still a fine mild day, but I was struck by the poor narrow road, and the isolation of the spot. Renee conceded that Sorley and she might well move out one day, if they became too old and frail, but for the moment it was good to be in Peinchorran, where his mother's people were, hard by the Narrows of Raasay. "As long as I can drive," she said, and bent to hiss conspiratorially in my ear — "Well, the *bodach* drives too, but I don't let him much now — he keeps looking at mountains instead of the road."

Sorley trotted up; he insisted that I sat in the front of the little white car, so that I might see better, and took his own place in the rear, sticking his head between Renee

Sorley MacLean by his birthplace in Oskaig, Raasay

and myself as we bowled up the road — the old high road, which was the one that Sheriff Ivory's taskforce took, over a hundred years ago. "It was a dawn raid, you see, so that they would take the people by surprise . . ." And as the car wound and twisted along the narrow tarmac trail, and the poet warmed to the tale, his chin bobbing on my shoulder, his moustache bristling with excitement, and Renee patiently dodging his gesticulating hand. "This is *Allt na Gobhlaig*," Sorley declared, as the road runs into a gorge and alongside a little burn, by some cottages: a fine place for an ambush. "Here the fighting really began in earnest. The people, with their flails and their stones . . ."

And so he unfolded the battle to me, as we drove from there up to a high point by cliffs, above *An Cuhmhan*, the narrows — "Stop!" said Sorley — where the crofters had their second line of defence, where rocks had been piled in readiness . . . "More men were coming as fast as they could from the *Allt*, and it was the worst possible place for the police . . ." And we continued on, with Sorley pointing at, recalling, describing, with a Gaelic name on every crag and a Gaelic name for every turn of every bend on the road, and what that dyke once marked, and who built that tumble of boulders that was once a home: and I realised that he was the last man in Braes who would know these things, that when he was gone we would be burying still more than a poet, even the greatest poet in Europe now living.

There is a monument to the men that fought at the Battle of the Braes, who turned the tide, who forced the Napier Commission and the Crofters Act. It is a little concreted stone thing, by the roadside, at the summit of the Gedintailor hill. We stop at the verge, and Sorley and myself leave the car and clamber up a little to view the inscription. "*Faisg air a'charn seo air an 9mh latha deug de'n ghibhlein 1882, chriochnaich an cath a chuir muinntir a'bhraighe air sgath tuath na gaidhealtachd,*" I read. "Near this cairn on the 19th April 1882 ended the battle fought by the people of Braes on behalf of the crofters of Gaeldom."

"I chose the wording," said Sorley slowly. I fumbled with my camera, wanting a photograph of the monument. There was a drizzle now beginning, a dull smirr on the hills and Raasay, silvering our jackets and bonnets. We looked at each other in the gentle wet, and I took my photograph; I was hoping to catch him in the shot, for I had a wide-angle lens, and I turned the camera a little, but he sidled away, self-consciously, and made for the car.

I had a new volume of his poetry with me, the first entire collection between two covers, and he kindly signed it for me, with his own pen, in Gaelic, because I asked for Gaelic. "There, now," he said, capping the pen, "but I'll just keep it for you a moment, and hold the page open, for the ink to dry."

L and.
 This is central to our identity, our past, our character: this land in which we are

born, and raised, that bleak and wet and rugged landscape of moor and loch and hill and mountain. But it is not one of unremitting futility, for much of our land is kind and fruitful. The lovely straths and plains of Perthshire, Inverness-shire, Sutherland; the little glades and clearings in the western seaboard, tamed by centuries of digging, dunged by a thousand generations of cattle. You might go to the Uists, or Harris, and see the west there: the rich and gorgeous swards of *machair*, the green pastures on beds of white Atlantic sand, limed and friendly, and look to the near slopes and gullies, and see the ridges of former cultivation, and perhaps the mounds of lost dwellings of lost communities, left by those who were cleared. But even if you then head east, to the hard rocky coast that faces the mainland, where no ocean brought the sweetening sand, you will still see where the Gaels have made good what was sour and dead: the *feannagan*, the lazy-beds, built on the rock by those dispossessed, who piled peat and seaware and manure into table-sized mounds, and wrung from each a sheaf of corn or a bucket or two of potatoes — "a harvest no man should despise", said Fraser Darling, the first man to write sense about Highland land-use.

For such a holding, dug and tilled by the sweat of his fathers, a man may know the acutest love. There are no novels written of this love for enclosed walls and a particular spot of earth; no picture or poem made of it, no paean from Hollywood. But this is his, and it is precious to him; precious, as we said before, because it has been made and held and wrung by the toil of his people, and the investment of their work, and this is the only right of ownership that we know.

Until the southern triumph: the cynical manoeuvres that followed the '45, to bring us to heel. Feudalism came to the Highlands, and a new concept of ownership: title-deeds, and cash moving from bank to bank, and a man taking a hold of some vast tract of Highlands or Hebrides, because he paid money, and had the paper, and the smiles from high of power and law. Not only did he own the land, but he held sway over all that was on it; and, until the Braes men wrought their humiliation on Ivory, he might be despot of what he possessed, claiming everything that swum or flew or worked or grew on those acres to which he had title. Crofting, once state-recognised and state-protected, kept the people from the worst of his depredations; crofting, if extensive on the estate, limited the operations of a landlord and limited his ambitions to sport. But the landlords still have great power to block and to paralyse, to spread a pall of depression and death over a community.

In these last twelve months, as I write, the eccentric and unpleasant proprietor of Eigg has successfully recovered the island from receivers, who had taken possession on behalf of his estranged wife. Islanders formed a Trust to buy Eigg for themselves; the dream was frustrated. Canna, another of the Small Isles, belonged for many years to a rare good landlord, John Lorne Campbell, a wise and far-seeing Gaelic scholar: he still lives on Canna, but years ago donated the island to the National Trust for Scotland. The National Trust, in a few short years, has alienated almost everyone on the island;

insensitive schemes for tourism have put Campbell on the record as regretting his gift, and the island's school has been closed.

Up the coast, at the Kyle of Lochalsh, the National Trust owns much of the surrounding beauty — reefs, islands, Kyle House and its policies at Kyleakin, the latter a recent acquisition. But it has offered no opposition whatever to the bridge now being built from Kyle to Skye, in the teeth of furious opposition from the islanders: for Miller Construction will be allowed to charge heavy tolls on this bridge for some years after completion, tolls of perhaps six pounds per car, to defray costs the Government would not meet. No other toll-bridge in Scotland sets a comparable tariff; and all serve only as a short-cut to a free alternative road. Yet Caledonian MacBrayne has been forbidden by the Secretary of State to run its car-ferry in competition once the bridge is open. The future of the Mallaig to Armadale ferry is uncertain, and it only runs in summer; the small private car-ferry at Kylerhea, also summer-only, may well be killed by the bridge. In winter the Skye people will have only this bridge for access; and the proposed box-girder design is exceedingly ugly. Yet the National Trust has granted the necessary land. And it has done nothing to save the magnificent view.

Gigha, "God's Island", off Kintyre, has also been in the news. Its speculative owner, Malcolm Potier, went bankrupt in 1992; he vanished for a time, leaving debts on the island unpaid, and then resurfaced, his bid for Gigha being the only one received by Swiss creditors. He was happy to talk of great plans for the island; an unhappy people will believe it when they see it.

Recent Highland history bristles with examples of arrogant and obstructive landlords. The same owner of Eigg, a sentimentalist, chose to declare a complete ban on all shooting, hunting or killing of any bird or beastie in his little empire. The late Dr John Green, a Sussex speculator, was able ludicrously to purchase Raasay House and other island properties from the Scottish Office at a bargain price in the early Sixties. Only twice did he briefly visit his new belongings; he bought some machinery for the Raasay Home Farm, and appointed a manager, but did little else. Raasay House was a magnificent dwelling, still very much as Herbert Wood had left it, packed with fine furnishings and carpets and china and bibelots; this, collected and shipped to the London auctions, would have earned Green a sum far over the cost of his Raasay purchases. He did nothing. The house declined, and mouldered; louts and tourists broke in, vandalised, looted, and by the time he died Raasay House was a gutted shell.

Like a vicious magpie, Green continued to buy property on the island that he never used and refused to let. A young local made a bid for Glen Lodge, where his late uncle had lived; Green outbid him and the house was left empty. In 1973 the beleaguered island was at last promised a long-desired car-ferry. The best site for a terminal was in Clachan Bay, by the boating-house of Raasay House. Only a quarter of an acre was needed for slip and approach-road. This Green refused to sell. The Highlands and Islands Development Board took him to law; he resisted, and appealed, and by the time the Board was vindicated the great Seventies inflation had struck, and costs had spiralled beyond budget. The Board settled for a much less suitable site at Suisnish, on the exposed south-west shore of Raasay. Green died in 1979; his wickedness exposed at last, to public incredulity, that the Board's powers of compulsory purchase — which William Ross had assured the House of Commons the HIDB would have — were sufficient only to take possession of a tiny property or lot. The Board duly sought proper authority to deal with selfish landlords; by the time it came to Government, the Tories were in office. And George Younger, new Secretary of State for Scotland, decreed that the HIDB should not gain stronger powers of compulsory purchase because it had never used those it already possessed.

Ian Noble, the pleasant and immensely wealthy laird of southern Skye — he bought it from the new Lord MacDonald in 1973, twenty-two thousand acres at five pounds each — has attracted much acclaim for his Gaelic zeal (he has learned the language fluently) and for assorted good works, such as financing the Gaelic college Sobhal Mor Ostaig by Isle Ornsay. But even he has been high-handed. Once the young oil-mogul successfully blocked a much-needed road improvement in Portree, until he had wrung a promise from the Council that the new road-signs would be both in Gaelic and English. Derek Cooper relates that he donated a building to the new *West Highland Free Press*, but "their attitude was uncompromising. They drew a parallel with the sale of the island of Gigha. 'Within the terms of the system,' commented the *West Highland Free Press*, 'the Horlicks of Gigha were "good landlords", but at the end of the day there is no such thing as "good landlords" because "good landlords" die or fade away leaving behind Hong Kong merchant-bankers or worse'."

West Highland land is cheap: the best agricultural land is held by crofters, and not "in hand" for the estate-owner, and the only sporting-rights of cash value today — salmon fishing — are often sold separately, so that a man may own both banks of a river without being able to fish in it. Hence, by modern standards, northern real-estate is a bargain. At the height of the London property-boom in the late Eighties, someone could sell a modestly large house in that city and buy thousands of northern acres with the proceeds. And many did. Some landlords are amiable romantics, like the pop-star Donovan; others unpleasant and shadowy speculators — like that recent scourge of Skye, Johannes Hellinga; some earnest New Agers; some bluff sporting characters; a very few men and women of genuine, though generally frustrated, good intentions.

But the concept is alien. The moral logic of such comings and goings in the Highland economy — with bewildered communities seeing themselves bought and sold like beasts at a fat-stock mart — is reprehensible. There is a hatred deep in the Highland psyche for all landowners, especially those who take to do at all with the lives or habitat of their tenants; and it is a loathing well justified by the realities of past and recent history.

And still we fall.

Others have been hated and sinister oppressors in the recent Highland landscape — the military, for one, with their rocket-ranges and torpedo-runs, and ear-shattering aircraft that crash periodically in some remote corrie — none has yet hit a house, or taken human life on the ground, but that day is inevitable, and it will come. For many years, after all, fishermen blamed the sudden disappearance of craft with all hands on the deadly tangle of submarines in nets; these, they argued, would not surface on exercise, and taut cables and wires may only be cut at great risk to men in the vicinity, and they were certain that some snared submarines did dive deep and take the helpless smacks with them. For many years those making such claims were contradicted, belittled and ridiculed, until at last the Royal Navy was exposed by the *Antares* tragedy, and forced to confirm what skippers had long known to be true.

A pretty tale might be told about military exploits in the Highlands during the Second World War: the germ-warfare experiments on Gruinard are infamous — the anthrax-laden island was not finally cleansed until 1986 — but less so are the many restrictions and privations brought on West Highland districts during the struggle against Hitler. Large areas were sealed off completely. Travel to Skye, Wester Ross, Lochaber or the Outer Isles was accomplished only with very great difficulty — if you were on some professional urgency, or had relatives in that immediate district. And in Lochaber, where the Commandos and the Special Operations Executive so famously trained during those six grim years, troops practised with live ammunition; I have met an old lady who recalled an appalling experience on the shores of Loch Eil — crouching helplessly behind a boulder, small children pressed against her, as bullets whizzed and smashed all around them; she was adamant, like many in Kilmallie, that dozens of soldiers were killed in these exercises and are secretly buried all over the area.

But that war is gone. And the Cold War too is over; the Americans have quit the Holy Loch, and in this strange new era of peace it is likely that the military presence in the Highlands will decline. The latest foe to the Highland and crofting communities is no longer be-khakied and armed, but be-Barboured and carrying a biology book. It is not bombers and soldiers who control our landscape now, and threaten our ways; it is the environmentalists. Not the good and wise environmentalists, I hasten to add: not men and women of the stamp of Fraser Darling and Morton Boyd, but the power-crazed single-issue fanatics who have become a genuine pest in the Highland economy.

Almost every new project that may offer employment or security to Highland villages is opposed by somebody on environmental grounds. The Dounreay atomic-power plant, at the centre of the Caithness economy and now scheduled for closure, has been besieged for years by the Cassandras of the anti-nuclear lobby. Friends of the Earth have attacked the proposed Harris superquarry with an extraordinary line in microbiological fascism: the project is highly dangerous, they say, because ships coming to load up aggregate will arrive laden with ballast-water and discharge this on site,

The Outer Isles: Airstrip One?

releasing non-native bacteria and plankton into the Minch, endangering the local Hebridean master-germ. For many centuries the men of Ness, at the Butt of Lewis, have sailed in autumn to harvest young gannets for winter food on the seablown islet of Sula Sgeir; this tradition has been sensibly protected by Parliament, and there is ample evidence that the gannet-colony actually benefits from culling. Yet every year bird-lovers rise in chorus to demand an immediate and final ban on the gannet-hunt.

Each new road, bridge or ferry-terminal, once proposed, is quickly seized on as a major threat to some abundantly plentiful form of wildlife. A Highland farmer, known to a friend of mine, decided to restore an old meadow and beautify the site before installing cows: he drained a bog, dug a little loch, and sowed clover. A nice lady came to admire his efforts after it had all taken shape; some weeks later, a letter came to announce that his pasture was now a Site of Special Scientific Interest, and cattle were on no account to be admitted.

Mug an old lady in Stornoway and steal her purse and you would escape with a fine. Disturb a nesting osprey, and you can be clapped in prison. The Royal Society for

STORNOWAY

Stornoway welcomes friendly bombers

Military-charity complex — RAF men stationed at Aird Uig, Lewis, on 'Meet the Peasants' outing about 1958

Plucking the "gugas", Ness, in the 1950s

the Protection of Birds has wrung astonishing powers from authority; on the pursuit of egg-thieves and bird-stuffers, they may tap wires and open mail and raid your home. And in this, as in much else, the nature-lovers work hand-in-glove with landlords happy to accommodate their views. For they both, proprietors and Greens, have this in common — a burning desire to preserve and protect the *status quo*. And, behind them both sounds the great and ready chorus of the millions in huddled England and the Lowlands, who look to the Highlands and Islands as their personal summer playground annually restocked with couthy natives.

"As more and more people set ever greater store by the opportunity to have access to such land," writes James Hunter, "so political pressure mounts for measures designed to ensure that it remains inviolate." Outlining the assorted bodies and designations now littering the Highland landscape — National Scenic Areas, Nature Reserves, Sites of Special Scientific Interest, Scenes of Outstanding Natural Beauty — he snaps, "Conflicts are inevitably exaggerated by the fact that conservation organisations, both official and unofficial, are often represented in the Highlands and Islands by individuals who have no knowledge of, and little interest in, the people with whom they have to deal. Crofting communities . . . find themselves ordered about, as they see it, by English-accented scientists whose manner is, at best, condescending and, at worst, downright dictatorial."

That such ecological groups and landowning interests are happy to network with one another is an incontrovertible fact. Jean Balfour, recently Chairman of the Scottish Countryside Commission and charged with preserving valued landscape, was with her husband the owner of the 6,900 acres of the prime Balbirnie lands in Fife — scarcely a neutral figure. In addition she owned lands about Scourie, in western Sutherland, which she once sensitively described as being "nothing but rocks and water . . . incapable of development or of sustaining significant employment". Her kind keep appearing on assorted public committees charged with investigating land-use or the safeguarding of nature. These landlords portray themselves as benevolent protectors, fearless guardians of moor and loch and river and mudflat from the villainies of Giant Progress. Those who run traditional sporting estates have already found a keen apologist amongst their number: Michael Wigan, whose book — *The Scottish Highland Estate* — *Preserving An Environment* — exemplifies my argument. Somehow, by ingenious ecological logic and sweeping generalisation, Wigan presents the traditional sporting Highland landlord as the warden of all that is good and true and Green.

That his book contains much that is interesting and wise does not reduce its impact on Gaelic blood-pressure. "The sporting estate has, I contest, with reasonable success, kept in good heart that large part of the Highlands given over to deer forest and grouse moor for well over a hundred years . . . Had [*the Clearances*] not taken place it seems certain that famine for a growing population unable to sustain itself would have been inevitable; the purses of the landlords would have emptied anyway . . . The crofting system has the look of a palliative sop, a gesture rather than a solution, to mitigate the effects of restlessness for a landless people . . ." He berates the western Highlanders who have burned away all their heather and left nasty green fell-land; happily, the moors of the east Grampians are thick with the stuff, and grouse. Later Wigan laments, "It is a sad anomaly that trout fishing is not a property right in Scotland." And "Planning in the Highlands is a mess", and even "A scene in which Highland rivers flowed to the sea unfished; lochs sported no rowing boats on dreich days; keepering, ghillieing, shooting and stalking came to a stop with the attendant closing of hotels, tackle shops, letting agencies is unthinkable". And there was myself with the champagne put by.

John MacEwen of Blairgowrie, who died in 1992 at the magnificent age of a hundred and five, was a keen scholar of Highland land-use who brimmed with contempt for such as Michael Wigan. A lifelong forester, he wrote of such nonsense that it exemplified "a sadistic obsession with game resulting in the almost complete degradation of millions of acres of our land", which largely remained "archaically run, unprofitable, under-capitalised and socially disastrous". And here we hit on a most important truth.

The West Highlands and Islands, beautiful as they undoubtedly are, are not a pure wilderness untouched by human hand. They are a man-made disaster-zone, environmental degradation on an epic scale. Naturally, this area should be similar to great wild places of Canada and the United States: mighty and ancient forests, dense scrubland, rich green pastures, rolling tundra. "The bald, unpalatable fact is," wrote Fraser Darling, "that the Highlands and Islands are a devastated terrain and that any policy which ignores this fact cannot hope to achieve rehabilitation . . . that is the plain primary reason why there are now few people and why there is a constant economic problem."

The Highlands were once almost wholly wooded, with softwood and hardwood native trees; even the windblown Outer Isles had ample scrub cover, of the sort you can still see on little midloch islands. Man, over the centuries, has systematically burned or chopped them down. With the noble exception of a past Duke of Atholl in the eighteenth century (who left the Perthshire Highlands with most of the old Caledonian Forest and much gorgeous scenery) none resisted this process until after the Great War. Then we formed the Forestry Commission: but, for far too long, that body has sponsored only vast plantations of uniform conifers. These acidify the soil, threatening salmon-fishing and altering the water-table; they have also proved a death-trap for deer caught above them in sudden snows. But the loss of native trees, with consequent erosion of topsoil by wind and water, was only part of the problem. There followed, down generations, repeated and thoughtless overgrazing and overburning. And finally, in the wake of the Clearances, there came intensive sheep-farming.

I have heard of fell-sheep being described approvingly as "the best parkkeepers in the Lake District". I cannot speak for Cumbria, but there can be little doubt that the explosion in Highland sheep-keeping was an ecological calamity of the worst magnitude. Cattle, the historic stock of the Highlands, eat almost anything; furthermore, they eat with their tongues, wrapping this round grass or weed and pulling food from the soil, and their dung has high manurial value. Sheep eat only grass, except when they break into your garden. Furthermore, they eat with their teeth, shaving pasture, gnawing to the quick of the earth, reducing grass to a flat trodden velvet; their dung has little value for the soil and their urine is acidic. In my own lifetime I have myself seen the impact of concentrated sheep-grazing on good pasture, especially in a place like Shawbost, where crofts have not seen horse nor cow in many years. The grass is cropped, and cropped, and never allowed to grow; rushes and thistles and silverweed and bracken, which cows demolish but sheep ignore, soon spread over the field. This was why the sheep-economy of the post-Clearance Highlands dwindled; for a decade or two great flocks could be kept in the fine hill pastures, dunged and nurtured by untold generations of cattle, but as that capital expired and the land deteriorated its stock-supporting abilities fast declined.

Fraser Darling wanted cattle back. He wanted an intensive programme of re-afforestation, of mixed trees, with plantations fenced for at least a decade against the ravages of sheep. In short, he wanted new ways and methods of land-use, a full-scale repairing and healing of a traumatised environment. But Darling is dead, his vision sustained only by a few Highland scholars. The environmental lobby has rejected his counsel, and made itself the enemy of all changes in land-use. "Instead of seeking to heal the wounds which have been afflicted on the land, too many conservationists are content to preserve Skye's landscape as it now exists," writes Hunter. "And since the Royal Society for the Protection of Birds, to name just one of scores of conservation groups, has thirty or forty times more members than there are people living on the island [*Skye*], this wholly negative approach may be the one which triumphs in the end." But there is a twist to that tale.

It is fashionable to make mock of modern crofting. A degree of cynicism is justified indeed: too many people, not least in the Western Isles, see crofting only as a convenient stepladder into a wonderful gallery of loans and grants and general protectionist goodies, and strive to obtain a croft for the many advantages in house-construction and finance. Many working crofters — notably in Lewis — work only with sheep. You can drive the entire west coast of that island and not see a single cow. The day of crops and hay-gathering is gone. The land about the houses is overgrazed, impoverished and sour. The objection by crofters near Stornoway to an extension of the municipal dump a decade ago — "it could destroy prime agricultural land" — raised black laughter amongst those who knew the crofts in question.

But in South Uist, Skye and elsewhere there are still young and not so young men working crofts seriously, rotating crops, keeping mixed stock, experimenting too in aquaculture. Land reclamation, as Fraser Darling outlined — sowing bog with shell-sand and clover, and rapidly creating sweet good pasture — has been done in Barvas and elsewhere with great success. A case might well be made for reform — stronger powers to transfer land from absentee tenants; a minimum of agricultural endeavour demanded before major home-improvement grants are awarded. But the total public monies given to all crofters in the Highlands and Islands are dwarfed by the state-subsidy of mortgage tax-relief in southern England. And this must always, and unanswerably, be said of crofting: unlike the great empty acres of East Lothian and Angus and the Mearns, it has kept people on the land.

This is our land, for which our fathers fought and bled and died; this is our inheritance, and we seek no other. Yet there is that bareness, that sense of despoilation and tragedy, the air of hill and moors weeping for great wrongs in the past. It was this that haunted a Canadian novelist, Hugh MacLennan, when he came to Scotland once to see the Kintail his great-grandfather had left a century before. Almost forty years have passed since MacLennan wrote these lines but the truth is piercing still: "This Highland emptiness, only a few hundred miles above the massed population of England, is a far different thing from the emptiness of our own North-west Territories. Above

Angus MacHattie, crofter, Waterloo, Isle of Skye

the 60th Parallel in Canada you feel that nobody but God had ever been there before you. But in a deserted Highland glen you feel that everyone who ever mattered is dead and gone."

We fell: and still we fall.

CHAPTER TEN

A Magic Tongue

October 1990: a bright and golden morning, and Inverness most lovely in the autumn. I was sitting by the bedside of a most remarkable woman, Catherine MacVicar, who had been born in a black house on the west of Lewis a hundred years before. She was small, fragile and housebound; she had not left her home for a decade, but she had bright eyes and a firm hand and a mind as sharp as a razor. For a time we talked of her childhood: of the shielings, of the Free Church triumph in the House of Lords in 1904, and — inevitably — of the *Iolaire*. And then domestic service in Glasgow, and Stornoway; nursing in Paisley and Stirlingshire, marriage and a child quite late in life.

Her world was a room, and her heart an ocean. She disliked television, but enjoyed the radio, though increasing deafness was making that hard. She had read a great deal in her life — history, biographies — and memorised much poetry and song; her sight was weak now, but her daughter read the papers to her. "She is very good to me, but then, amn't I very good to her?" And she laughed, and squeezed my hand, and we talked politics for a while. "We are all very staunchly Labourite in this house. I have always been Labour: how could you not be, when you come from a crofting place? I never saw a necessity for the poverty around me in my young days, and the older I get the more I am sure of that." I asked what she made of the present Tory troubles (Sir Geoffrey Howe had just quit the Government). Catherine frowned. "I am *glad* of Thatcher's troubles. Maybe it will stop her uppityness and arrogance!"

I put to her the question inevitably asked of those who attain great age: how do they do it? "I don't think many of the present generation will live to be a hundred. Life is too busy for them, I think. There is too much on. When I was about we always kept early hours; I did not like to be late out of bed. And I lived a very good life, in the outward sense, because I became a Christian when I was sixteen. But we were so contented when I was young . . ."

There was a short, reflective silence. Her wiry hands worked with the quilt for a moment, and then she said, "I was last in the islands about fifteen years ago, and there had been many changes, but all really for the best. I suppose the Gaelic language is going down, which is a pity, because it is such an expressive language. We have a proverb in the Gaelic — '*Se sud an canan bha 'n garadh Eden, nuair thubhairt Adhamh "Mo gradh" ri Eubbha'*; which means, 'That was the language in the garden of Eden, when Adam said "My love" to Eve . . .'."

And how had Gaelic been regarded in her childhood, in school? She smiled, "Oh, by my time there was no rule against speaking Gaelic, though we were very much encouraged to speak English. Of course the teaching was all in English," and Catherine folded her hands, and looked pleasant and sensible — *"but that was the way the world was."*

Catherine MacVicar is still living as I write two years later: still alert, still radical in her hundred and third year. Even in that short space of time her native language has declined. In the course of her long life, spanning a generation unique in history for the scale of change and turmoil it was born to see, the Gaelic language has suffered astonishing reverse. In the eleventh century, you will remember, it was the dominant Scottish tongue: the language of court and nobility, spoken in almost all mainland districts and every western island, even briefly flickering at some points south of the Border. But by the fourteenth century Gaelic, and Gaels, were already in decline. By the fifteenth, Gaelic and its speakers were stigmatised as backward, uncouth, dangerous. The decline was slow, irregular. There was Gaelic spoken in Galloway, of all places, even in 1700; perhaps understood by some as late as 1759. Galloway today has more Gaelic place-names than Lewis, where most topographical labels are Norse. (Spoken Norse may have survived in some Lewis communities until the seventeenth century.)

When Catherine MacVicar was born, in 1890, Gaelic was still a living language in communities less than twenty miles from Glasgow — Roseneath, Arrochar, Drymen, Loch Lomondside. Gaelic was spoken on the islands of the Clyde: Bute, Arran, Cumbrae. Around Queen Victoria's Balmoral playground, Gaelic was still spoken and sung; there was Gaelic throughout Perthshire, Stirlingshire, Tomatin, Daviot, Dores. Gaelic was spoken, in that space of one living memory, throughout Argyllshire — Inveraray, Kintyre, the Kyles of Bute, Benderloch, Appin and Lorne. And it was spoken, in 1890, on every Hebridean island and almost every mainland parish north of the Firth of Lorne, the Moray Firth and the Great Glen. When the Free Presbyterian Church was born, only two congregations — those at Wick and the south side of Glasgow — did not hold regular Gaelic services, and even Wick had to employ a Gaelic missionary for the herring-girls in summer. For many years, until well after the Second World War, some parishes in the Free and Free Presbyterian Churches never heard an English sermon.

Yet even the nineteenth century had witnessed great decline. A survey by the Rev John Walker, published in 1808 and thought reasonably reliable, reckoned the Gaelic-speaking souls of Scotland at 289,000 — twenty-three per cent of the population, and this figure was for those who spoke *only* Gaelic, excluding the bilingual. But the census of 1901 listed 202,700 Scots who could speak Gaelic — only 28,106 being Gaelic monoglots, and the whole body but four and a half per cent of all in Scotland. In half a century this total was more than halved: in 1951, a mere 93,269 Gaelic speakers lived in Scotland, making 1.8 per cent of the national headcount. After nearly seventy years of compulsory education throughout the realm, only 2,178 Gaelic monoglots survived — some pre-school toddlers, most very old and largely female. By 1971, when the question was last put, there were just 477 people who could speak nothing but Gaelic — though the overall tally, in a strange blip, was actually higher than the 1961 figure: 88,415 to 80,004. The 1981 census, still the basis for presently available analysis, counts Scotland's Gaelic-speaking (and, for the first time assessed, Gaelic reading and writing) minority at 82,620, 1.6 per cent of the population.

The first astonishing plunge in numbers — between 1800 and 1900 — is most readily explained by the Clearances, which threw thousands of Gaels out of Scotland, and drove many more from pillar to post throughout the Highlands, destroying communal and cultural identity. The second great drop — numbers more than halving between 1911 and 1951, a fifty per cent decline in forty years — occurred over a time of less calculated disorder: much emigration, two world wars, the dawn of wireless and the tightening fingers of forced English monolingual schooling. But these questions, of how and why, are yet matters of fierce debate.

The lifetime of Catherine MacVicar has seen zealous and increasing hysterical efforts to arrest the dying of the Gaelic tongue. An Commun Gaidhealach — the Gaelic Council, born in 1891 — held the first National Mod in 1892, at Oban, and the competitive festival of Gaelic music and arts has been held each peacetime year since. By the end of the First World War many enlightened Highland teachers were giving their pupils some Gaelic instruction. Gaelic broadcasting is almost as old as Scottish wireless itself, and the BBC has for many years provided musical and religious radio-broadcasts. The century has seen a growing interest in Gaelic from without — each census indicates an increasing mass of learners, and books for such students now make a long list. Gaelic television programming is near as old as myself; Gaelic is taught as a subject in every Highland school, and the Scottish Examination Board has long set Gaelic O-Grade and Higher syllabi — both for native speakers and, since 1967 (after a formidable campaign by Sorley MacLean, then headmaster at Plockton), for Gaelic learners.

In the last twelve years we have seen the great expansion of Gaelic broadcasting, especially in the realm of news and current affairs, culminating in the 1990 creation of the Gaelic Television Fund with nine and a half million pounds of Government money a year; the rise and rise of Gaelic nursery-schools, *croileagan*, throughout Scotland — one of the most successful is at Tollcross in the heart of Edinburgh; the dawn, at long last, of Gaelic-medium education, with children being taught general subjects through the Gaelic language — the first class opened at Breasclete, Lewis, in 1986; and we now have Gaelic offered as a secondary-school subject, at least somewhere in its authority, by each Scottish regional council.

The Sixties saw the creation of the Highlands and Islands Development Board, which had as one of its specific aims the renewal of Gaelic identity. The Scottish National Party emerged as a significant political force, seizing the Western Isles constituency at the 1970 General Election, adding Argyll in 1974 and polling strongly throughout the Gaidhealtachd. The Seventies also brought the *West Highland Free Press*, a new radical Skye-based weekly paper formed by a co-operative of young and rather groovy left-wing graduates; Gaelic writing has been a regular feature. In the same year, some mild island youths of musical leanings formed a dance-band called RunRig; their first album, in 1978, was entirely of Gaelic songs and instrumentals, and — slowly but surely — they emerged as Scotland's premier rock-group. In Skye, too, at this time, Ian Noble founded the Gaelic College by Isle Ornsay, teaching business and technical subjects through the Gaelic tongue.

The BBC carved off Gaelic radio from the Scottish Home Service and established Radio nan Gaidheal, headquarters at Stornoway, with the local opt-out Radio nan Eilean arriving in 1979. Stornoway was also the seat of the new Western Isles Council, Comhairle nan Eilean, who now took control of local affairs in the Outer Hebrides from alien squires at Inverness and Dingwall, and soon strove fervently to promote and strengthen Gaelic in schools and beyond. The Comhairle adopted a bilingual policy. In recruitment, Gaelic speakers are consistently favoured, especially in those jobs involving contact with the public. The Comhairle has, over the years, done much to encourage and fund research into Gaelic education; interpreters are on hand to translate Gaelic speeches into English for English-monoglot councillors; for some years, with much attendant confusion, all island road signs outwith Stornoway and Benbecula — of these, more shortly — have been solely in Gaelic. At least one of Stornoway's small but respected Pakistani community has become a fluent Gaelic speaker.

A nd yet, despite all this endeavour, and all this expenditure of time and labour and money, and the spawning of a dozen and more Gaelic lobbies and quangoes and pressure groups, the language of Eden has declined and continues to do so. And here I must make a distinction between what is called "community" Gaelic — Gaelic spoken indigenously in districts, parishes — and "network" Gaelic, as spoken by the Highland diaspora in towns and districts beyond their homeland, and also by scholars and learners.

The retreat of community Gaelic has been astonishing both in its scale and its speed. By 1879 the demographer Ernst Georg Ravenstein was able to confine community Gaelic beyond a distinct geographical line, now known as the "Ravenstein boundary" — a line remarkable in three respects. First: even in 1879, one could truthfully say that the great majority of Scots north and west of this boundary were Gaelic speakers. Second:

even into my own lifetime, all principal districts beyond the Ravenstein boundary contained at least a few native community speakers. And third: it follows, remarkably closely, the boundary set in 1966 for the territories to benefit from the Highlands and Islands Development Board.

The Ravenstein boundary is drawn from Campbeltown, heading up the Firth of Clyde to cross Bute and Cowal and fix on the mainland at Arrochar; it cuts across Dunbartonshire and Stirlingshire, leaves the greater part of Perthshire in the Gaidhealtachd, just takes in the edge of Angus, and bends north and then east — roping in the western extremity of Aberdeenshire, the southern tip of Banffshire, a slice of Moray and a hunk of Nairn: a town described in 1870 as at the very border of the Gaels. The western neck of the Black Isle was still Gaelic, and only one coastal strip on the Cromarty Firth was marked out as non-Gaelic from the rest of Ross-shire; finally, the boundary bisects Caithness and chews into the most north-easterly point of Sutherland. Apart from these very few bites — Alness and Evanton, Wick and Thurso and lands about — all the Highland counties, all the Hebrides, all of Argyll and old Dalriada were still solidly a Gaelic heartland. So, for that matter, were such districts as Crianlarich, Tyndrum, the Trossachs, Rannoch, Breadalbane, Atholl, Deeside and much of Speyside.

When I was born, a little over a quarter of a century ago, native speakers from all those places were still alive. Gaelic might be heard in shops and corners about the Kyles of Bute, Benderloch, Ardgour, Lochaber and the remotest corners of Perthshire — Balquhidder, Glen Lyon. My father, then a minister in Lochaber, could still hold Gaelic services about Loch Eil and Ardgour and attract a few hearers. When he was a minister in Partick, Glasgow — a specifically Highland charge of the Free Church, for the area held a large exiled Hebridean community — he kept, as recently as 1980, three Gaelic services a week. And I remember, just two decades ago, congregations of five hundred people and more filling the church for the Gaelic Sabbath evening service of a Communion weekend; and, in the summers on Lewis, hearing school-age children playing and talking with one another in the old language.

Not now.

The last speaker of Aberdeenshire Gaelic, a very old lady, died in 1983. The last certain speaker of Perthshire Gaelic, Petrine Stewart, died last year, though correspondence columns of the Scottish press briefly fizzed on the question. Gaelic has completely vanished in Dunbartonshire, Stirlingshire, Moray and Nairn, and the glens of Inverness-shire east of the Great Glen; I am fairly certain there are no Gaelic native speakers to be found anywhere on the mainland south or east of that magnificent fault. Black Isle Gaelic, Easter Ross Gaelic, Caithness Gaelic and East Sutherland Gaelic are quite vanished; some native speakers still survive from western Lochness-side — Glen Urquhart, Glen Moriston. In truth Gaelic, as a language of community — day-to-day conversation, public worship, and so on — is virtually extinct on the Scottish mainland, apart — just possibly — from one or two villages in Morvern and Moidart. Native speakers may still readily be found in such areas as Arisaig, Glenshiel, Lochcarron, Applecross, Torridon, Gairloch and Assynt; very, very few ever use it. The understanding has survived; the speech has not.

Of the southern Hebrides, only Islay still boasts a true Gaelic community. Other islands, like Mull or Tiree, still have some native speakers. In Skye, community Gaelic is confined to the northern parishes — Bracadale, Duirinish, Snizort and most strongly in Kilmuir; in Sleat, Gaelic is preserved by the deliberate efforts of Noble and others in the schools and elsewhere. It is only a little better in Raasay. The last true heartland of Gaelic in Scotland is the Western Isles, though Stornoway and Benbecula are heavily anglicised by military and other influences, and the language is not in good heart in such areas as Barra and Broad Bay. There is much futile inter-parish conflict on the niceties of which had the best and purest Gaelic. Still, Stornoway had in 1981 a good seventy per cent showing for Gaelic speakers; Gaelic-speaking in the Western Isles as a whole approached ninety-five per cent, and in some areas — such as Scalpay, or Ness — a healthy ninety-eight per cent.

Such figures masked realities, realities as old as man: birth and death. Every week perhaps two dozen native Gaelic speakers pass away; of babies born in their communities that week (and few enough there are), only a handful will be raised as Gaelic-speaking children in Gaelic-speaking households. Biological arithmetic is not on Eden's side. And the 1981 census, which showed the Western Isles still strong in Gaelic, followed but a few years after the arrival of a full television service; most of those under eighteen in 1981 had grown up with only the programmes of BBC 1. By the late 1980s, four TV channels poured their delights into virtually every island home. Satellite television has rapidly caught on; from far above the mountains, the picture quality is much better for island communities.

There were many hints by 1990, straws in the wind that should have been heeded. You began to notice that children did not speak Gaelic in the road anymore, though Mammy put them in front of the TV and *Padruig Post* each morning, and nice Miss Macleod in the school taught them by Gaelic computer and the colourful *Leabhar Mor Spot* — "Spot's Big Book", a picture-dictionary for thinking tots. You heard churchmen murmuring about the difficulty of finding Gaelic supply. The Church of Scotland, for many years now, has struggled to find enough ministers for all its Gaelic congregations; many vacancies are only filled when they reluctantly change status from "Gaelic Essential Charge" to "Gaelic Desired Charge". The Free Presbyterians presently have four vacancies meriting a "Gaelic Essential" label — Glendale in Skye; North Harris; Ness and North Tolsta in Lewis. Of the three divinity-students now training, only one has Gaelic: the Ness and North Harris congregations have been pastorless for seven years.

In 1944 a noted professor of linguistics wrote that the Celtic languages had "more of the structure of the ideal auxiliary language" than any other he knew. My source comments acidly how it is then passing strange that the Celtic languages have given way at every turn. But Gaelic is a most curious language, notoriously hard to learn; though it has many Latin (and increasingly, many English) loan-words, it resembles no other European tongue, save its Celtic sisters, and of these it is much closer to the Gadelic (Irish Gaelic, and Manx — extinct as a living language since 1977) than the Brythonic (Welsh, Breton and Cornish).

Written Gaelic has an alphabet of eighteen letters; there is no *j, k, q, v, w, x, y* or *z*. Gaelic orthography — spelling — defies the phonetic norms of English and presents another barrier to the learner, though the phonetics of the language are more clearly and regularly expressed in writing than is the case in English. Gaelic grammar, like most European languages, has masculine and feminine nouns to which pronouns and adjectives suitably adapt; it also preserves the distinction, which modern English has lost, between *you* singular and *you* plural — the *thou-you* form of the Authorised Version — and, like these other tongues, one uses the *you*-plural form when courteously addressing a superior or stranger, besides addressing a multitude.

The key to understanding Gaelic pronunciation is to recognise the most striking feature of spoken Gaelic — heavy aspiration. There are very few hard consonants, with aspiration repeatedly softening the conclusion and beginning of words, giving spoken Gaelic its striking liquidity — and, again, impenetrability to the non-native. In Gaelic orthography, the letter *h* is employed as the sign of aspiration. "Mh" and "Bh" are pronounced as we pronounce the letter *v* in English; they, and the other aspirants, feminise an adjective — hence "Calum Ban" and "Mairi Bhan", Fair Calum but Fair Mary — and mark the genitive and vocative — "tigh Mhairi", house of Mary; "O Mhairi" — oh Mary. "Dh" is said as we say the letter *y*; "Ph" and "Th" usually have our *h* sound, and "Fh" is completely silent . . . but I have said enough to show the obstacles before the blithe Gaelic learner, though it must be said that many (like my younger brother) have learned in adulthood, and attained remarkable fluency.

All of this makes spoken Gaelic a very different noise from spoken English; the old language demands palatal and glottal effects which modern English has either discarded or never employed. The initial *L* in Gaelic is a thicker sound, palatal rather than alveolar — that is, the Gael puts his tongue about the sides of the roof of his mouth, and not against the alveolar ridge behind the upper front teeth. The glottal sound, concluding *ch*, presents non-Scots with a famous problem — "Lock Ness!"; the *chd* sound — "loch . . . k"! (*sic*) is not found in English at all. Vowel combinations and sounds also vary from English — and we have not even left the complexities of Gaelic sound to consider what we are saying in the first place. Certain numerate mechanisms — telling the time in Gaelic, giving the date — are more complicated than giving these in English; most Gaels, outwith the ranks of Gaelic zealotry, would today tell you the time in English — "*Tha e four o'clock.*"

Standard English has developed over centuries, with a huge boost from the printing-press; Chaucer, Shakespeare, Bunyan and — critically — the Authorised Version of the Bible confirmed a standard of formal, literary, governing English nearly four centuries ago. Not until 1801 was there a complete translation of the Gaelic Bible; not until after 1820 was it readily available and affordable, and this version has seen several revisions — a modern printing, with new orthography, has just been issued. Hence Gaelic remains a much less uniform language than English; though English accents vary far and wide, real dialectic variance (unless you dare to count Scots, or American) has practically disappeared. But Gaelic has ten significant dialectic divisions: though six of these — Perth, Aberdeen, Banff, Moray, Nairn and Caithness — are extinct, some speakers of Sutherland Gaelic are still spared, and three Highland county dialects — Argyll, Ross, Inverness — are yet strong.

The advent of Radio nan Gaidheal, following on the Gaelic journal *Gairm*, has done much to flatten out such variance to create a very formal, literary and — frankly — rather artificial Gaelic, if one understood by all native speakers. Yet this network Gaelic is not a living language, not the Gaelic of hearth and home or even of the pulpit; on the ground, spoken Gaelic remains highly colloquial — and divided. At the extremes of the Gaeltachd — Ness to Islay — are significant differences in pronunciation and vocabulary; even a Gaelic apologist has to plead that "an *educated* Scots Gael [*my italics*], once his ear is attuned, should have no difficulty in conversing the length and breadth of Gaelic Scotland". Yet, in one community, there can be striking variations from parish to parish. The Gaelic of Lewis is distinct in many respects from the Gaelic of Harris — though they are geographically the same island; it also varies widely from that of North Uist, South Uist and Benbecula, at the opposite end of the archipelago, though it is oddly similar to that of Barra in the extreme south. Even so, Lewis has eight Gaelic sub-dialects, each with its own unique features, words and pronunciation — Ness, West Side, Uig, Broad Bay, Stornoway, Point, North Lochs and Park. And I need hardly add that the speakers in each district consider their own brand of Gaelic superior to any other.

Consider these difficulties. Consider that Gaelic, unlike Welsh, has never been recognised by the British state; that it has no official status, and that for many years after 1872 it was systematically ground down by the educational system, well into my own lifetime. You went to school in Lewis, even in the last decade, perhaps without a word of English — but from the day you entered, you were spoken to in English and taught arithmetic and reading and writing in English. You would be taught more Gaelic, in its slot, than your parents; they were perhaps trained to sing in a Gaelic choir. Your grandparents may well have been strapped for speaking Gaelic in school. With the sole and noble exception of the Presbyterian churches, no form of authority or officialdom recognised the Gaelic tongue; and Gaelic became the language of hearth and home, of the kitchen and the byre. You saw it had no other usefulness, and you grew up to doubt the validity of the native tongue of your people.

Consider how, after a century and more of such teaching, Gaelic has progressively weakened even amongst fluent native speakers: the vocabulary shrinking with each generation, the increasing import of English words and structures. Consider the ongoing depopulation of outlying Highland districts. Consider the rise of the mass-media, the improving surface-communications that brought all manner of entertainments and goodies to even the furthest islands. Consider now, with television, that over ninety-five per cent of Hebridean and West Highland homes have a garrulous English speaker in the living-room every evening. Not only does television primarily — and, until the last decade, well-nigh exclusively — talk with an English tongue; it also sophisticates, and glamourises. Hebridean youngsters are much more socially aware than their big brothers of the late Sixties; much more "hip" and "with it", but more conscious too of the tinselled delights of the world beyond. The delights of that world are English, and their apostles — Jonathan Ross, Paula Yates, all the tacky little princelings of the world of rock and "yoof" — are most English and exciting; Gaelic is the language of dusty old Bibles, and slow Granny, and overkeen Miss Macleod at the school, and the wild writer by the loch, and the mind-numbing sermons of the red-faced minister.

As I write these lines, early in November 1992, the Highland and Gaelic establishment is reeling from the first shock of the 1991 census figures for Gaelic, which numerals were released three weeks ago. It was widely expected that the April 1991 survey, which followed a decade of fervent and innovative activity to protect and revive the Gaelic tongue — Gaelic-medium education, Gaelic nursery-schooling, the Gaelic Television Fund to name but three — would show a final arrest of the Gaelic decline, consolidating Gaelic speakers at seventy-five thousand to eighty thousand, and perhaps even registering an increase. For, though the cold sweep of death continues through the Highland community, there has been a huge resurgence of interest in Gaelic, and a host of people flooding to learn the language, and much belated cash-support from local and national authorities; surely now the tide would turn?

The first statistics — we still await a detailed breakdown and analysis of census findings — have come as a brutal shock. Gaelic-speaking has plunged from seventy-nine thousand to sixty-five thousand in Scotland; Gaelic speakers now form less than one per cent of the population. "The truth is that we are dying faster than we are born," wailed Torcuil Crichton, Lewis-born reporter at *The Herald*, on 16th October 1992, but he added defiantly, "The mortality of man, however, does not deter the development agencies working for the revival of Gaelic. Educationalists, development officers, parents and enthusiasts are convinced that the 1991 statistics signal a bottoming of the decline. Recovery, they are sure, is around the corner, or at least near the end of the decade . . ."

Well, they would be, would they not? For, as we shall see, many have staked much on the campaign to protect the Gaelic language. Yet Crichton and his friends should be truly alarmed by another, and much less publicised, figure from the 1991 census. It is now an official fact that less than half the children of the Western Isles can speak Gaelic — only forty-nine per cent of all under the age of eighteen — and if that is true of Gaelic's last stronghold, and if it cannot be rapidly reversed, the Gaelic language is finished. Crichton does obliquely address this question. "On Eriskay . . . a depressing number of children are not fluent despite having Gaelic-speaking parents. The previous generation's mistaken assumption — that the language would be passed on somehow, almost genetically, against a barrage of counter-culture from television, school and peers — has still to be overturned."

Television is now robed by some as an angel of salvation, but Crichton identifies it as "the single most powerful agent of destruction", and rightly queries its potential for deliverance: even if, from 1993, we will have ten hours a week of Gaelic goggle-box financed by benevolent Tories at nine and a half million pounds a year. "No-one really knows what will happen when Gaelic television hits the screens next January, but it is certain that, on its own, it will not save the Gaelic language. Securing . . . Government funding to provide the service was a masterpiece of political campaigning which gave an enormous boost to confidence and the profile of the language. The downside is that it has engendered a degree of complacency and may stifle development in other areas. Inevitably, glamorous Gaelic TV has found a fertile recruiting-ground in Gaelic radio, now denuded of much of its staff. It has also had the unbalancing effect of drawing on the small pool of young speakers who might otherwise end up as teachers . . . the success in obtaining the TV service leaves little steam for demanding more education funding, the lynchpin of recovery."

Now Torcuil Crichton is a gifted writer, a dedicated investigative reporter, and stands out amongst all the holy huddle of the Highland chattering-classes for having some independence of mind. But here, though hitting upon much that is true, he misses the central issue completely.

Gaelic has dwindled steadily over the last century, from over quarter of a million speakers in the year my Shawbost grandfather was born — 1891 — to sixty-five thousand today. In the short lifetime of Crichton and myself, Ravenstein's watershed has shivered and slid. Community Gaelic is all but gone on the Scottish mainland, surviving only in tiny pockets on the western edge; the vast bulk of community Gaelic is today found within the bounds of two small local authorities — Skye and Lochalsh District, the Western Isles. Only a handful of very old people speak the Gaelic language in its true purity. Of these sixty-five thousand, a good many are Gaelic learners, including a number who can read and write the language but not truly speak it; many native speakers are conversely illiterate in Gaelic; and many of these supposed native speakers will actually be more fluent in English, and use it as their language of choice.

That is the dark message of the 1991 census. This is a dark message from the hearts and minds of the Gaelic establishment — the speed and venom with which they have leapt to decry the census figure, and query its accuracy, and pour scorn and abuse on all who dare to question the long-term prospects of the Gaelic tongue. Here is one very human and very terrible fact that must surely convince you of Gaelic's plight — the last known true monoglot, of adult age and normal intelligence, died on the Isle of Scalpay off the east coast of Harris in January 1991. And I am now resigned to seeing in my own lifetime the disappearance of Gaelic as a living language of real communities.

Why? Why this long grim march of language-death? Education is certainly a factor, from the conscious repression of the Gaelic tongue by teachers in the last century, to the benevolent trivialisation of our own — sing it, kids; act it, kids; go to the Mod and win a medal, kids; but don't expect to be taught anything of relevance or importance in the Gaelic tongue, never mind the history of your own people and culture.

Television: oh yes, dread television, that glowering eye of modern ennui, flattening all before and around like a great cultural steam-iron, filling our hearts and minds with images of improbably delicious sex and sanitised death and sterilised politics and the mindless trivia of the night-club and the market. But the biggest enemy of the Gaelic language and the Gaelic outlook and the Gaelic world is not education, nor television: it is what it has always been, the systematic stripping and clearing of the Highland glens.

Why is Gaelic dying? It is dying because Mull is empty, and Moidart is empty, and Torridon is empty, and Sutherland is empty, and St Kilda and Soay were evacuated; it is dying because Skye is empty, and Uist is empty, and Harris is empty, and Mingulay and Taransay and Scarp long depopulated, and Park is empty, and Uig is empty — straths long cleansed of their cumbersome inhabitants, islands obligingly helped to close down and move out by nice officials, villages (like Calbost, a lovely little township in the Park district of Lewis: present population two) that had perhaps two hundred people at the turn of the century now hold only a handful of elderly widows. And at night they put on the television, for comfort, and do not look out at other lights, because there are none that burn in ruined or shuttered homes.

Gaelic is dying not because there was no-one to care for the language itself, but because so little was done to uphold and preserve the communities in which it had to survive. A car-ferry here was delayed, and delayed; a road was not built in time to save the last family moving out; it was cheaper to evacuate the St Kildans than to provide a regular supply boat (oh, St Kildans, had you been missile-trackers and the Ordnance!); because, even in recent years, the honoured heads of honourable bodies charged with Highland regeneration put all their energies into massive and prestigious developments employing hundreds at significant centres, and not into spawning and supporting a hundred little ones that might have kept young people and life at the heart of a township, at the end of a headland.

Keen and zealous have been the bodies labouring for the Gaelic tongue; and yet even they bear witness to its battles and its ailing. The *West Highland Free Press* and the rock-group RunRig fight for Gaelic: but the *Free Press* is an English newspaper, and RunRig in their greatness average but two Gaelic tracks an album. In a last and dreadful irony, those who labour to find solutions to the Gaelic crisis are fast becoming part of the problem. Gaelic threatens to suffocate under a surfeit of worthiness, as all from teachers to agitators to poets to journalists stress and stress and stress its importance, its uniqueness, its beauty, its trouble: they have made it a political issue, and — with much ill-veiled intolerance — a moral issue, and the public switch off, and the children yawn. Jean Paul Sartre wrote of the fighting Basques in Spain, speaking their own language rather than Spanish, that "It is a revolutionary act". For a time, two decades ago, speaking Gaelic became just that: RunRig sang, and the *Free Press* scandalised, and Nationalism terrified the British establishment. But now these radicals, aging, are themselves the Highland establishment, and they have made Gaelic square, and the young turn off in droves.

The cry of battle is heard, as voices from An Commun and Commun na Gaidheal and Sabhal Mor scream of impending disaster for the Gaelic language — like a Regency whore in a Gillray cartoon, squeaking, "Oh my good sir have mercy!" and "Help!" and "Murder!". And then you hear the same voices gloating over Gaelic renaissance, and recovery, and renewal; and later hear them calling the census a lie and the realists race-traitors, and you may be forgiven if you are overcome by cynicism.

What is lost if Gaelic dies? A great deal, at one level: a language, ancient and precious, not like any other, with its greatness a vast vocabulary, words and words with tiny and powerful shades of meaning, encapsulating observations and truths that no English equivalent can hold; a language that was complex and true in poetry, gorgeous and warm in song, in its noise and music sonorous, lilting, resonant with power — a language that was fearful in battlecry, most seemly in love. Still, a language is only a language — an unpopular truth, but a truth nonetheless. A language is a collection of sounds and marks to describe realities, convey meaning and probe truth. Our own century has seen philosophers like Wittgenstein and Russell and Ayre wrestle with such profundity: the relationship between language, truth and logic; the connection between words and facts. Facts, truths, insights, things and works of beauty — these are the dynamic of the mind and soul, the glory of creation. Language is but a tool — less: a channel, a conduit — by which these things are wrought.

Gaelic is failing; Gaelic is going. Living Gaelic is now only to be found in the islands, and creeps away even there; every week the obituary columns of Highland newspapers record the passing of native speakers, and every year brings new evidence and anecdote of Gaelic's weakening grip on the young. Network Gaelic, strangely, is growing: an urbanised, educated, socially aware élite of people who have deliberately seized on and honed their Gaelic, or acquired it in learner's classes, and who now deploy

An Lanntair Gallery, and friends. This island culture-shop opened in Stornoway in the mid-1980s

it to their own ends in Gaelic academe, journalism, broadcasting. But, like all armies in a desperate cause, they include many erratic and obsessive and highly unpleasant people. And their glasshouse Gaelic is not a living tongue. It is a standardised, bastardised, westernised uniform argot that was never spoken by honest Gael on land or sea. Its southern learners read and speak Gaelic but will ever think in English; Gaelic television-shows, and their accounts, and their committee-meetings, and even their post-canning post-broadcast parties, are directed and produced and budgeted and processed and seen off in a chatter of English. At Radio nan Gaidheal in Inverness, the prospects-board on the newsroom wall is written in English. And southern learners are southern still.

Sorley MacLean wrote, many years ago: "I do not see the sense of my toil, putting thoughts in a dying tongue." He went on writing Gaelic poetry, to our blessing, because — as Iain Crichton Smith shrewdly said — he had no choice; his poems came to him in Gaelic anyway. But, these days, few native speakers share Sorley's command of the Gaelic language, or the breadth of his vocabulary. His poems now appear with parallel English translations — his own translations — and these are magnificent poetry in their own right for assonance and rhythm and sound; but they are only great — as Sorley himself is only great — because of the power and vitality of the concepts addressed and explored, the agonies laid bare, the great might of an imagination and integrity that transcends all barriers of race, or any dying tongue.

Gaelic has long been deemed central to our identity as Hebrideans and Highlanders. But is this true? Is not our Gaeldom as much racial, and psychological, as linguistic? And is Gaelic not so much the core of our identity as a badge of our difference? In truth, should we not now acknowledge Gaelic as an external, an instrument outwith our identity — quaint marks, lovely sounds, but nothing more than a language, and a language heading for the abyss?

This is not a view I will be thanked for advancing. It is not a view that is popular or politic, or fashionable. I have already been condemned, in such debate, for daring to address the central questions of Gaeldom and the Highlands without a fluent knowledge of Gaelic — "just taking the easy bits, John, the portable bits" — and been forcibly told that I may know nothing of my own culture, nor write with any authority thereon, nor face its concerns, because I am not a Gaelic speaker. Such bigotry is unpleasant: it is also highly dangerous, because it ignores what is manifest reality. The Gaelic language is in inexorable decline. It is being propelled to extinction by forces of fantastic power and inhuman scale, forces of history and commerce and culture and psychology. Those who defy those forces, or belittle their significance, arraign themselves as Canute against the tide. And those who simultaneously press the Gaelic cause on learners willing and unwilling, while poisonously portraying themselves as the keepers of a cave of gold, and it entered only with a magic tongue, make themselves the foes of Gaelic ways and the Highland culture. We have much to give the world beyond: but no right to demand that they first learn Gaelic. And if we do, we will make ourselves a clique and a ghetto; we will screw down the coffin-lid from inside.

Language is a tool: a tool of living, and growing, and relating, and creating, and weeping, and rejoicing, and community and conquest. By language we bond with each other; by language we come to know and understand our place in this world, and to enjoy its fruits. Gaelic is no longer up to this task; that is why the wise should shed no tears, and why it is doomed to die. And it is high time to cast off those who seek to bind the Highland soul and Highland credibility to a fading tongue, and set to the pressing task of shaping a post-Gaelic Highland identity.

CHAPTER ELEVEN

A Troubled Tribe

January 1991: a clear and coldly calm winter's day in northern Harris. It is a little over forty-eight hours since Sorley and Renee MacLean deposited me back in Portree, after my walk over the *Leitir* and my tour of the Braes, and his low strong voice is still heavy in my mind: it, and him, and the dignity and grandeur of what they represent will make the evening's events seem the more sinister.

It is Friday, with the early winter night approaching, and I am spending some days with friends in Tarbert, staying with the Maciver family in the Church of Scotland manse. The young Macivers are just coming from school, and the house has that air of Friday-night excitement, the sort you have when lessons are over and the weekend looms, a buzz of spirit you lose when you grow up. Even Rex, the family spaniel (and a more docile, easy-going dog I never saw) is happy, or at least looking as happy as a pug-mouthed King Charles spaniel ever can. But he trots about the warm kitchen in excitement, and as daughter and each son troop in he flings himself against each in soul-melting affection, rising on his hindpaws, pleading for titbits with Bambi eyes.

Norman, the head of the house, says he will now take me for a promised drive to Luskentyre, the beautiful delta-sands on the west side of the island, a splash of green and white below its barren rocky flanks, on which the people of Harris are buried. So we announce that we will be away for an hour or so, but back for tea, and we walk out to the garage. The Tarbert street-lamps are glowing; the clouds are dark in a slaty sky. The car growls into life. We bowl down the drive, on to the pier car-park, and in by the new shore road to the Tarbert junction. Right is for Lewis and Stornoway; left is for South Harris. We go left, roaring up the steep Caw brae, and the lights of Tarbert, its shops and pier, twinkle on the water below.

We talk pleasantly as we weave along the main road, into the encroaching night, the ghastly beauty of this tortured and stony landscape. Many Hebridean islands can be captured in a word: Raasay — verdure; Skye — mountains; Lewis — peat; South Uist — machair. Harris is, emphatically, rock. Here great glaciers paused to rest, and gladly dumped their stony load. Northern Harris is strewn with boulders and rubble, stones great and stones small. Eastern Harris — Tarbert, Kyles, Finsbay — seems nothing but one great rock, rippled mass of gneiss, dotted and lined with apologetic scraps of peat and thin heather, the stone scarring the land like the ribs of some decaying beast. Only on the coastal fringe, by fishing and toil, could a man feed his children here. And, though in deep peaty Lewis the rivers must go brown and dark as Indian tea, in Harris the streams run clear.

Near Stockinish there is another junction: left to join the Golden Road down the bare east coast, right for Glen Luskentyre and the machair of the west. We go right. Glen Luskentyre is a bleak broad valley, steep and empty, terrifying boulders like monsters at the roadside, impossible cuttings and gorges of rock. Lochs shine feebly in the twilight. A sickly sun sets in a pinking sky. I ask Norman to stop now and again, and leap out to take photographs. At one lonely bend we see a little brown dog trotting along, and exchange curious glances, for we are miles from habitation.

I have spoken ill at times here of the Church of Scotland, but Norman Maciver is a good man: a minister of character and conviction, a solid doctrinal preacher, a pastor who would adorn any church that had him. He is the sort of man that has strong principles, that does not harbour illusion or self-deceit, who would say it to your face if he saw you going wrong — but never to another behind your back. This toughness, though, is veiled most of the time by a gentle manner. He smiles a great deal; his voice is the lilting accent of the Point area in Lewis. If you met Norman, you would think him very shy.

We reach Luskentyre. It is now more night than day, but a deep light is still light, and the tide has ebbed from the bay to leave a great expanse of wet and shining sand. At the graveyard we stop and get out, walking about for a time amongst the lairs; the rows of modest plain memorials, the Atlantic roar in our ears. We return at length to the car, and put it round, and head in the direction of home.

We see the lights simultaneously as we ascend Glen Luskentyre: twin orange beacons, flashing on and off, rhythmically, and I say, "Roadworks . . . ? But I don't remember . . .", for there were no lights when we passed down this road not fifteen minutes before. "Oh dear. I wonder if there's been an accident," murmurs Norman, and he accelerates; we storm up the road, in and out of bends, and crest a summit, and there is a forlorn young woman standing by her car and the hazard-lights of it beep-beeping in the darkness.

We stop. "Can we help at all?" asks Norman, and she looks at us in wooden relief to say, "Yes, there has been a crash. I think it is three lads . . . I was just down the road phoning for the Tarbert ambulance." My eyes catch the bashed front of her own car, a little blood on the mangled grill, and then Norman and myself see her turn to look up the road, and there is a youth staggering towards us, dizzy, bleeding.

"It is quite all right," he says blearily, "but if you could find my shoe I'd be grateful. A training-shoe, I lost it in the bog . . ." Norman and I are already running, past him, up the brae to the scene of trouble, where another car has just drawn up, and two older men sliding out with their wide eyes fixed on something off the road. We are with them in a second or two, following them on to the peat. The moor is quite clear at this point — none of these nightmare-rocks nearby, and the wreck of an old yellow estate-car lies lopsidedly in a bog. Beside it sprawl two bodies — "Norman," I say nervously, certain at once of spilled guts and appalling injuries — and about all is an overwhelming smell of petrol.

Fortunately, one of the corpses sits up as we approach. He is a thick-set youth with empty eyes, staring about, and he reacts only woozily when one of us grabs him by the shoulders to enquire for his welfare. Blood streams from his cut face, soaking into his casual jacket. "Cold, cold, cold," he repeats, "it's so cold, it's so cold." But the other fellow is lying very still and straight, in what you would almost think was the start of a grave, because he seems to be in a hollow just the shape of himself. He is also quite alive; he is perhaps thirty, in denims, with a thin sharp beard. But he stares up straight ahead, into the night, not looking at us, the eyes hard, and says, "C'mon, give us a smoke. Just a smoke, that's all I want," and he curses and swears as we eye him doubtfully. There are one or two small contusions on hands and face, but he is not so bad to look on as the other fellow, and it is only the rigid stillness of him that is worrying. He is as impassive as an elder at the door of a kirk, as if there is nothing in being thrown from a car at high speed in the winter of the January moor. Instinctively, we all sniff: petrol, indeed, but not the only spirit in the air.

"We can't give him any smokes until the doctor comes." "No, indeed. Not with that petrol so thick," say I, profoundly. But there is no explaining this to Beardie on the ground. "For any sake!" he snarls, and swears ripely. "There's smokes in my jacket pocket. Come on, I'll even *pay* you guys if you just give me a light, even. All I want is a smoke. There's my car, just wrecked there, and I've nothing left in the world at all . . ." The accent is Stornoway: hard, thick, almost obscene in the murmur of Harris voices. "Cold, so cold," says the lad with the cut face, and Norman leads him away to shelter in his car. The dusk is on us now, almost night; I splash into the bog about the car, feeling the icy water soak into my socks, and peer for a training-shoe. This banger is banged, right enough. The wheels bow from bust axles; the glass has crazed in each window, the front is knocked in and even the door pillars dented under a rippled roof. The car clearly left the road, and overturned, and rolled and righted. There is some blood on the seats. There is no sign of a shoe.

I rejoin the little huddle standing solicitously over Beardie. Someone asks how he is. "Never you mind," spits he, "just give me a smoke, bwana." "But the petrol . . ." Eff the petrol, says Beardie: why will we not let him have a smoke? And have we seen his dog? "I've lost my dog. It was in the car with us, a lovely wee brown beggar of a thing. Like a Wispa bar." He is genuinely upset; almost weeping. "But we saw a dog," chorus Norman and I, "brown, too." 'Aye, that's him, the little mutt," says Beardie with pathetic eagerness, and tells me to find him, and says he will pay me if I find him, but will I first not give him a smoke? "If you just come up to the road I'll give you plenty smokes then," I snap, and wince at my brutality. "Er — are you hurting badly?" "What do you think? Of *course* I'm hurting badly. Didn't the car roll on top of me?"

"Was it yourself that was driving?" asks one of the old men slyly. "Ah, now. You'll not catch me at that. I'm saying nothing."

At this point a car pulls up and the doctor gets out: James Finlayson, from Tarbert. I know James well, and our meeting is most ironic. This winter, and indeed the previous winter, I have written ferocious articles on the rising problem of teenage-drunkenness in Stornoway: how, in the small hours of a weekend night, the centre of town fills with hundreds of young people, some as small as twelve or thirteen, many smashed out of their skulls, and drinking prodigiously in the dark secrecy of the Castle grounds. These pieces provoked an outcry as vicious as it was irrational: the leaders of community, big fish in a small pool, uniting not to address the problem but to attack myself. A *Stornoway Gazette* editorial, before Christmas, said I was out to "do down my own island". I even had the first (and to date, only) death-threat of my career, from a well-spoken island lady who rang my house and withheld her name; but I had seen it all with my own eyes, and, alone of Hebrideans, James Finlayson had spoken up to say he could vouch for every word.

So here we meet again, in the island of perfect young people where nobody sins, and we eye each other significantly, and he dumps a vast case on the ground and crouches to examine Beardie, who is now a fearful colour of white. "Will you just move your toes? Can you move your toes for us?" asks James in his best Newtonmore accent; Beardie responds with rich speculation on our paternity, intelligence and sexual preference — and Norman before him, dog-collar and all! — but at length deigns to roll his elegant cowboy-boots a little. James unfastens his collar for pulse, undoes Beardie's belt; the prone figure comments foully. "Go down to the Luskentyre road-end, Norman, and 'phone for the Northon ambulance," said James at length. "We'll need a special stretcher for this boy, and it'll take all the room in this one." For the Tarbert ambulance has drawn up at the roadside.

A queue of cars now sits patiently along the road, cars for South Harris returning after a day of work or shopping in Tarbert, Stornoway. It is as well for the boys that they crashed during the island equivalent of rush-hour. Late at night, and they might have lain out here for hours, undetected, unaided: the cold, cold wind, the ice forming and tinkling in the pools of the black lonely moor. A nurse emerges from the ambulance, a big motherly lady; she cradles Beardie's head and sighs sympathetically at his petulant pleas for nicotine. The ambulancemen come with a spinal stretcher, two halves of metal and canvas frame. Two peaked caps glint in the ambulance light, and burly Tarbert policemen join us.

"Well, *hell*, it's the law," says Beardie. "Here to help you, boy," says one officer with gruff kindliness.

"*Ha!* You're not getting a thing out of me tonight." The policeman groans. "I see — you're just waiting on your solicitor, eh?" Doctor, nurse, ambulance-crew and policemen help to work the bits of stretcher under and over Beardie's inert form and slot the tubes together. The journalist picks up the doctor's bag and follows them up to the road. This is his sole contribution to the rescue. Norman stands talking with the girl who found the accident, and we both console her. "Ach, the nuisance of it," she mutters. "I just had the car back from the garage on Wednesday, and look at it now." I said that I hoped the boys would be insured for it, and she looks at me in surprise. "Oh, they never hit me at all. They'd gone off the road when I saw them, and I drove on to 'phone for an ambulance, and . . . well," she grimaces, "I hit a sheep on the way." We commiserate as best we may. I feel guilty for so abandoning her to rush and comfort the beauties in the bog.

The other boys are warming up in friendly cars; James inspects them, and decides they must all go to hospital, and that one too should be in a spinal stretcher. As he organises this, I retreat down the road, wanting a smoke myself; as I pass cars, heads pop out seeking details of the night's carnage. "What . . . ? Well, now. Isn't that dreadful. These people from Stornoway . . ." I light up at length, and relax and enter the night: the stars gleaming in a velvet sky, the moor a realm of mystery, strange birds calling. The boom of the Atlantic on the coast, a thump and hiss of surf regular as a ticking clock. I walk back up, and rejoin the commotion; I catch Norman, his collar white in the dark; we hear the chorus of voices, giving orders, demanding smokes, seeking the story, questioning the delay. The emergency folds into a cortege. Our cars, one by one, trickle home to civilisation.

It all ends happily enough. None of the boys is badly hurt; they leave hospital the following day, sober and in their right minds. The dog, I learn much later, turns up safe and well. The yellow car lies there for many months, rusting in peace, until in mid-June it is removed. All Harris soon hears about the bad boys from town coming drunk to the south and smashing their car and swearing at Mr Maciver, and him a minister.

My afternoon with Sorley MacLean is one image of the Gael, and perhaps closest to the image we would seek for ourselves: courteous, scholarly, ever humble, always gracious — bards and sages to whom the land is precious and the past is dear. The experience fits one romantic type of the Highlander as held abroad; but my close encounter in Glen Luskentyre is the sort that fuels another and less flattering myth of the Gaels, still held in high places, still beloved of the cheap Tory press — the fly, sly, drunken Teuchter; the feckless incompetent, the irresponsible rascal. This patronising view was already popular with *Punch* cartoonists in the last century: in the twentieth, with varying degrees of malice, it has gained credence through popular book and film — Munro's well-oiled *Para Handy*, the memoirs of Lillian Beckwith, the novels of Compton Mackenzie, the films of Alexander MacKendrick.

Murdo MacFarlane, the Melbost Bard: a colourful and radical Gaelic poet, he died in 1983

Sorley does represent a genuine strand of the Highland psyche, one now almost extinct — the bearer of tradition, the muse of the clan, the fiercely proud exponent of Highland art, and to Sorley might be added his remarkable brothers, like Alasdair and the late Calum Iain, or the late Murdo MacFarlane, the "Melbost Bard", or the Barra singer Flora MacNeil. There are many other Highland writers, poets, musicians, folklorists; but few today, very few, who have not joined a self-conscious and urbanised Gaelic set, who yet remain in their native communities and abide by their values. So, yes, Sorley is of an authentic breed. And so, unfortunately, were those moronic louts we found in a Harris strath two cold winters ago.

They are, as I said before, of a lost generation. Go to Stornoway on a Friday or Saturday night, and you will see dozens — no, hundreds — of others like them, who pour into town in afternoon and early evening, and go a-bopping in the discos and clubs, or buy a "carry-out" of alcohol (often, if they are under eighteen, persuading an older youth to buy it for them: not that some Stornoway licensees are particular) and sneak off to consume this in a shed, or bus-shelter, or under a bridge. Solvent abuse goes on about Stornoway — when I first wrote of the problem in 1989, sniffing fire-extinguishers was then the fad — and youngsters use soft drugs, pills or cannabis. I have myself seen, at perhaps nine-thirty at night, a group of fifteen-year-old girls sharing a joint in the swing-park (the smell was unmistakable); and, the same memorable evening,

I photographed several spectacularly under-age teenagers drinking in a Stornoway hotel. (The management eventually threw me out.)

It is, however, not until the small hours that the night becomes sinister. Then everything shuts, and the party-goers and drinkers pour into Stornoway's very small town-centre, so that by one-thirty in the morning Cromwell Street may actually be busier than at the height of Saturday shopping the following day. Stornoway's pathetically tiny police-force can do little more than drive round and round town eyeing all suspiciously. I should hastily make plain that, of the host jamming into the "narrows" of the town-centre, most are relaxed and friendly, most are not visibly drunk, and only a minority are taking drugs. But some are drunk, and some are high, and some are violent: there are periodic fights, and bouts of vandalism, and smashed windows, and there have been several near-riots — on one memorable night, a gang storming the police-station after a mate was arrested. Though rape is infrequent, and murder unheard of (there has only been one in Lewis this century, when I was very young, and it has never been solved), tragedy comes with depressing regularity. For many of those youngsters — some as small as twelve — hitchhike into town; there are no buses running after midnight, and few can afford taxis, so they hitchhike back or even walk. Hence, every so often, someone dies: there is a car accident, or they fall drunkenly in a ditch or field and succumb to exposure.

I would not claim that Stornoway's problem in this regard is worse than any comparable town on the mainland. But, like much else on the Western Isles, it is spectacularly visible. (I might add that island youngsters, by mainland standards, are comically dated: jackets and hairstyles *circa* 1983 are still to be seen about Stornoway, and many teenagers are heavy-metal fans, with the long hair and "Satan's Army" garb that quit this side of the Minch a long time ago.) It leads to repeated heartbreak and anguish: a situation that would be no less evil on any scale in any society, but is particularly horrifying in a community justly famed for its human warmth and devout religion. Yet the appalling truth is that, for a long time, local leaders in Stornoway and Lewis denied that any problem existed. Two pieces I wrote caused a great to-do; denials and abuse were showered about me, and the local Member of Parliament said of one that "to comment on this article would be to give it a dignity it did not deserve". And the execrable *Stornoway Gazette* denounced yours truly as one "out to do down his own island".

Others, however, knew better. Volunteers began running a late-night coffee-bar to provide teenagers with somewhere warm and safe, and in the autumn of 1991 — after a succession of outrages that even the *Gazette* could not ignore — the Chief Constable of the Northern Police insisted on meetings with community-leaders throughout the island to discuss the crisis.

What has brought about such a state of affairs? One cause is economic: the growing recession, which has bitten deep into the Outer Isles, with the fishing industry ravished

Stornoway and a lowering sky — land of salvation and sin?

and the Harris Tweed trade in free-fall and the BCCI disaster knocking Council spending for six. There are few local jobs for school-leavers, and the plight of the nation as a whole has reduced opportunities elsewhere. So they stay in the islands, bored and demoralised, and battered by the continuing twists of Government unemployment policy. These days teenagers are denied benefits unless they join employment-training schemes. So unemployed young islanders, many most personable and talented, are forced to sign on in trades of mind-numbing boredom — catering, electrical repair, hairdressing — to work dog's hours for a pittance a week.

Such training is provided only on a regional basis, not parochial, so youngsters from such places as Vatersay, Barra and Benbecula are forcibly uprooted to Stornoway, a town they do not know on an island which, religiously and otherwise, is very different from their own. They are poor, homesick and lonely. Is it not understandable when many such, in frustration and pain, take to delinquency and addiction?

But the problem of island youth is more complex still. For this generation, born in the Seventies, are a Gaelic race reared with television and video and all the treats of this present world; they are the children of a previous line, born in the Forties and

Fifties, who reached adult life amidst unprecedented island prosperity: they have come from the black house to the kit-house, from the lavatory of the dung-channel in the byre to a world of double-glazing, fitted carpets, gadget-cluttered kitchens and four-door cars, electronic entertainments and holidays abroad. It is impossible to overstate the shock of such new wealth and comfort on island life and society. It has threatened, and largely broken down, the traditional classless structure of Hebridean life. It has brought, in its train, competition and snobbery and greed and stress. Octogenarian grandparents, who once lived in a Lewis of fearful destitution and hardship, now watch their children live lives of what for them would have been unthinkable luxury; and they are seeing those children succumb to the stresses of debt and the green eyes of jealousy, and their grandchildren — many unemployed, poor, without hope of independence or access to the pleasures of big spending — turn critical, envious and angry.

This is the first non-Gaelic generation, another barrier and wall of stress between their parents and themselves: though a good minority of island teenagers still have Gaelic, all are more fluent and confident in English. This is the first generation which has grown accustomed from the cradle to seeing the outside world, and its riches, and its sophistication, on the flickering box in the living-room: my father was ten before he saw a train, and his father still older, but Hebridean children today see London and New York and the surface of the moon before they even reach school. The city and the city-people are mesmeric and glamorous to them. And, as teenagers, they yearn to join that anonymity and flee the ever-watching eyes, the storm of gossip, the frown of elders.

Hence a related problem: notoriously, islanders going to university on the mainland — even youngsters who profess religion — frequently plunge into heavy drinking and hard living, both because of a certain naivety, and because they have never been equipped or prepared for the perils of urban civilisation, nor — in a society where all is seen and nothing goes unreported — have they had to learn the self-discipline required for life on streets where no man knows his neighbour. And those problems must increase in a culture undergoing massive change. Never before, and never again, will parents and children in the Outer Isles be so divided by an accident of social history. Yet, as nervous older islanders confront the perceived Sodom and Gomorrah across the Minch, their own defensive responses serve only to make things worse.

The dominant church on Lewis, the Free Church of Scotland — to which some eighty-five per cent of islanders adhere — threatens to become an intolerant gerontocracy, where aging and ill-educated elders hold the whip-hand, and a tightening process of fixed calls and Presbyterial bossism has brought them ministers of ever-diminishing independence and guts. Hence all too many preachers in Lewis find themselves attacking, again and again, "worldliness" — always defined as the pleasures of youth: dancing, concert-going, record-buying, sex, and never as the true vices of this world — materialism, bigotry, slander and gossip. And the Free Church, outwith Stornoway, remains stubbornly and irrationally Gaelic. Most of the Communion-season services are held in Gaelic, and — absurdly — all but one of the *orduigean beagan* meetings, bi-annual week-long series of supposedly evangelistic services, which the unconverted stopped attending a long time ago.

Politically unable to address the realities of modern life in a fallen world, ministers and kirk-sessions repeatedly oppose the granting of liquor-licenses. So there are today only three bars in the island outwith Stornoway, and those seeking drink must converge on town, an exertion driving many to drink or buy more booze than they need, and forcing the happy on to the roads. Even worse, Free Church leaders have a lamentable track record on encouraging healthy leisure pursuits in the local township. In days past every alternative entertainment to formal religion — be it badminton, table-tennis, football, ceilidh-dances, social evenings, Gaelic concerts, night-classes or the Highland Film Guild — was denounced from the pulpit and blocked from the community. In Wester Ross and Skye, where such conflicts burst vehemently forth after the Second World War, short-sighted clergymen must carry much of the blame for alienating the young, depopulating villages and emptying their own churches. The cause of Christ must legitimately question the opening of alcohol outlets, and teach young people of the dangers of irresponsible partying and casual sex. It has no authority to pronounce anathema on harmless and enjoyable leisure activities, far less to make the name of the Saviour one of mocking amongst the ungodly for His followers' folly and harshness. But it has: and so the Free Church in Lewis is a body of believers unjustly — but increasingly — rejected by the island's underclass.

The Free Church in Lewis still has great privileges. Comhairle and community figures are largely its adherents, and the Free Church has much power over local education. But, despite the complacency of those who proclaim Lewis and themselves as the "last stronghold of the pure Gospel", attendances are now in rapid decline. The church is visibly losing its grip. Even in the last three years, the "Lewis Sabbath" has receded, with more and more islanders out and about at assorted carnal activities. The day will come when islanders will wake up and see the Free Church is done, and almost overnight the Church will be stripped of civil and political authority.

Fear: fear of change, of the future, of the present. Unease: in themselves, in their community, in their lives. These drive men and women into bunkers, into regimented gangs and collectives, into a striving to keep up with the status and wealth of those about them — these bestow identity and security at the price of individuality. Yet the insecurity grows: financial worry, because so much is on credit; obsessive secrecy, because the telephone now relays your troubles and gaffes around the island and not just the village; and a paranoid rending of any who criticise or threaten the new island order.

"The 'narrows' becoming a no-go area at weekends for law-abiding citizens", ran the headline on the *Stornoway Gazette* of 2nd November 1991, interspersing a long and belated report of the juvenile time-bomb with such phrases as "the usual breach of the peace, violence and anti-social behaviour", "nefarious activities", and "mob rule". "The kind of person most likely to be involved . . . is male, seventeen years old and drunk," observed the writer, and quoted Murdo Alex Macleod, minister of Stornoway Free Church, as saying, "The breakdown of family life affecting us here in the Western Isles is the same as in the rest of Scotland."

The police, declared the *Gazette*, now had "the unenviable task of maintaining law and order in an area being overrun by drunken youths". And an editorial solemnly pronounced: "The situation in Stornoway at the weekends with hooliganism is horrendous . . . Other young folk — from the Greenock area — said that they . . . were terrified with the goings-on in Stornoway at the weekend and said they had never witnessed anything like it . . . parents MUST accept their responsibilities and make it their business to know how their youngsters are spending their weekends, for if the present situation is allowed to continue, there is little doubt it will end in a fatality." But to comment further on this article might give it a dignity it does not deserve.

A people on the western edge, before the surge of the south. And there are other strands and cords in Highland response to the death of the Gaelic world, and in the crisis of that death. One grouping I have alluded to already: and, just last week, I sat with three of their number, in the close bright heat of a Glasgow television studio. It was a programme called *Night Flyte*, of the five-incredibly-brainy-people-talking-late-at-night-on-Channel-4 variety, all pink sofas and gesticulating hands and ruthless interruption.

It was fun, though a little intimidating, for it was a free-ranging debate on the future of Gaelic after the new census figures. There were three of us on this sofa, and I was in the middle. On the couch opposite, by chairman Donald MacCormick, was Glasgow novelist William McIlvanney, a clever man, faintly dishy in a Seventies sort of way, who agreed with all I said and re-framed it much more competently. And beside him was a different creature altogether: Rhoda MacDonald, sometime Rhoda MacLeod, Head of Gaelic at Scottish Television, that franchise-holder that won most of the lolly in the Gaelic Television Fund, and hoovered up so much of Scotland's freelance Gaelic talent.

Rhoda MacDonald was thirtysomething: small, dark-haired and gorgeous, despite heavy make-up and tired lines. She had a pretty face and a Jackie Kennedy suit in shocking pink, and a quick tongue and a deadly blend of sexuality and charm. On my right was Donald MacAulay, Professor of Celtic at Glasgow University, slow-spoken and ponderous, a middle-aged Lewisman who was also a very fine poet. And on my left was Brian Wilson, founder and sometime editor — now publisher — of the *West Highland Free Press*, and longtime radical Highland activist: now Member of Parliament for Cunninghame North, and a coming man on Labour's front-bench. No-one has done more than Brian Wilson to revitalise Highland thinking and Highland strategy; he cannot be underestimated at any level, moral or intellectual, but I have never met anyone more complex in our public life, and Wilson was — for reasons best known to himself — an old and personal enemy.

He sat there, prickling, small and plump and casually clad. So we debated, and one by one I shot off my points — that Gaelic was practically dead already; that the Gaelic Television Fund was twenty or thirty years too late, and just a ploy to win votes for the Tories; that the real need in the Highlands was not cultural but economic regeneration; that Highland values could still be preserved in a non-Gaelic world. It was great fun, for each new nostrum roused howls and squeaks of protest, and in no time at all they were on my territory and discussing Gaelic on my terms. But it became increasingly difficult to amplify these themes, for as tempers rose the voices flared. Again and again I was shouted down. McIlvanney was wonderful, for he was much older than I, with a deep strong voice and much experience of television, and he rescued my argument time and again and would not let the others lock it away. So he and I had a sub-plot going over the fake coffee-table: but it was against an incorrigible trio.

MacAulay was pleasantly ponderous enough to be hard to derail, and as an academic he was allowed to voice long and wandering expert opinions. Wilson was a politician: rowdy debate his world, and television his daily arena, and so he launched into interruption-proof non-falsifiable orations. And Rhoda, the only woman, had an inestimable advantage. She interrupted, again and again and again, and side-tracked, and belittled, and trivialised, and only once did I really have the better of her, when I announced something I was not supposed to know — that Scottish Television have scripted their looming Gaelic soap-opera ("Drama serial!" declared Rhoda firmly) around a fictitious Gaelic college, to explain the varying fluency and dialects of actors recruited from the very small Gaelic pool. MacCormick threw this straight at Rhoda: she panicked and lost her way, and stuttered, and finally went on a wonderful roll about how clever the college idea was because it showed Gaelic as hip and happening.

But mostly Rhoda trumped the rest of us, because she was in a studio in her domain. When McIlvanney proved too tough to interrupt and when he made a telling point that she objected to, she unwisely shrieked, "You've *got* to let me come back on that!" after McIlvanney said something rude about Scottish Television, and he flashed a spider-and-the-fly smile, and murmured, "Sure. You can come back for three hours if you want." It all ended happily; the moment the cameras switched off, and the video was in the can, we suspended hostilities and repaired upstairs for a happy and reasonably sober ceilidh. Rhoda, at the end, kissed us each goodbye. But I left this gathering (and so, I think, did McIlvanney) feeling as if I had just been done over by urban-jungle soccer-casuals, and that left in the metaphorical pool of blood about me was a cheaply printed calling-card saying, "Congratulations! You have just been visited by the Gaelic Mafia."

The Gaelic Mafia is that web of activists in the Gaelic language and cognate concerns. These three are in it — MacDonald, MacAulay, Wilson — and many others, like the neo-Essens at Sabhal Mor Ostaig, and the pet-singers of RunRig, and the beautiful people of An Commun Gaidhealach and the Mod, and the wheelers and dealers in Gaelic broadcasting — Radio nan Gaidheal, Grampian Television, and the sprouting fungi of new independent media-units and production companies like Eolas and Media nan Eilean and Abutele; poets, like Iain Crichton Smith and Aonghas Mac Neacall; zealots, like Dr Finlay MacLeod; and politicians, like Wilson and Calum MacDonald; and lobbyists, like John Angus Mackay of Commun na Gaidheal — whose brilliant campaign created the Gaelic Television Fund, and ended up with him running it.

This is another significant bloc of the modern Highland psyche: not mystic, nor religious, nor amassing, nor riotous, but a jolly crowd of people doing very well out of Gaelic and the Highlands and who have invested much in the struggle to defend and repair what they regard as our heritage. They are our self-appointed leaders, our enthusiastic spokesmen, our tireless friends with friends in high places. And they are a network, and do network, endlessly and enjoyably, sharing out the publicity and propping up their own importance. And I must make plain that they do not include some Highlanders of equal zeal and energy, but of truly independent mind and will — the likes of Sorley MacLean, James Hunter and John Farquhar Munro are not of this clan.

They are characterised, the Gaelic Mafia, by several striking and risible curiosities. For one, precious few of them live in the islands and glens they noisily represent: the Mafia is urbanised, working in universities and broadcasting stations, living in Glasgow and Inverness and Edinburgh and even Aberdeen. They are polished, sophisticated people who dress very well and speak deliciously and party a great deal: why, dear reader, once our ruling-set in the Highlands was be-tweeded, and now it is Armani'd.

Almost all of them are indifferent to religion: at worst, they seethe with hostility to Highland Presbyterianism and its works, and they have ensured that the Free and Free Presbyterian Church and their common faith have been locked out of the Gaelic broadcasting media. Some of the Mafia — I am thinking especially of Iain Crichton Smith, Finlay MacLeod, and John Murray — seem to blaze with a hatred against religion. Crichton Smith has written that he so detests the power of the Church in Lewis that, on seeing a minister walking along the other side of the road, it is all he can do not to dash across and punch him on the nose.

It is scarcely surprising, then, to observe how far many individuals in the Gaelic Mafia have moved from the personal and moral values of the villages that gave them birth. At their most vulgar level, in the overweight and Burton-suited types who haunt the National Mod, they are infamous for drunkenness and rowdiness and being sacked from their jobs. At a higher level substance-abuse persists; there is also a heartbreak tangle of broken marriages. Below the cosmetics and nose-jobs and Grecian 2000 they lead driven and desperate lives, neglecting spouses and families, some from sincere passion for the Gaelic cause. And others, despite the conspicuous affection and cheek-pecking, would boil their grannies down for glue; they gossip and backbite, and claw opponents and *quondam* friends to the dust if they dare to stand between them and some goal, position or honour.

Still, they network. They are a peculiarly incestuous bunch, ever attending one another's parties, plugging one another's books, licking the same shoes and bending the same ears. Again and again you see them at it: Peter MacAulay interviewing Rhoda MacDonald, Rhoda MacDonald profiling singer Mary Macinnes, Mary Macinnes interviewing Peter MacAulay. I have even watched the great and grand Anne Lorne Gillies, Italian-trained Gaelic singer and La Pasionara of the Gaelic struggle, appear on MacAulay's late-night Grampian TV news-magazine *Crann Tara* pretending to be one hitherto unknown "Ann Friziel". (She was then married to BBC Scotland's Neil Fraser.)

The Gaelic Mafia, foot-soldiers and officers, work as one in a realm of luvvies. They have sought, and in large part succeeded, to persuade the world that they are the true faces of Gaeldom and the high priests of its heritage. They are the best known, and most powerful, and most dangerous strand of Highland society today. For, posing as wardens of Highland ways and Highland values, some are in truth its imperturbable foe. For the real battle to safeguard that inheritance, and the real heroes of that army and its crusade, we must look in conclusion elsewhere.

CHAPTER TWELVE

But Still We Sing

We are survivors.

We have to be, we Gaels and Highlanders, for we have lived for many centuries as a tribe on the edge of a rich and powerful civilisation which has long viewed us with indifference and on occasion with genocidal ferocity. And our land, though beautiful, is a hard land; a land of peat and rock and poor thin soil, mountainous, wind-blown, repeatedly soaked with drenching rain, riven by steep glens and deep long fjords, so that we are not only well-separated from the south but well-separated from one another. And, though great improvements have come in our communications, these roads and bridges and ferries have been centrally planned, to lead south and east and out, so that it is easier to leave our glens and islands than to move around within them.

The land is poor; and crofting, our primary land-use, was deliberately devised two centuries ago to ensure that none of us would have enough of it to keep ourselves and our children, so we would be more readily persuaded to gather our landlord's kelp. And the day came, of course, when the kelp failed that had made them great, and they had to look for other means to sustain themselves in wealth and comfort. In the name of modernity and improvement, then, we were gathered and harried and hustled here and there, and thousands at length were driven from the land of their birth, by sticks and dogs and the might of the law, to drowning on the high seas, to hardship in the Empire. This is our holocaust; but, till very recently, it was a forgotten history, a tale denied to children in our schools, and repressed by communal amnesia.

But we have survived.

We are still here, in good numbers, out on the western ridge of Scotland, in Torridon and Skye and the Outer Isles, in cluttered little townships with their little plots of land, and we have been good to our land, for we are not intensive reapers and raiders. Here, the corncrake still grates in the evening; it was not ourselves that emptied the seas of all that swam, or built towns of concrete and stone that saw only sky and denied the earth. And, if our children still leave, we yet have children who will stay, and even those that go are strangely drawn to return, and not to repudiate their roots amongst us; and the day is past when a clever youth can find no place amongst us, or that all left on croft and *machair* think of the migrants as doing well and of themselves as failures.

Abandoned cars, Isle of Lewis

We survived, because we fought. Not that we raised arms in rebellion against the rulers of the state — we tried that game, and it was nearly the finish of us, and that calamity is yet only three human lifetimes of memory away. But, broken and scattered, we came to ourselves in the new order of Highland religion, and that gave us in due time the dignity and the self-belief to stand. So, in Bernera, and Glendale, and the Braes, it was ourselves that became a ribbon of fire: and we made a spark between us and the minds of Britain beyond, and ever since — though they are still a tedious, patronising crowd at times — the larger country has held us in a little esteem, and forced our Governments to be good to us.

Neglect, folly, incompetence, tunnel-vision, forcing square pegs at round holes — oh, they are up to that yet, and still exploiting where they can, and still experimenting, and still with their bombs and torpedoes and grouse-shoots and preservation orders, but they will never again tell us to shut down, nor make us move out, nor deny us the right and the freedom to go on living and pursuing our own happiness in the land for which our fathers bled. Still we sing: and we survive.

We survive, we Gaels, because we are very good at making the most of our circumstances. Compromise, adjustment, adaptability — these are part of us now, well-honed in our experience, and so we abide and, in a manner, prosper. Crofters are still far from shops and towns, needing to be careful with money, not surrounded by skilled tradesmen. So we do what we can for ourselves. We are, most of us, competent mechanics, adequate joiners, bankable stock-men, imaginative builders; we can, when pressed, wire and plumb and paper and paint, or run a small boat, or keep a van on the road, and we are very good at keeping our accounts, in cash, and in kind, and in generosity to one another.

We survive, despite the myths you all so stubbornly hold. You think we do not value nor enjoy our land, and that all we say is "You can't live on scenery", and that you are giving us a good example when you come a-holidaying amongst the blooming heather and silver lochs and crisp air and glowing evenings. But we love the earth and rocks about us; no-one appreciates the scenery more than those who live here. You like to think we are laid-back and slothful; but if we were, these hills and Hebrides would have been empty long since. You say that we are especially prone to mental illness; that we have a very high rate of drunkenness and alcoholism; that we go in either for manic boozing or manic religion. These are tabloid fantasies. Our religion, which still impacts our communities, seems preferable to your own non-religion that does not. So our elders burned fiddles? But your bishops burned people. And there is no statistical proof whatever that we are any more prone to depression or addiction than yourselves.

We see things differently; that is why our community life survives, while yours in the south is largely dead. We have time for people, for children; for strangers: time to smile or wave or stop for a crack in the road. We remember the widows. We revere our old. We entertain strangers. We care about our islands and villages and what becomes of them; we know little of other villages, far less of other Hebrides, but we know our own intimately and we love it passionately. We think of time, and we are most conscious of it — not in the hypertensive, rushing, frenzied sense of shortage that bedevils your world, but in its great and majestic and humbling sweep, time gone and time now and time to come. So we carry tradition and wisdom from our past, and preserve the memory of our people and family-lines, and look to preserve it and the land for our children and their children, and we watch the tide and the passing of seasons, and think how little in ourselves we are.

You come to our townships and complain about our "junk" — rusting old cars and tractors, heaps of scrap, mouldering sheds crammed with this and that. But to us these things are beautiful in another way: faithful old motors that served us well, that deserve to rust in peace, and can remain a communal resource for spare parts and useful bits of metal. You mock our Sabbath, where we still honour it: but you would enjoy it, if you were not always wanting to dash and to do, and entered into that rest and felt it give rhythm to your days and renewing to your bones.

We have survived. We know the weather, and the moor, and the sea, and the rocks; we know how things are done, and who should be doing them, and our communities hum about you with unseen energy and efficiency: watching, talking, deciding, acting. We have survived: though many must leave, many will return, and in the meantime they support the old ones at home, and link our township with its shadow in the great city, that urban tangle of Gaels, in churches and in the ballrooms.

We are in a new world now. It is one that combines the comforts and technology of the modern with the human values of our past. Though we may at times combine it badly, and suffer the stresses and tensions of change, we are getting there. To function in this world, we need — and use — English, because language is a means to communicate, and everyone now speaks English, and gey few today have Gaelic, and the most of them better in English anyway. Do not expect us to stick with an outmoded tongue — man, you would have us back in the black houses if you could, the more quaint for you on your summer holiday. And do not make a moral issue of the thing, as if we were murdering a body; linguistic despotism is never pretty.

We have survived, though persecuted and belittled; we have survived in this land, and survived the attentions and tyrannies of yourselves. To be sure, we have fallen in great number, and still we fall; but though we fall, we shall rise again. And the day may come when the tide will turn.

I am in Harris, of January 1991, and the community is in uproar over the latest decree of Caledonian MacBrayne, that from May the Tarbert ferry will be sailing to and from Skye on the Sabbath, and the company will not be moved on the matter, though almost all the community oppose the innovation, and there is a great frenzy of letter-writing and petition-drafting and questions from Calum MacDonald in the House of Commons. But on the evening of the Friday that we retrieve the boys from Glen Luskentyre, there is a meeting in the modern community-hall at Tarbert, and the car-park jammed with buses and vans and cars from all over the island. It is a prayer-meeting, chaired by Norman Maciver; the other Harris ministers, Free Church and Church of Scotland and Free Presbyterian, take turns to precent Gaelic Psalms. And man after man, Christian after Christian, is called on to rise and pray that these plans may come to nought. Never before, outside a funeral or wedding service, have the three Presbyterian churches in the island come together in this manner.

A week later there is another meeting in the community-hall, public but not officially religious, though a minister is asked to pray at the beginning. It is chaired by John Murdo Morrison, forceful and popular manager of the Harris Hotel: with him on the platform are Comhairle leaders, and the Western Isles MP, and assorted dignitaries. Powerful speeches are made from the platform, and the floor, by James Finlayson and others; not a voice is raised in the hundreds-strong gathering in support of Sunday ferries, and the vote taken is unanimous. Besides, there are fishing-boats tied at the pier, boats from Scalpay that have brought the Scalpay men to the meeting, and their leading master now declares to Tarbert and the world that they will blockade the harbour on the Saturday night before the first Sunday ferry, so that the boat will be unable to leave the narrow inlet the following day, unless the Royal Navy be deployed to blast the fishermen aside before the gathered media of the western world.

The Secretary of State for Scotland, Mr Ian Lang, hears of the meetings and of this declaration. A few weeks later, in evident chagrin, Caledonian MacBrayne are forced to announce a humiliating retreat. There will be no Sunday ferries this year or the next.

I am in Raasay in July 1992. It is a soft and warm summer over that green island; the waters of the Clarach as silvered glass, Glamaig and the Braes in haze. I am in the Free Presbyterian manse, which stands over one of the finest views in Scotland, across the Sound of Raasay and the Clarach to gaze up Loch Sligachan, at Sgurr nan Gillean and Beinn Dearg Mor and Bla Bheinn, and along the bay of Inverarish and the slopes of Suisnish, and all out beyond the flower-strewn meadows and wooded policies of Raasay House. We have just supped in the manse, after a Communion Sabbath, and I am in the sitting-room with James Tallach and George Hutton and their most senior colleague, Donald MacLean.

He is in his seventy-eighth year; there is a certain stiffness in his walk, and a kiss of grey hair at his temples, but the tough old fellow still stands as tall and seems as ageless as ever he was. And he is in bubbling good humour, benevolent, and as we relax about him Donald MacLean glows in his tales and anecdotes, and leans back, and waves large long hands about to expand a point, and he talks of old days and old people in the Free Presbyterian Church. He remembers preaching at open-air communions in Shieldaig, and Applecross, and elsewhere, in the days when no church could hold the gatherings that came, and they sat outside on the green with the ministers at a portable pulpit. He remembers boyhood summers in Raasay, and the day that Sammy MacLean and himself — "well, Sorley, as we know him now" — were chased by a lively calf belonging to one "Box", until they were rescued by Donald's formidable aunt, to whom a playmate had gone crying, "Box calf eat Sammy!".

Gaelic. Why is Gaelic going down? "Because of the decline of family worship in the home, and because the Gaelic catechism is no longer taught. Do you know how I learned Gaelic? Well, when I became a student of the ministry, I spent time with the Rev John Colquhoun, that was minister in Glendale — and every morning we started studying Gaelic at nine, and broke only for meals at which I had to talk Gaelic all the time, and we'd go on like that till midnight."

R. R. Sinclair, in his ninety-fifth year, now APC, has retired at last from the ministry after sixty years at Wick. "I thought of writing to him," says Mr MacLean, "I really did, because we were once friends, you know . . . gone to the Rhodesian mission-field together, as deputies, and we were close in those days. But I suppose it would be too late now: he retired in March, after all . . ." He falls silent, and drums his fingers on the arms of the chair, and his mouth tightens in lonely thought. There is a grandeur yet to this old and remarkable Glasgow Highlander: and also a certain pathos.

I am in Assynt, in spirit; though I have never seen that landscape, I know it is very similar in geology and topography to that of eastern Lewis, all gneiss and peat. They are very attractive, these ports and townships: Lochinver, Stoer, Drumbeg, Achmelvich. In the spring of 1992, that part of Assynt in the North Lochinver estate was put on sale by the liquidators of Scandinavian Property Services Ltd, who had bought the land some years before from the unlovely Vestey family. These delightful people sacked a gamekeeper, not so many years ago, because he preferred his own home to the tied house they provided; they still retain the mineral rights. The SPS showed little sign of understanding crofters and their place in the universe; the people on the estate are weary of living through the vagaries of international land-speculation. And so the Assynt crofters have made an audacious bid for the land.

Under the 1976 Crofting Act, which granted to every crofter the right to buy his holding for a maximum of sixteen times the annual rental — an Act framed by the Heath Government and passed by Wilson's, and which has served hitherto as little more than a white settlers' charter — the men and women of Assynt can take over much of the North Lochinver estate for a rather cheap £39,000. But this is a fall-back option: they want the lot. The SPS demand £475,000. A survey commissioned by the Assynt crofters suggests a realistic sum might be half of that. And the recent Kinlochewe judgement in the Court of Session has uncovered a loophole in crofting law; if the Assynt crofters, having bought out their holdings, transfer them to a third party — they create one, called the Assynt Crofters Trust — they need not then pay the landlord a mighty chunk, as the law would oblige them if they sold their crofts.

The Assynt Crofters Trust prepares to bid for the estate. It could give them their land and their future: they could deploy its scenic and sporting and environmental assets to create jobs, build chalets to let to tourists on the common-grazing, supply low-cost sites for young couples to build affordable housing — the young folk presently being repeatedly outbid by holiday-home seekers and new white settlers. So the Trust makes a public appeal for donations. They fire the imagination of the land. By every post, cheques and cash pour in. The local MP, Robert Maclennan, promises £1,300; the *West Highland Free Press* £1,000; the boys of RunRig, £1,000. Two Government ministers bless the venture. In the event, the Assynt Crofters Trust makes a substantial bid — £250,000. It is the highest offer received by SPS, and the only one for the whole estate — but they decline to sell.

Spinning for Harris Tweed, about 1955. Today almost all Harris Tweed is woven from factory-yarn produced in Stornoway or Shawbost

The crofters, though, are not done yet. They will own this land, one way or the other. They repeat the offer. It is rejected again. But the SPS are running out of time to find a rival purchaser; the prospect of crofters invoking the 1976 Act to rip much of the property from a future owner's control deters other would-be lairds of North Lochinver. After weeks of haggling, on 8th December 1992 the SPS cave in. The North Lochinver estate has returned to its people. The Assynt Crofters Trust is the new landlord.

Alan MacRae is Trust chairman: his great-grandfather was cleared last century to make way for a sheep farm. "It seems we have won our land," he says, "a moment to savour, but my immediate thought is that some of our forebears should have been here to share it. It is a historic blow for people on the land throughout the Highlands and Islands." "For the first time since the post-Great War raiders staked their claims, and thus forced government to intervene," comments Brian Wilson, "fresh substance has been given to the inalienable theory that the land does indeed belong to the people."

I am on the West Highland Railway, between Fort William and Mallaig, rolling through the most dramatic autumn scenery: it is September 1992. There, on the other side of Loch Eilt, runs the narrow and inadequate highway, the worst trunk-road in Europe. But the people of the west, of Arisaig and Morar and Mallaig itself, are sick of the decades of unfulfilled promises to widen and update this artery. In a mad but highly successful publicity stunt, local drivers and residents recently blocked the highway completely — for a little while, no more — to draw attention to their plight. Something, this time, should be done.

I am in Portree, two days later, a Friday lunchtime, watching the children snack about Sommerled Square on their break from studies at Portree High School. This gaunt grim concrete complex, two decades old, is dirty and leaking and dangerous: the playing-fields are of abrasive blaise. Conditions are, comments the local teaching-union secretary, "nothing short of barbaric"; but a vast crowd has now jammed a hall in town to demand action. Months ago, when the Highland Health Board announced the forthcoming closure of the little geriatric hospital at Gesto and the transfer of its elderly patients to a private Portree nursing-home, there was a great outcry on the island: so large was the crowd that converged on a conceded public-meeting to discuss the closure, that the police had to be called to disperse it — the mass of bodies contravened fire-regulations. There was, later, another meeting: Highland Health Board backed away. Gesto remains open.

It is true, observes *Herald* reporter David Ross in his account of these incidents, that the people of Skye have had a high-toll, free-enterprise bridge foisted upon them. "It is, however, equally true that the first toll has yet to be paid," he darkly observes.

There is now an influential Highland policy-group manned by Highlanders and meeting in the Highlands. James Hunter has established Barail, the Centre for Highland Policy Studies: it is a small but devoted group of people who, in David Ross's words, "care deeply about the Highlands and are tired of all policy affecting the area being formulated outside it". And this same Hunter is the man who rediscovered our history for a popular readership, and energised much else: the new Scottish Crofters Union, formed in 1985, was first directed by Hunter, and born in part by his suggestion.

I am at my desk in Edinburgh, with a large and glossy brochure by the keyboard. It is titled *Crofting and the Environment: A New Approach*, and it is splendidly printed and illustrated. This strong case for the crofting economy comes, of course, from the SCU; but — would you believe it? — in association with the Royal Society for the Protection of Birds. This is new and skilled wisdom: crofters and environmentalists forging ground in common, and reaping the benefits of fighting together. The conservationists gain West Highland goodwill; the Highlanders have a powerful new ally, whose voice is heard in the high affairs of this land.

The study calls for rationalisation of crofting grants and subsidies; measures to reduce over-grazing and de-emphasise sheep; the creation of new Environmentally Sensitive Areas — like that of the Uists and Barra machair, where crofters are paid not to disturb wildlife; woodlands grants, to encourage re-afforestation; community conservation plans; new direct-income payments to elderly crofters who agree to assign their holdings to younger ones — and much else that is sensible, useful and true. But it abounds also in exquisite photographs, of busy townships and fat cattle and shy corncrakes and ruddy children and industrious weavers. And, most cleverly, it provides examples of how traditional low-intensity crofting safeguards rare birds and flowers and valued landscape, while keeping people in the West Highland communities and providing stable social organisation.

There is a dream too in this brochure; not much of a dream as yet, but one that may yet fan into flame. In a boxed inset a writer demolishes the "wilderness fallacy" we have already noted, advising, "Almost every landscape in northern Scotland bears the mark of human influence. Many of the most unpopulated localities were once thickly peopled — their populations having been expelled forcibly by the landlords responsible for the Highland Clearances. Crofters still aspire to win back these lost lands. There is no environmental reason why a measure of resettlement should not recur. Indeed there would be every reason to welcome reforms which made it possible to combine an element of resettlement with, for example, woodland regeneration and other measures designed to rehabilitate habitats which have been seriously degraded in the period since the Clearances."

Though much is taken, much abides.

School's out: Achmore, Lewis

A Monday night: April 1992. I am in Harris again, on a damp evening, with friends in the hamlet of Lingerabay. After a jolly meal, I excuse myself and go for a walk up the road; I take the little bridge over the river, and climb up by tatty sheds and ruined homes. It is a narrow and twisting road, single-track, though I am fortunate: twenty years ago there was no such road at all, and you had to come to Bayhead and Lingerabay by a rough track from Finsbay. The drizzle is earnest, but not a nuisance. The Minch is green and choppy, slapping into the reefs of the shore under low cloud. On a clear day I would see Skye — Trotternish and Duirinish, but today there is no view to speak of, except of Lingerabay, and the battered heath and grass of a moor in spring, and — of course — the rocks.

I reach the main road, and turn left. In half an hour, tramping steadily, I would come to Rodel: but tonight I am looking for the quarry. This is up on the bouldered flank of Roineabhal, which huddles high over the road, its round peak in misty mystery. Roineabhal is grand and bare, the heather curiously dark to see, and you have to think a while before you realise it is only in contrast to its rock. The rock of Roineabhal — and I should say that the hill is perhaps the best viewpoint in the whole Outer

Hebrides — is not the standard Lewissian gneiss; it is a rock of a different sort and value all together. Once a little quarry worked this deposit, but it closed nearly three decades ago. A track still remains, running down from the main road to the shore, a white scar in the peat, strewn with lumps and chunks of the valued mineral.

I reach this track; I pick up a fragment. It is rather heavy for its size, and dense — not crystalline, sugary, like gneiss. There is a white soapy texture to it, though the prevailing hue is a very light green-blue. It is very, very hard. It is anorthosite, the solidified melt of an ancient South Harris volcano. It is made largely of feldspar, which gives the whitish appearance; it is only found in inhospitable places — Siberia, Greenland, northern Canada, Norway. Yet anorthosite is a precious rock. It is uniquely strong, and impervious to water; rain will not leach, the tide not rot, the frost not split this stone. This makes anorthosite a valuable building-aggregate — a foundation for roads and bridges, a base for piers and quays.

And they want it. They want it badly, this hard soapy rock with the green flecks that you have in your hand. And they, Redland Aggregates, a mighty mining concern, are coming to take the anorthosite of Lingerabay away: a proposed extraction of hundreds of thousands of tonnes, over decades of toil, in a scheme projected to take sixty years before completion. It will leave Lingerabay with a deep broad sea-loch where now there is land: the highest cliffs in Europe, and a hole in the ground big enough to hide the Empire State Building. Half of Lingerabay will disappear, and much of Roineabhal; the new superquarry will, the people of Harris are promised, provide sixty to eighty-six local jobs. And it will earn Redland Aggregates thousands of millions of pounds.

A piece of rock in the palm of your hand.

The company is moving in tandem with the landowner, son of a fading hotel dynasty, and a speculator in possession of the mineral rights. The superquarry will be the biggest ever seen in Britain, a mighty hole in the coast of the Hebrides, shaking daily with the bang and rumble of explosives, the roar of haulage-vehicles, the chug of big ships coming and taking tons of Harris away to build North sea harbours and German autobahns. Harris is an aging community, with little by way of employment to keep the children at home: in an island of 2,450 souls, eighty-six jobs matter. But — oh, woe — there are the environmentalists, Friends of the Earth and all their kind, talking crisis, preaching apocalypse. And the white settlers, of whom Harris has many, being pretty and poor — incomers with bright smiles and clipped vowels and fat vans and shaggy children, rats from the rat-race.

And the churches, striving for the Sabbath as well as for the material wellbeing of their people. And the Comhairle: not that its stock is presently high, after the BCCI debacle, when the Council lost an improperly invested twenty-four million pounds in the dodgy multinational bank. And the media: television crews desperate to film overalled crofters with grizzled hair and bright eyes, not to mention apple-cheeked grannies spinning at the doors. All seething and flapping over Lingerabay and Redland Aggregates and the quarry: for a community whose population is one-sixth that of Morningside, and on account of the hard and dusty rock in the palm of my hand.

But there is a Harris Action Group, chaired by Morag Munro, a youthful and strong-willed lady, and the group most cleverly composed: on this group sit, amongst others, Murdo Smith (local Church of Scotland minister); Mary Anne MacDonald (Lingerabay resident, mother of two pre-school children, and the wife of the Free Presbyterian missionary); a young local crofter; the popular Leverburgh headmaster; and Ian Callaghan, white settler supreme, owner of the famous Scarista House Hotel.

Tuesday night: I am in a crowd of at least two hundred people, in the hall of the Leverburgh school. Murdo Smith presides. All the members of the Action Group, in turn, rise and speak. Views are invited from the floor. Naturally the white settlers insist on talking longer, and more frequently, than anyone else: almost to a man they oppose the project, for it threatens their playground and the beauty of the environment about them. But, as James Finlayson roars in a fiery speech, "Never mind the lovely landscape of Harris — think of the lovely people. What happens if there's no jobs? What's the point in a fine land with no people?" And there is tumultuous, foot-stamping, cheering applause. The white settlers, unabashed, rise to twitter once more.

The people of Harris are still campaigning, and most skilfully, buoyed by their triumph last year over Caledonian MacBrayne. They seek two things — a cast-iron guarantee that there will be no Sabbath working at the plant, and the creation of a Community Trust Fund for Lingerabay and South Harris, into which Redlands must pay a small levy per ton of rock. The company, so far, refuses to rule out the docking of ships on the Lord's Day; and it offers the people of Harris — out of a projected sixty-five million pounds annual turnover at Lingerabay only a token five thousand to twenty-five thousand pounds a year. "Not peanuts," runs the local joke, "but one peanut!"

It is an issue typifying the troubles of the modern Hebrides. It is the looming creation of a classic Third World exploitative development, of a kind that would be unthinkable in the Home Counties, and would certainly be stopped by authorities there — but here, in this economic black hole, very few native Harris people will stand against it. There is a dreadful irony in the struggle. When Lord Leverhulme pulled out of Lewis and transferred his hopes to Harris in the early Twenties — he was the founder of Lever House, a soap-baron with far-sighted dreams for the Hebridean economy but little local empathy — he offered the people of Lewis and Harris outright ownership of the island. Apart from Stornoway (where, to this day, the Stornoway Trust owns and administers town and policies), the islanders turned him down. Leverhulme left his name on the model-port of Leverburgh, but little else. "Had the people of Harris taken their land," writes David Ross, "they would today be the ones controlling the mineral rights. They would have had total control over a superquarry project which in sixty years will turn over some £3,900 million. Instead, they have eighty-six jobs and £25,000 a year or so dangled in front of them."

By the end of 1992, Redland Aggregates were dropping strange hints of withdrawal: that they might not take up their option on Lingerabay's anorthosite after all, that — even if they did — it could be several, even many years before operations began. The recession, claimed Redland Aggregates, had sent demand for road-metal tumbling. It remained to be seen if the company were genuinely quitting Harris, or if this was their latest — and cynical — negotiating tactic.

I am near the end of my story. Has it not been, at many levels, a most weary and depressing one? We have followed in broad sweep the great developments of recent Highland history. We have studied the psychology, and nemesis, of personalities and politics in a very Highland institution. And we have explored, in the broadest outline, some of the central themes and groups in the collective myth of Highland identity.

There are lessons that seem at once to spring from these studies. Again and again, we have stumbled on the central issue of Highland identity and Highland angst — the ownership, and holding, and use of Highland land. Highland land is impoverished, right enough, but it is land of astonishing natural beauty, and happy societies survive elsewhere in the world in much more hostile terrain. Highland land is dominated by crofters and the crofting institution. That was devised, as we have seen, in deliberate measure to control and manipulate the Highland people, but yet — for all its limitations — has kept people in the west and in the islands.

It has also preserved flora and fauna of great value and charm, fragile forms of life long vanished from the rest of Britain. The corncrake alone, an evocative bird often heard but seldom seen, was in 1939 to be found across all of Scotland, Wales and western England. By 1979 it was confined to western Scotland. By 1991 it was exclusive to the West Highlands and Islands, and the great majority of breeding pairs were to be found in Tiree and the Western Isles; elsewhere, modern mechanised harvesting has annihilated the fowl. Even in the Hebrides, the species is dwindling. Fifteen years ago you heard the corncrake about Stornoway, not now; stocks have been ravaged by a peculiar island threat — mink. These were reared in a Lewis fur-farm some decades ago; when the project folded (the climate was too warm, so their fur was too short) the creatures were stupidly released into the wild. Feral mink now overrun Lewis and Harris, slaughtering poultry and devouring the eggs and young of wildfowl, and they are said to be a main factor in corncrake decline. But this is by the way.

Highland land, in large degree, is still owned and sold and disposed of in disgraceful secrecy amongst a set of barons and sportsmen and foreign syndicates from beyond the Highland region. And these men and women have repeatedly blocked much that would have benefited their luckless tenants, on whom they look at best with apathy and at worst with meddling contempt. Little can be done to address the central problems of the Highland economy, and to further the wellbeing of Gaeldom, until a national register of land-ownership is established and the relevant authorities of local government and development are granted full powers of compulsory purchase. In the long term, parochial land-ownership and land-control — as already practised by the Stornoway Trust, and newly won by the people of Assynt — is the key to solving most Highland problems.

Such bodies could reduce the white settler menace. I have no wish to appear an alarmist, but the uncontrolled flood of strangers into Highland districts and townships has proved a disaster of the worst magnitude. The incomers swamp local community, take control of local society, have voices that drown out those of the indigenous people about them, and are frequently most hostile to the traditions and values of the communities unfortunate enough to be honoured by their presence. There is good proof, for instance, that these invasions destroy Gaelic-speaking interaction within a very short period of time; yet all who matter in the Highlands, and all who vaunt themselves at the head of the Gaelic crusade, are inexplicably and utterly silent.

With communal land-ownership comes communal control, and power. The BCCI debacle in the Western Isles has been hugely distorted and misunderstood, discrediting the competence and ability of Gaels to administer their own affairs. This is manifestly unjust. Wherever Highlanders have been entrusted with responsibility and power in their own affairs they have used it well. The BCCI disaster was not the work of malicious and wicked men in the Hebrides; it resulted from the villainy of overseas financiers and the incompetence of Government at home, and the Western Isles paid dearly for the bad luck and one mistake of overworked officials in an unhealthily secretive council environment. Yet Comhairle nan Eilean, the Western Isles Islands Council, has ruled the Outer Hebrides with general success for nigh on two decades, and has left the islands much better than it found them. Comhairle rule has brought a full refuse service, support for the aged, fine modern schools, a grand new hospital, far-sighted education policy, improved harbour facilities, wide strong roads and bridges, and better ferry links: it is a cruel fate, even by the harsh standards of contemporary journalism, to be remembered for one fiasco and not for numerous achievements.

As the Highlands and Islands near the end of the twentieth century — a hundred years of improvement to a level unthinkable ten decades ago, but years also of upheaval and tragedy — the people of Gaeldom now sense new opportunities to assert their own authority. For many years Government bodies, expert agencies, and optimistic quangos have strode north and west to direct and guide and to implement various hopeful schemes for prosperity. These, largely, have come to nothing. As I write, I can only think of four things that have brought substantial benefit to Highlanders — the availability, for many years, of public monies to improve housing; the construction and arrival of better transport links — the big coastal bridges, air services and of roll-on roll-off car-ferries; the big post-war push to provide all Highland districts with electricity; and, above all, imperfect but greatly beneficial, the 1886 Crofters Act.

We have seen one truly successful new industry in the modern era — the

The delights of civilisation: Stornoway shopfront, about 1980. Island prices are substantially higher than those of the mainland

manufacture of Harris Tweed, a living ideally suited to Hebridean character and values, and ruthlessly but well protected by its trade association. Even so, the great cloth is presently in deep recession; only one milling-concern now survives. Too often, we have seen development that proved disastrous and stupid. The great manufacturing plants at Invergordon and Corpach were ill-conceived and never truly viable. The 1976 Crofting Act, which provoked the resignations of several important Labour Party activists in protest at its terms, conferred a right of owner-occupation on crofters which they had never sought and which most refused to exercise. Or the rise of fish-farming, a hapless business, bristling with environmental and ethical horror, and increasingly quit by such men as grew weary with the constant battle against storms, infection and vermin.

The Salmon Act of 1986, a wretched centenary-present for the great law before, flew in the face of Highland values and has gratified only landlords. And there are dozens of smaller, equally wretched examples: island council-houses built to a national standard in peat-burning communities — without chimneys. Bad piers, like an infamous Victorian example at Petersport on Benbecula that looked fine on a bureaucrat's map but proved useless when built — the cove was ringed by reefs. A Wester Ross trawler-

Lewis Stokfisk Ltd, at Breasclete on Lewis, one of many expensive HIDB projects
to flounder and fail. Today, a pharmaceutical company uses the plant to produce
fish-oil capsules

skipper, who faced the loss of his livelihood when much of the local waters were seized
for a torpedo-range — he was told that he would be given a job with the range, as a
deck-hand. Or the standard absurdities of pronunciation and fact, from those who will
not trouble to learn. The British Tourist Board booklet describing Barra as uninhabited.
The newscasters and weathermen who say "Kyleekin" and "Mallaig".

We have learned, we survivors, not to look to such for salvation. We want only
the possession of our own land — in the name of its resident people, as the Lord always
meant it to be — and the freedom to administer its development and affairs, in
consultation with all entitled interest-groups, as we Highlanders see fit. We want to see
the modest funds and counselling resources necessary to launch small-scale economic
projects. And we want, too, funding for our transport links and more control over such
agencies as Caledonian MacBrayne. Our freight and transport charges are far too high;
and such as CalMac seem to be working not for the Highland people but for those who
want to visit them.

You ask: what right have you strange people to public monies and aid out of my
taxes? We Gaels will not indulge in moral blackmail and plead three centuries and more
of external persecution. But the fact is that you like our land, and you value us as

people: were it not so, you would not be reading this book. And we are happy to preserve our environment as a fresh and open space for the whey-faced citizens of your world; we are a lung for a choking country, and custodians of your refreshment. You may never have seen the Highlands, and perhaps you never will. But is it not good to know that we are there? And, learning of our struggle to survive in these far-flung territories, as we once trooped away to fight for you on disproportionate scale in two world wars, will you not agree that we are entitled to your support? Or is it, indeed, no great mischief if we fall?

The Highland people have further tasks ahead. It is imperative that we accept the inevitable and looming disappearance of Gaelic as a living language, and cease to waste time and funds in denying that reality. Yet the loss of Gaelic community need not mean the loss of Gaelic knowledge, nor indeed of the Gaelic world. When was Latin last spoken as a language of real people doing real things in real places? But Latin is still accessible to those who want it: and the lost Roman Empire, its laws and concepts and practical principles, is yet the foundation of western European civilisation. Too much can be made of language. One in eight Scots is still a regular, church-going Christian. But how many can read Greek and Hebrew?

Gaelic has become a millstone round the neck of the Highland people: not because the language itself is backward and a nuisance, because it is not — if it were, we Gaels would never have attained such status in other societies as we did — but because Gaelic, and its ruling élite, draw away attention and cash from the problems that truly affect Highland lives. And the tragedy is that, in fighting vainly to save a tongue, we risk losing both Gaelic speech and Gaelic values. Yet these values transcend Gaelic. And they may, and must, survive its passing.

A love-affair, and bonding, with our land and landscape. A keen sense of the past, and of coming posterity. A wise concept of time, as a river, not an ocean. A serene belief in Providence. A love of kin: a grasp of the ties of blood, an awareness that is not individual, but tribal. A sympathy for children, an empathy with animals, a wondering at the sea and the stars and the gentle sleep of death. These are things that the going of a tongue need not take from us. These are things on which we may build an abiding but new identity, and preserve them in our communities, in the tending of the soil and the practice of our faith, in a reaching out and caring for our kinsmen and our neighbours and our friends. We are indeed hardy, and intrepid; we have suffered much from the evil deeds of strangers and the vagaries of progress; but the greatest struggles are over, and the foulest foes are gone.

That age may come indeed when the empty straths are tilled once more, and the ruined homes rise again. For such a time, we must at once forsake the passive joys of victimhood. These are our Highlands, and it is our future; look you to your duty, and the day will come — I promise you — when our seed may yet be told a very different story all together.

To Shawbost Shore

Midsummer: midsummer in Scotland, and no night in the north to speak of, no night but the soft half-light of the high turn of the year. And there is this half-light over the Outer Isles and Lewis, and down the west side, where tonight there is no wind or rain: the half-light of solstice on Shawbost, and the sheen of dipping sun on the deep and green new growth.

We stand for a time on the croft of my grandfather, and become part of the evening. The house is shut and glum, without noise or light of its own, for my uncle is not staying at present. There are no sheep grazing about us, for they are on the hill. There is dew on the silverweed, wet on the leaves of buttercups as we amble. A rabbit starts at our approach, and bounds for the fence and the long secret grass about it. There is just a breath of wind, enough to keep the midges down, though it is early enough to see them. Come in August, on a night as mild and a shade more still, and we would be eaten alive.

"There's an old saying — kill a midge, and a hundred'll come to the funeral," says the Cousin.

"Well, they must be away to a wake tonight," I say jocularly, "or perhaps to a Cleg Convention. Motion — Big Blood is Best Blood . . . or Speed, Not Bulk."

"Clegs are stupid," says the Cousin, "though they've got one mean bite — it itches and swells, and leaves a scar for ages . . . but at least you've got the satisfaction of killing the beast. Sits on your arm for ages sucking . . . you know?"

"Quite."

We look about us. Lights on in the houses up the street; the friendly flash and flicker of television. A snipe drumming somewhere. The faraway rumble and mumble of the sea. The hum of a car going into town. A door slamming on Church Street. The distant laughter of boys at the Gate. The houses at the Gate, and on Church Street, and across our own street, in outline against an eggshell sky.

"No old houses now," says the Cousin.

"No," I muse, "not even our own." We have reached the foot of the croft, by the concrete garage where my grandfather kept his bus and his lorry. There is nothing else now. No peat-stack, nor the black patch where it sat. No old house, nor oldest house.

They were cleared efficiently by Council workmen, a few months after my grandmother died — every last stone and stick — and carried away for found for a road. Their scar is hidden now, under grass and docken and silverweed. Even the rhubarb patch has disappeared.

"The tribal land," I say, and we turn to look up the park. The tumbling stones of the dyke at the head, along the ridge of Druim Tortomar. The broad beds of the *feannagan*, ribs that once grew corn and oats and turnips, that grow nothing now. The fenced square of my uncle's vegetable-plot. The whispering willows in the corner, and the tumbling fence-posts, rotten, sagging with wire, that I watched my grandfather erect and strain two long decades ago. The clean green land, fallow, overgrazed, dotted with clumps of rushes and the drying dung of sheep; the rabbits playing in its further reach. The land that our long-gone progenitor broke and tilled and made his own, a century before ourselves. Him hauling and heaping and breaking the stones. Him with his children and the Gaelic Bible in the old house, where the smoke curled, where the breath of cattle was sweet and warm, on such a night as this.

"You know why I prefer Shawbost to Ness?" I announce. "It is because here I feel that the old people, the ancestors, are but sleeping; in Ness, you know fine they're dead."

He smiles, a little tightly, and I feel uncomfortable, as if I have made some *faux pas*. We do not open the galvanised gate. We scrabble over it, on to the road, and find ourselves walking up towards the Gate and the crossroads and Baile Stigh and the shore. Quite without meaning to, we are walking in step. Slowly. Measuredly. Past Poko's, and Maggie's, and the ugly new bungalows, and the solid wall of an old but roofless house, and meadows today that hold no cows and yield no hay. To the Gate: a light on at Murchadh Ghobh's, youngsters about the old and shuttered shop that closed before the most of them were born, where the young people met in my grandfather's youth, and no doubt long before that.

They eye us with pink and humorous faces; cigarettes glow, denims huddle. "Aye, aye!" say the girls coyly, and "Aye, aye," say I back, with a quick tilt of the head. We keep walking. Into Baile Stigh, the township to the shore; this is a much older part of Shawbost, and the houses look older — solid, traditional, not much of flash modernity — and huddle by each other and very close to the road, as the houses of fishermen do, though there are no fishers in Baile Stigh now. But some of the houses are derelict and boarded, and there are many ruins of old black houses. We can see the shore to our left, broad crescent of ocean on sand and rock, and hear the sighing of its waves.

"'Time, the deer, is in the wood of Hallaig'," says the Cousin. "You know that poem, don't you? Sorley MacLean. That's the epigraph he put at the start of it. And that was what the poem explored: Time, romping and leaping through a place, bringing change and death and removal. Hallaig is beautiful, John. And Hallaig is empty."

"I was there three weeks ago," says myself. "I've read the poem, and seen the movie. And I've walked to Hallaig from Fearns. And from Screapdal. Och, aye — it was a lovely place indeed. But the poem is not at all easy to understand."

"It's Time, and what it does to a place and its people," says the Cousin. We reach the turning for the shore; we turn, hard-left. Around us now are beds of flags, still flowering, in the marshy terrace about the little burn from Loch na Miulne to Loch a Bhaile. Loch a Bhaile, the loch of the township, is right in behind the beach, separated only by that bank of sand and shingle and great round stones.

"Trees and people — Sorley sees the trees as like the people, standing, but changing, and yet beyond change. In the folk-memory, or something . . . ?

> *'The men lying on the green*
> *at the end of every house that was,*
> *the girls a wood of birches,*
> *broad their backs, bent their heads . . .'"*

"Yes, very romantic, I'm sure," says the Cousin. We are at the shore; we cross the tiny bridge over the stream from loch to sea, a bridge without walls to a road without tar. "But that was his fantasy. You can leave Time in your imagination; but you can't stop Time, can you? You can't suspend it or deny it, not even you. You can escape outwith it and write nice stories. But what's reality? Time is reality, and the forces of history, and against them not you nor me nor anybody else is going to prevail."

"I know that fine, my cousin. Wasn't there always change? Wasn't Hallaig empty before it was settled? And wasn't there a people, centuries and centuries ago, with a tongue older than Gaelic and ways that were old when they built the standing stones? Isn't there always change now, even in our own lives, even between ourselves?"

"So why write the poem?"

"Why write my book?"

"I shudder to think. Money. Kudos. The Whitbread Prize. Giving out autographs at Melven's. Or, perhaps, some quaint and couthy piece of homage to ye departed friends." He strikes an attitude; he puts a bardic hand to his brow and mimics a bad Highland accent. "They may be dead, but we can sing their song!"

"Yes," I say. "That's part of it. But it's our song too. We're still Gaels. We've got Gaelic in our soul; we've had good Lewis grannies, we like it here. Well, most of the time. I dare say we're no less hardy and intrepid than they were themselves. We'd better be. There's still plenty of folk about that think Teuchs like us are expendable."

He pulls a face. We stand without speaking. There is a strange, rhythmic grating noise in the land behind — *erk-erk, erk-erk* — and I say, "Hey, that's a corncrake." And another one starts up then, somewhere in the nearer flags — *erk-erk, erk-erk*. They boom to one another, grinding like the two old halves of a rusting gate. "They're still here. And two pairs!"

"And precious scarce," says the Cousin. "Progress has got most of 'em. Combine harvesters. Short-stem grain. No nice long rails of corn, cut by sturdy sickle-wielding peasants. Nothing to keep a decent honest corncrake alive these days at all." He wheels about, and looks at the sea. The sea, silver and grey in the twilight, very still, though the current roars at the distant reef; a deep light over the land, and darkness in the crags of the Beinn behind us. The Cousin frowns, rather sadly, and says, "Gaelic is dying. You've admitted that. The old houses and ways have gone, and the hardship and sickness too — you can't want that back. And, yes, the old people are dead, and will die. And what can you do about it?"

"Tell the story," I insist. "Tell what happened to our people, and why it happened, and write it for our children, so that it won't be forgotten. Tell the Highland people. Take a good look into ourselves. How have we responded to our hardship? Have we not grown passive and bitter? Is it not time we took a hold of who we are, and what we can be?"

The Cousin beams; his face crinkled, his teeth very white. He turns to gaze at me. "And stop the clock? Like Sorley? Shoot the deer with a bullet from the gun of Love?"

"'. . . his eye will freeze in the wood, his blood will not be traced while I live'," quote I, and I chuckle too, and I add, "No, and I don't think Sorley would stop the clock either. But I think he was speaking to people like you."

"Eh?" The Cousin glances curiously at me.

"Aye, that's what he means. People who like to talk of vast strong impersonal forces, great powers without moral accountability or reason, because it covers up their own refusal to take responsibility — and the deeds of bad men. Don't you see? It was history that murdered the clansmen after Culloden. It wasn't progress that fired the thatches. It wasn't time that emptied Sutherland, or South Uist, or Hallaig. It was people. Bad people. Wicked men, like the Duke of Sutherland, or George Rainy, or Colonel Gordon. That's the ones who wrought the heartbreak — the heartbreak of the tale. And the lazy ones, who sigh and say, 'Ah, material advancement' and, 'Agricultural tides then sweeping Europe . . .' and, 'Well, what can you do?' — and they did sod-all. Didn't stand. Didn't speak up. Didn't fight. And they either stay here, in the islands, and pile up the comforts and let their minds rot and their wills atrophy, or they go to the mainland and they sell out!"

The smile has gone. "But I . . ."

"Aye, Cousin. Choices. People make choices. And you'll make your choice. You can go off and get westernised; you can get a grand job in Glasgow and a big house in Bearsden and fill it with goodies and get into debt up to your oxters and meanwhile make babies with some wee blonde pagan from the Deep South. Or — well, you could come back. Or step back, over your father's generation, and make your living here. Or somewhere like it. You can even get a croft, work it in your free time. But even if you didn't do all that, even if you preferred to stay south, you can keep the faith. Remember the old ones. Keep their story. Remember the roots, the fathers . . . you know? But for Pete's sake, *care* about who they were and what happened to them!"

"That's wild talk," says the Cousin, "a fool's talk." He is going from me, the eyes shuttered now; he is retreating, into the twilight, into the green and dim, and the noise of the corncrakes.

"Choices," I cry foolishly, "I was talking about choices . ."

"I had them. So do you." The sound is distant, fading, and I look for him; but there is nothing there, not a sign of a soul. He has never been here. He never will be. He is but a shade from the irrevocable past, and I cannot now hear his voice. There is only myself and the island night: the grating of an unseen bird, and the sound of the sea on the shore.

Further Reading

This list of readily available books on the Highlands and Islands is by no means exhaustive. What are given here are merely those I found myself consulting in the actual writing of this book. I also made use of other materials, not least the published records and journals of the Free Presbyterian Church: copies of these may be consulted by arrangement in the Library of that denomination at 133 Woodlands Road, Glasgow. A most important source for my account of the Mackay affair was the nightly journal I kept at that period, noting events and conversations of the day.

If I could recommend but four books on the Highlands, these would be the *Collected Poems* of Sorley MacLean; the wonderful travelogue *The Highlands* by his late brother, Calum I. MacLean; and the two popular histories by James Hunter, *Skye: The Island* and *Scottish Highlanders* — notwithstanding his religious prejudices. These three last are to be had from Mainstream Publishing. American academic Susan Parman's lively anthropology text, *Scottish Crofters*, is based on her field study of Shawbost society in the early Seventies; she lived in the village for several years and maintains local friendships to this day.

A. D. Cameron, *Go Listen To The Crofters*, Stornoway, 1986
Derek Cooper, *Hebridean Connection*, London, 1977
Derek Cooper, *The Road to Mingulay*, London, 1985
David Craig, *On The Crofters' Trail*, London, 1990
Alexander Fenton, *The Island Blackhouse*, Edinburgh, 1978
James Shaw Grant, *Discovering Lewis and Harris*, Edinburgh, 1987
James Shaw Grant, *Highland Villages*, London 1977
Ian Grimble, *Scottish Islands*, London, 1985
James Hunter, *The Claim Of Crofting*, Edinburgh, 1991
James Hunter, *Scottish Highlanders*, Edinburgh, 1992
James Hunter, *Skye: The Island*, Edinburgh, 1986
Kittiwake Press pub., *Outer Isles Handbook And Guide*, Darowen, 1989
Bruce Lenman, *The Jacobite Risings in Britain 1689–1746*, London, 1980

Donald J. MacDonald and others, *Free Presbyterians and the Requiem Mass*, Glasgow, 1989

Calum I. MacLean, *The Highlands*, Edinburgh, 1961

Fitzroy MacLean, *Bonnie Prince Charlie*, Edinburgh, 1988

Sorley MacLean, *From Wood to Ridge: Collected Poems in Gaelic and English*, Manchester, 1989

Frank McLynn, *Charles Edward Stuart*, Oxford, 1988

Frank McLynn, *The Jacobites*, London, 1985

Alexander McPherson ed., *History of the Free Presbyterian Church of Scotland 1893–1970*, Inverness, 1975

Susan Parman, *Scottish Crofters*, Fort Worth (USA), 1989

John Prebble, *Glencoe*, London, 1966

Scottish Crofters Union pub., *Crofting and the Environment: A New Approach*, Broadford, 1992

Richard Sharp, *Raasay: A Study In Island History*, London, 1982

Alexander Stewart and J. Kennedy Cameron, *The Free Church of Scotland 1843–1910*, Edinburgh, 1910

Stornoway Gazette pub., *Sea Sorrow — The Story of the Iolaire Disaster*, Stornoway, 1972

John Tallach, *A Plea Against Extremism*, Fearn, 1989

S. Fraser Tallach, *One Is Your Master*, Fearn, 1989

Francis Thompson, *Harris and Lewis*, Devon, 1968

Francis Thompson, *The Western Isles*, London, 1988

Derick S. Thomson ed., *The Companion to Gaelic Scotland*, Oxford, 1983

Michael Wigan, *The Scottish Highland Estate*, Shrewsbury, 1991

Charles W. J. Withers, *Gaelic in Scotland 1698–1981*, Edinburgh, 1984

Index